PARTY ACROSS America!

PARTY ACROSS
America!

 OF THE **GREATEST FESTIVALS,**
SPORTING EVENTS, AND
CELEBRATIONS IN THE **U.S.**

MICHAEL GUERRIERO

AVON, MASSACHUSETTS

Published by Adams Media,
an F+W Media Company
57 Littlefield Street, Avon, MA 02322. U.S.A.
www.adamsmedia.com

ISBN 10: 1-59869-816-8
ISBN 13: 978-1-59869-816-9

Printed in the United States of America.

J I H G F E D C B A

Library of Congress Cataloging-in-Publication
Data is available from the publisher.

This book is available at quantity discounts for
bulk purchases. For information, please call
1-800-289-0963.

This publication is designed to provide accurate and authoritative information with regard
to the subject matter covered. It is sold with the
understanding that the publisher is not engaged
in rendering legal, accounting, or other professional advice. If legal advice or other expert
assistance is required, the services of a compe-
tent professional person should be sought.
—From a *Declaration of Principles*
jointly adopted by a Committee of the
American Bar Association and a
Committee of Publishers and Associations

Many of the designations used by manufacturers and sellers to distinguish their product are
claimed as trademarks. Where those designations appear in this book and Adams Media was
aware of a trademark claim, the designations
have been printed with initial capital letters.

Many efforts have been made to ensure the
accuracy of addresses, phone numbers, prices,
and other information in this book. However,
phone numbers and addresses change, prices
go up, and schedules that were accurate during
the time of writing are modified. Readers must
call or e-mail ahead of time to confirm all information for themselves. The author, editor, and
publisher are not to be held accountable for any
issues that arise as a result of information con-
tained in this book.

dedication

Love frequently sparks inspiration.
This book is dedicated to my wife,
best friend, and the greatest person
on the planet, Jennifer. Without
her encouragement, patience, and
support this project would have
never come to fruition.

*"And in the end, it's not the years in
your life that count. It's the life in
your years."*

—*Abraham Lincoln*

CONTENTS

SECTION 2 — THE SOUTHEAST

SECTION 3 — MIDDLE AMERICA

SECTION 4 — THE WILD WEST

SECTION 5 — THE WEST COAST

SECTION 6 — ALASKA, HAWAII, AND THE SUPER BOWL

INTRODUCTION

The greatest parties in America have never been organized into a thrill seeker's travel guide, or a party hopper's bible—until now.

The events in this book are the reigning kings of raging celebrations. They're annual extravaganzas that attract thousands upon thousands of revelers. They occur in the same place year after year, and nearly every state in the country is represented. Whether you're a working stiff who wants to blow off some steam, a fun-loving retiree with free time on your hands, a college student shopping for spring break destinations, or a best man or maid of honor planning the perfect bachelor or bachelorette trip—this book will become your friend.

It's fairly common knowledge that the social scene at Mardi Gras and the Kentucky Derby is extraordinary. However, the reality is that our country is teeming with parties that are comparable in both energy level and attitude. These spirited gatherings take the idea of a weekend getaway to the next level and are a surefire way to celebrate life in the United States.

The "commercialization of America" has resulted in nationwide uniform strip-mall landscapes that contain the same fast-food joints and repeating chain retail storefronts. In fact, it's often difficult to distinguish one town or city from the next. What you cannot learn about a place by looking at it, you can learn by partying in it. There are unique cultural traditions and festivities hovering just below the radar in every area of the country. Many events tell a fascinating story about the city or region in which they occur, and the people in attendance are always full of jovial spirit. There's more to these gatherings than beer drinking and uninhibited behavior (although that's usually at the forefront)—they help to weave the social fabric of our country. So get out there and party across America, from sea to shining sea.

HOW TO USE THIS BOOK

This book is written like a traditional travel guide, the destination being an event as well as a place. Each profile contains a description as well as how to get there; where to stay; what to bring; and phone numbers, ticket information, and special instructions. Use this guide in conjunction with the Internet—many websites are listed for planning purposes.

It's organized into six geographic regions—The Northeast, The Southeast, Middle America, The Wild West, The West Coast, and Alaska, Hawaii, and the Super Bowl. States are alphabetically arranged in each of these regions.

Description

This section outlines the most important aspects of the event and the schedule, providing guidance to the party. Read about the history, the number of people who attend, and discover helpful hints about the area.

Transportation

Find the most convenient airport and navigate the local public transportation. Driving directions from the airport to your destination can be obtained on *www.map quest.com*. In most cases you'll use the hotel's address as your MapQuest ending location. Each airport code is given, as is the airport website, which contains car-rental agencies and their phone numbers. The locations of Amtrak and Greyhound Bus stations are listed—visit *www.amtrak.com* or *www.greyhound.com* for schedules, rates, and further information. Local taxicab phone numbers and airport shuttle information are included.

Accommodations

In an effort to stay inside of people's comfort zones, easily recognizable chain hotels are featured as often as possible. These include Holiday Inn, Marriott, Fairfield Inn, Best Western, and Days Inn, to name a few. Phone numbers, starting room rates (which do not include tax) during the event, and addresses for each hotel are provided. You can find further hotel listings by searching on Google for the city's visitor's center. Many of these parties are so huge that every room in town will sell out. Make your hotel reservation as soon as you purchase an airline ticket!

Tickets

If tickets are necessary, this is where you'll look. Many of the parties are sporting events, music festivals, or other ticketed events, and they often sell out. You'll find out where to go, whom to call, and how much tickets cost. Just be warned: The prices are current at the time of writing, but they're guaranteed to go up each year.

What to Pack

Some of the items listed are a joke, but many are not. Furthermore, not every single necessity is listed—just the items that aren't too obvious.

Travel Deals

Many people book their travel and hotel arrangements online, and this book is structured for that purpose. However, *Party Across America!* has partnered with a travel agency to make your party-hopping that much easier. Their name is Aggie Travel Points International, and they will often beat any online price for airfare and hotels to the events in this book. Give them a call at 970-482-1235 and mention *Party Across America!* for the best rates.

Visit

www.partyacrossamericabook.com

to share your own party experiences, to meet the author, and to blog about which celebrations you'd like to see in the next edition.

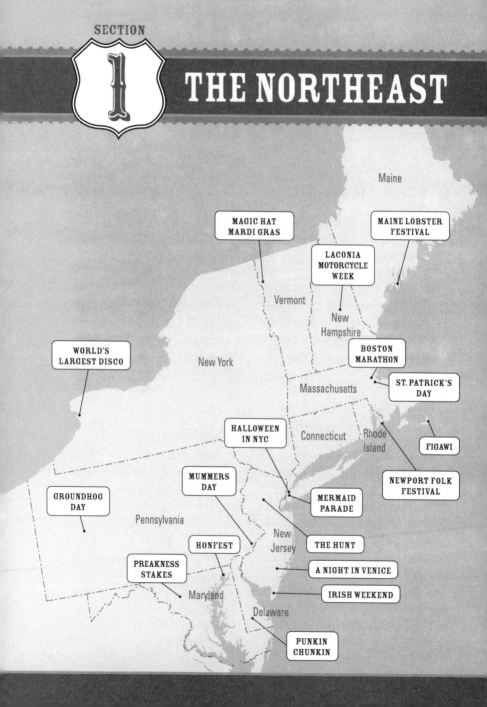

SECTION

1

THE NORTHEAST

Maine

MAGIC HAT
MARDI GRAS

MAINE LOBSTER
FESTIVAL

LACONIA
MOTORCYCLE
WEEK

Vermont

New
Hampshire

WORLD'S
LARGEST DISCO

New York

BOSTON
MARATHON

Massachusetts

ST. PATRICK'S
DAY

HALLOWEEN
IN NYC

Connecticut

Rhode
Island

FIGAWI

MUMMERS
DAY

NEWPORT FOLK
FESTIVAL

GROUNDHOG
DAY

MERMAID
PARADE

Pennsylvania

New
Jersey

HONFEST

THE HUNT

PREAKNESS
STAKES

A NIGHT IN VENICE

Maryland

IRISH WEEKEND

Delaware

PUNKIN
CHUNKIN

Delaware

PUNKIN CHUNKIN

★ Bridgeville, Delaware
First weekend in November
www.punkinchunkin.com

Have you ever wondered what happens to all those unpicked pumpkins after the Halloween season has passed? Some lie rotting in fields, others find their way into freshly baked pumpkin pies, while a select few are placed into gigantic catapults and launched over a mile through the Delaware sky.

The annual Punkin Chunkin World Championships has been taking place for over twenty years. The contestants who enter this most unique of long-distance volleys have gone so far as to genetically engineer the perfect white pumpkin, with a thick skin that resists breaking apart upon countdown sequence (believe it or not, an ounce of these seeds costs $80). This three-day party has grown each year at an astounding rate, with reports of 50,000 in attendance in 2007. The celebration has

evolved into the second-largest annual gathering in the entire state and was recently relocated from a 300-acre field to a 1,000-acre field to accommodate advancements in punkin chunkin technology.

The catapulting begins at about 8:00 A.M. and ends at 2:30 P.M. The contestants tend to be local engineers, many seemingly unemployed, who enter one of several different classes. The machines resemble life-size erector-set models, and they hurtle pumpkins so far that you lose sight of them with the naked eye. Over 100 of these produce-slingers are put to the test each day while a variety of chili, pie, and pastry cook-offs are held outside of the ropes.

This "sporting" event takes place in a field, the atmosphere being that of a massive tailgate party that rages on long after the day's contests have ended. Beer is not sold on the premises, but it is permitted, so bring your own. A stage is set up for live music, which takes place all day Friday through Sunday. Friday night is when the headlining musical act plays, and recent performers have been the Marshall Tucker Band and Charlie Daniels. On Saturday night, fireworks replace pumpkins as the skybound objects during the dramatic closing ceremony.

TRANSPORTATION

✈ **AIR:** Book flights into Baltimore / Washington International Airport (BWI / *www.bwi.com*) located seventy-seven miles away. There is also a smaller regional airport in Salisbury, Maryland, located thirty miles away.

ACCOMMODATIONS

🏨 **HOTELS:** Seaford, just five minutes south of Bridgeville, is the closest town with accommodations. The Holiday Inn Express (210 North Dual Highway / 302-629-2000 / $118), Hampton Inn (799 North Dual Highway / 302-629-4500 / $129), Days Inn (420 North Dual Highway / 302-629-4300 / $80), and Quality Inn (225 North Dual Highway / 302-629-8385 / $75) are options. If Seaford hotels are booked, then try a hotel in Rehoboth Beach by visiting *www.rehoboth.com*.

🔥 **CAMPING:** Setting up a campsite is permitted from 10:00 A.M. Thursday to 10:00 A.M. Monday, and costs $150. One vehicle, two tents, and four campers are allowed per site, although additional parking passes are available. A camping form must be downloaded from the event website and mailed in prior to arrival. No water or power is available, although port-a-potties are. No fires and no sleeping in cars.

🚐 **RV:** Beginning in 2007 the Punkin Chunkin has opened itself to RV campers. There is plenty of space on the new grounds. Check-in begins on Thursday at 10:00 A.M. and checkout is 10:00 A.M. on Monday. Visit *www.punkinchunkin.com* to download an RV parking form and mail it in prior to arrival. Showers are not available.

TICKETS

The entrance fee is $7 per person and a single car parking pass is $2—both are available upon arrival. Three-day camping and RV parking passes cost $150 and $200 respectively, should be purchased ahead of time, and include entrance to the festival.

party tip

The technical wizards who design the launching devices take extreme pride in their performance, but once in a while a "dud" pumpkin will be shot from a catapult. When this occurs, the gooey pieces of ammunition drop from the sky just a few feet away and zero points are awarded. At this point the crowd will yell "pie in the sky!" at the top of their lungs.

What to Pack

- Warm clothing—army camouflage jackets make a strong showing during the Punkin Chunkin
- A flask to fight off the November chill
- A tent, warm sleeping bag, and plenty of giant-size wet wipes (no showers for campers)
- Binoculars
- Your appetite for comfort foods (pies, starches, crispy things)

Maine

MAINE LOBSTER FESTIVAL

⊛ Rockland, Maine
Late July to early August
www.mainelobsterfestival.com

Crustaceans residing in New England waters begin to shake in their shells each summer as the world's largest "lobstaah" party approaches. This gathering is one of New England's greatest, most delicious, and totally unique summer events.

The festivities take place in Harbor Park, a beautiful area right on the bay. Over 100,000 bibbed visitors infiltrate Rockland, population 7,600, throughout the five-day shell-busting brouhaha. It has been growing by leaps and bounds since its start over sixty years ago. Visitors from all across the country, as well as international lobster lovers, consume over 20,000 pounds of buttery sea meat—think about the sheer number of claw crackers involved.

Plan to spend a considerable amount of time underneath the Main Eating Tent. Succulent lobsters are fired out of the largest steamer in the world at an astounding rate, as are fresh mussels, clams, and shrimp. Coleslaw and corn are served alongside the single-, double-, and triple-sized lobster plates. They range from $15 to $35. A smart idea is to fill up at the absolutely fantastic all-you-can eat $5 blueberry pancake breakfast (held Thursday through Sunday, 7:00 A.M. to 11:00 A.M.), skip lunch, and then gorge yourself on seafood at dinnertime.

Organizers place as high a value on entertainment as they do on food; there are fantastic events all day long to satiate the eyes along with the stomach. High noon on Wednesday signals the start of a constant crackling sound that doesn't end until Sunday. The previous year's Sea Goddess along with King Neptune and his court begin the opening ceremonies in front of the Harbor Master Building. Merchants, artists, jugglers, cooks, musicians, and stilt walkers fill numerous tents and booths in the park. Take a tour on the USS *Nassau*, which is docked in the bay. Separate tickets are needed for the Friday and Saturday night concerts, which tend to be acts that are typical of a medium-size venue. Over 25,000 people line the streets to watch the big parade at 10:00 A.M. on Saturday.

The highlight of the festival is the Lobster Crate Race, which takes place on Sunday. Hordes of onlookers line the docks to watch participants run across a string of fifty floating lobster crates as they bob up and down in the bay. He or she who can navigate the most crates before falling in the water wins. The all-time record is over 3,000 crates, and the secret is to run fast. Sign-ups begin at 7:00 A.M. on Sunday, and any brave soul may enter.

TRANSPORTATION

AIR: The closest major airport is Bangor International (BGR / *www.flybangor.com*) located fifty miles away. Car-rental agencies are available.

You may also fly into Knox County Regional Airport (RKD) if you own a private plane.

BOAT: Many people sail their way into Rockland Harbor for this event. It's one of the state's largest ports and the harbormaster can be contacted at 207-594-0312.

ACCOMMODATIONS

HOTELS: A stay in a historic New England inn adds even more flavor to the weekend. Among the nicest are Berry Manor Inn (81 Talbot Ave. / 207-596-7696 / $115), Captain Lindsey House (5 Lindsey St. / 207-596-7950 / $136), Limerock Inn (96 Limerock St. / 207-594-2257 / $110), and Old Granite Inn (546 Main St. / 207-594-9036 / $80), which overlooks the bay. Available rooms are limited at these beautiful properties, so call well in advance. The two hotels in town, Trade Winds Motor Inn (2 Park Dr. / 207-596-6661 / $89) and Navigator Motor Inn (520 Main St. 207-594-2131 / $95), are basic and less expensive.

CAMPING: A couple of beautiful campsites are located about five miles from Rockland, in Thomaston. Lobster Buoy (*www.lobsterbuoy campsites.com* / 207-594-7546) is a private site, located on the seashore. You can pitch a tent or hook up an RV, swim in the ocean, and build a campfire. Saltwater Farm Campground (*www .saltwaterfarmcampground.com* / 207-354-6735) is a wide-open grassland that overlooks the Saint George River. It also accommodates tent campers and has RV hookups.

TICKETS

Opening Wednesday is free. Thursday through Saturday, 9:00 A.M. through 3:00 P.M., costs $7 at the gate. Tickets for 3:00 P.M. through 10:00 P.M. must be purchased separately for $10. Sunday is $7 all day. Four-day passes are available from June to late July via the event website or may be purchased at the gate for $25. Seated tickets for Friday and Saturday nights' musical acts must be purchased separately and are priced according to the act. Arrive early to tour the USS *Nassau* because the line can get lengthy.

party tip

Many people love lobster but have no idea how to properly attack the meat. You can use the caveman approach, which usually leads to the loss and destruction of good food, or you can do it the right way. Arch the back of the lobster until it breaks, and then yank off the tail. Gently break off the tail flippers, leaving plenty of space to insert a fork and push the tail meat out. Next, unhinge the outer shell from the body. Notice the green area, which is considered a delicacy. Pull the body apart, cracking the shell, and notice the meat where the legs meet the body. Finally, the claws are some of the best eating; break them from the body and open them with scissors or pliers.

Maryland

PREAKNESS STAKES

★ Pimlico, Maryland
Third Saturday in May
www.preakness.com

Pimlico Race Course, a Victorian-style structure built in 1870, is home to the Preakness Stakes. It is located in a residential neighborhood thirty minutes from Baltimore. The Preakness is one of the three major horse races that comprise the famed Triple Crown. The history of this race dates back over 130 years, to a time when gentlemen attended in a top hat and jacket, and women donned their finest dress. Times have certainly changed because the Preakness is now far from prim and proper. While many top horse races still cater to refined upper-class fans, the Preakness encourages people from all walks to bring a twelve-pack into the race and take a spot on the most rowdy infield on the eastern seaboard.

Over time the Preakness has evolved into a rite of passage among Maryland's hardest partiers, many of whom return year after year. As a "fan" you have your choice of seating, which ranges from grandstand bleachers all the way to posh skyboxes complete with all the amenities. These are great seats if you plan on actually watching the horses, but the infield is where the real fun takes place!

On Saturday arrive at 7:00 A.M. or earlier for the world-class tailgating outside of the Pimlico Race Course. Be there on time, as the gates open up at 8:00 A.M. and the infield fills very quickly. The crowd at the Preakness numbers just over 100,000, which is small compared with the Kentucky Derby. However, the Preakness infield is much more rowdy due to the fact that beer and wine are permitted, along with 60,000 fans.

The actual race doesn't begin until 6:15 P.M., so this will not be a short day. Expect to experience slip 'n' slides, frozen T-shirt contests, and twister—all in the name of horse racing.

Security prohibits kegs and hard alcohol inside the gates, but you can bring as much beer and wine as you can carry on your person. For this reason you can expect to see people going to great lengths to attach alcohol to themselves.

TRANSPORTATION

✈ AIR: The nearest airport is Baltimore Washington International (BWI / *www.bwiairport.com*), located a half hour away.

🅿 PARKING: Parking in Pimlico can be a bit of a hassle, and if at all possible you should visit the Preakness website by January to obtain a parking pass. These range from $30 to $125 but usually sell out by February. Since the track is located in a residential neighborhood, you can also pay a resident about $25 to park on his or her property.

🚊 LIGHT-RAIL TRAIN: If you do not have a designated driver, then it is best to take a train from any number of local light-rail stations in the Baltimore area. The train station in Pimlico has shuttle buses running back and forth from the train station to the racetrack. Call 410-539-5000 for schedule and train information.

ACCOMMODATIONS

🏨 HOTELS: The closest hotels to the Pimlico Race Course fill up early, and it is best to book a room by January. Nearby hotels include the Hilton (1726 Reisterstown Rd. / 410-653-1100 / $249), Ramada Inn (1721 Reisterstown Rd. / 410-486-5600 / $185), and Radisson (5100 Falls Rd. / 410-532-6900 / $215). Visit *www.preakness .com/Admissions/HotelsMotels.htm* for a complete list of hotels ranging from three miles to ten miles from the racetrack. If you do not have much time to plan, then you will find plenty of rooms in Baltimore, which is just a short train ride away.

TICKETS

Tickets to the infield can be purchased on race day, but purchasing tickets beforehand can save some money. Visit *www.ticketmaster.com* for tickets—the ticket prices online prior to the race are about $15 less expensive.

What to Pack
- A folding lawn chair for the infield
- A raincoat for cloudy skies
- A wad of cash for betting
- Duct tape (to secure wine bottles to your torso)

party tip

The black-eyed Susan is the official drink of the Preakness Stakes. If you bring a pitcher of B.E.S. then you will be an official participant. Just be sure to finish them in the parking lot because security will confiscate liquor.

Official Black-Eyed Susan Recipe
1 part Finlandia Vodka
1 part Appleton Estate V/X Rum
1 part Pepe Lopez Triple Sec
1 part pineapple juice
1 part orange juice

Serve over ice, garnish with a cherry

HONFEST

★ Baltimore, Maryland
Second weekend in June
www.honfest.net

This is the rare occasion when letting your hair down is not cool, because the beehive is back in a *big* way, hon. For one glorious weekend in June, 50,000 hipsters in "Bawlmer," pack "The Avenue" in celebration of everything that's great about the Waterfront City. At the top of this list are the unique dialect, food, and music of a quirky town that's clearly got more to offer than Cal Ripken and a great aquarium.

Honfest takes its name from 1960s-era women who called everyone "Hon" (short for honey)—from their husband to the encyclopedia salesman. With equal single-mindedness they caked on layers of blue eye shadow, crammed their legs into leopard-print pants, and spent untold deaf hours with their heads beneath plastic salon globes. This dressed-up block party, taking place since 1994, is quickly shedding its "locals-only" skin as the East Coast masses are discovering the fun that lies beneath its shagadelic beehive.

The two-day art, music, and food festival takes place in Hampden, one of Baltimore's swankiest and most revered neighborhoods. Covering four city blocks along Thirty-sixth Street, Honfest requires partygoers to dress for the occasion and groove like the first wave of the British Invasion just hit. Local storeowners set up shop on the streets, bubblegum is chewed at an alarming rate, and the bars and restaurants are packed on Saturday and Sunday—so be sure to leave a little extra room in those tight pants to indulge in famous Baltimore crab cakes and meatloaf "sammiches." Café Hon (1002 W. Thirty-sixth St.) is the perfect place to grab a bite. Owner Denise Whiting is the creator of Honfest—her mantra is "the higher the hair, the nearer to God."

Highlights of the festival include a Hula Hoop contest and

the live music and dancing on Saturday and Sunday evenings showcased at the Beehive Lounge. Semifinalists for the Best Hon Contest are selected on Saturday, with the finals taking place on Sunday. Don't sweat it if you don't own Hon apparel. The Hon Boutique has feather boas, cat's-eye glasses, and false eyelashes galore, and the Glamour Lounge will do your hair while spackling your face with brilliant eye shadow.

And Hon, if youse git firsty at Honfest, the Bawlmer wooder is great!

TRANSPORTATION

✈ **AIR:** Book flights into Baltimore / Washington International Airport (BWI / *www.bwiairport.com*), located thirteen miles from Hampden. Car rental and taxis are available.

🚕 **TAXIS:** Baltimore's public transportation is notoriously unreliable and almost nonexistent. The good news is that downtown is only a ten-minute car ride from Hampden, so you can take a taxi. Cab companies include Yellow Cab (410-685-1212), Checker (410-235-0300), Royal Cab (410-327-0330), and Blue Cab (443-524-9000).

🚌 **BUS / 🚆 TRAIN:** The Greyhound station is located at 2110 Haines Street, and Amtrak is at 1515 North Charles Street.

ACCOMMODATIONS

🏨 **HOTELS:** If you can afford it, a hotel on the waterfront makes for excellent scenery. A great option is the Marriott-Baltimore Waterfront (700 Aliceanna / 410-385-3000 / $259). Other hotels in the inner harbor include Wyndham Inner Harbor (101 W. Fayette St. / 410-752-1100 / $144), Radisson (20 W. Baltimore St. / 410-539-8400 / $159), Hyatt Regency (300 Light St. / 410-528-1234 / $219), Holiday Inn Inner Harbor (301 W. Lombard St. / 410-685-3500 / $183) and Days Inn Inner Harbor (100 Hopkins Pl. / 410-576-1000 / $144).

What to Pack
- "Greaser" attire for the guys
- Leopard-print anything and everything
- Thick-rimmed glasses
- Fifteen packs of Bubblicious Bubble Gum
- Enough hairspray to slightly thin the ozone layer

party tip

Out-of-towners can't leave Baltimore without having paid a visit to the aquarium. This world-renowned building houses some amazing wildlife and is beautifully situated in the Inner Harbor. Be sure to check out the rooftop rainforest and multiple-story shark tanks.

Massachusetts

ST. PATRICK'S DAY

✪ Boston, Massachusetts
March 17
www.boston.com/ae/events/st_patricks_day

Saint Patrick would be proud to see an entire East Coast metropolis pay tribute to his existence so wholeheartedly. The patron saint of Ireland would be further honored if he had a penchant for drinking Guinness from sunrise to sunset while wearing a Red Sox hat. There's definitely whiskey in Boston's jar—the Irish capital of America unleashes the most brilliant Saint Patrick's Day celebration anywhere.

It doesn't matter if you're Asian, Hispanic, Protestant, or Hebrew, everyone in town is honorary green during this holiday. The crowd, which is estimated at 600,000, is a bit smaller than other major U.S. cities' St. Patty's Day extravaganzas—however the spirit is unequaled. You won't have to look hard to find the crowds, as you'll be immersed in a sea of green all night long. The party overflows from each watering hole onto the streets, resulting in a combination pub crawl and street party. The Black Rose (160 State St.) is a Quincy Market favorite that opens at 8:00 A.M. on "The Day" and features live music. Grafton Street Pub & Grill (1230 Massachusetts Ave.) is another hot spot, with world famous leg of lamb and shepherd's pie plus live music. You can also head to Doyle's Café (3484 Washington St.) for live bagpipers, or to the Blarney Stone (1505 Dorchester Ave.)—the first U.S. bar to serve Guinness—for Irish step dancing and a live DJ in the evening. Other lucky pubs include the Kinsale Irish Pub (2 Center Plaza), J.J. Foley's (21 Kingston St.), the Publick House (1648 Beacon St.), and Crossroads Irish Pub (495 Beacon St.).

The Dropkick Murphys, Boston's most famous Celtic punk rock music group, always play a few concerts in town during St. Patrick's Day weekend. Their electric Irish rock has been featured in Martin Scorsese's *The Departed*, as well as *Fever Pitch* starring Jimmy Fallon and Drew Barrymore. An energetic stage show and huge Beantown following make these concerts a guaranteed great show and a St. Patty's Day must. Visit *www.dropkickmurphys.com* for their tour schedule and ticket links.

Don't miss the parade held on the Sunday closest to the 17th in South Boston—the city's most Irish Catholic neighborhood. Referred to as "Southie" by its inhabitants, this section of the city has played host to the parade since 1804 and continues to overflow with onlookers on Broadway Street every March. Check the website for the exact date of this 600,000-person street fair.

TRANSPORTATION

AIR: Book flights into Logan Airport (BOS / www.massport.com/logan). There is no need to rent a car—just jump in a cab for the short ride downtown.

SUBWAY/TROLLEY: The T is Boston's most efficient means of transportation. To get from downtown to South Boston, hop on the Red Line and exit at the South Boston Broadway stop.

TAXIS: Cab companies include Boston Cab (617-536-5010), Checker Cab (617-536-7000), City Cab (617-536-5100), ITOA (617-825-4000), Metro Cab (617-782-5500), and Town Taxi (617-536-5000).

BUS / TRAIN: The closest Amtrak station is located at 145 Dartmouth St. in Copley Place. The closest downtown Greyhound station is located at 700 Atlantic Ave.

ACCOMMODATIONS

HOTELS: Boston Hotels include Sheraton (39 Dalton St. / 617-236-2000 / $249), Radisson (200 Stuart St. / 617-482-1800 / $189), Marriott (110 Huntington Ave. / 617-236-5800 / $249), Courtyard Tremont (275 Tremont St. / 617-426-1400 / $100), Doubletree (821 Washington St. / 617-956-7900 / $199), Hilton (89 Broad St. / 617-556-0006 / $240), and Best Western (1650 Commonwealth Ave. / 617-566-6260 / $130). A nice website, *www .boston.hotelscheap.org* has a good selection of discounted rooms.

What to Pack
- Green Red Sox hat—referred to as the "Boston Red Sox St. Patrick's Hat"
- Terry O'Reilly Bruins jersey—no gloves needed
- Larry Bird jersey—short shorts needed
- Dropkick Murphys' *Do or Die*

party tip

A visit to Boston wouldn't be complete without going on a Duck Tour. You'll head down the streets past the city's many historical sites before plunging off a boat launch for a tour up the Charles River. Visit *www.bostonducktours.com* for reservations.

BOSTON MARATHON

★ **Boston, Massachusetts**
Third Monday in April
www.bostonmarathon.org

The Boston Marathon is one of the most prestigious of races worldwide and draws over 20,000 participants who've trained for months, sometimes years, to earn the right to jog the most famous twenty-six miles in sports. Many of the half million spectators who flood the streets and finish line each year furnish support to family members and friends, offering words of encouragement, much needed splashes of water, and post-race congratulatory hugs. Another large contingent of Bostonians who congregate downtown do so because the finish line of the Boston Marathon is a "wicked" party.

The marathon takes place on the 3rd Monday in April, more commonly referred to as Patriot's Day. This holiday comes and goes without the bat of an eyelash from 99 percent of U.S. residents. However, Boston gives Patriot's Day the celebratory status that ancient Rome bestowed upon Julius Caesar's birthday. The Red Sox play a 10:00 A.M. home game, while the marathon serves as the festive spark that ignites thousands of New Englanders—even those who wouldn't be caught dead in a pair of Nikes.

The first wave of 10,000 runners begins at 10:00 A.M., and another huge wave takes off at 10:30 A.M. The elite women's group and wheelchair participants leave earlier, at around 9:30 A.M. The Boston Marathon's grueling reputation is due to the infamous series of hills that begin at mile sixteen in the town of Newton. One of these, commonly referred to as "Heartbreak Hill," is a half-mile ascent at a point in the marathon where racers have little left in their tanks, causing countless athletes to crash and burn. For an unforgettable experience, get to the hill, which is just a short train ride from the finish line, in time to shout words of encouragement alongside racer's families.

The finish line is located on Boylston Street, between Exeter and Dartmouth Streets, next to the Boston Public Library. This area, known as Copley Square, hosts myriad parties, which begin as early as seven o'clock in the morning. Check out the Pour House Bar and Grill (909 Boylston), the Cactus Club (939 Boylston), or Dillon's (955 Boylston) for some morning cocktails. Or get to Vinny T's (867 Boylston) early and grab an outdoor patio table. These prime, albeit limited pieces of real estate are typically claimed in the morning and seldom surrendered.

Other notable Marathon Monday hot spots include Boston Beer Works (61 Brookline Ave.) and the Cask & Flagon (62 Brookline Ave.). These two sports bars are havens for the pre– and post–Red Sox game crowd, which exits Fenway Park in time to watch the last mile of the marathon. Copley Square hops all day long and into the evening, so keep a healthy pace and avoid shin splints.

TRANSPORTATION

AIR: Book flights into Logan Airport (BOS / *www.massport.com/logan*). There is no need to rent a car—just jump in a cab for the short ride downtown.

SUBWAY/TROLLEY: Boston's T is the preferred public transit. The T system is very easy to navigate, and runs into every area of the city. To get to the marathon finish line from the airport, take the "Blue" Line to Government Center and transfer to the Green Line heading toward Copley. The Copley Square stop is closed during Patriot's Day, so get off at the Arlington or Hynes Convention Center stops. Trains typically arrive every five to ten minutes.

You can also take the T to Heartbreak Hill. Take the B train on the Green Line to the Boston College stop on Commonwealth Ave. Walk west down Commonwealth until you arrive at the hill.

Visit *www.mbta.com* for a complete T schedule and information.

TAXIS: Cab companies include Boston Cab (617-536-5010), Checker Cab (617-536-7000), City Cab (617-536-5100), ITOA (617-825-4000), Metro Cab (617-782-5500), and Town Taxi (617-536-5000).

TRAIN / B BUS: The closest Amtrak Station is located at 145 Dartmouth St. in Copley Place, just a short walk from the finish line. The closest downtown Greyhound station is located at 700 Atlantic Ave.

ACCOMMODATIONS

HOTELS: The city becomes very crowded on Patriot's Day, so getting around takes longer than usual. A reservation close to Copley Square or Fenway Park is recommended. Try Howard Johnson Inn Fenway Park (1271 Boylston St. / 617-267-8300 / $240), Boston Hotel Buckminster (645 Beacon St. / 617-236-7050 / $279), the Sheraton Boston (39 Dalton St. / 617-236-2000 / $389), Hilton (89 Broad St. / 617-556-0006 / $459), Marriott (110 Huntington Ave. / 617-236-5800 / $240), or the Best Western (1650 Commonwealth Ave. / 617-566-6260 / $229). Make reservations by January.

TICKETS

If you'd like to purchase tickets to the Red Sox game then do so when tickets go on sale in mid-

February. The game is usually held on opening day, and sells out within hours. Visit *www.redsox.mlb.com* for ticket purchases.

party tip

While scores of tourists head to high-profile watering holes like Cheers, pay a visit to the Union Oyster House on your post-marathon pub crawl. Cheers may be the place where everybody knows your name, but the food is marginal and Sam Malone is never working the bar. Union Oyster House, the oldest continuously operating restaurant in the United States, is the place where nobody cares who you are, but the oysters and clam chowder are unmatched—even by Norm's standards.

FIGAWI

⊛ Nantucket, Massachusetts
Memorial Day weekend
www.figawi.com

Drop an anchor in Nantucket for a full-throttle boat race party that's more popular onshore than it is at sea. This Memorial Day nautical fest is a spring break for both young sailors and weathered captains alike. It's the largest sailing race on the East Coast and signals the official beginning of summer.

Figawi has been taking place since 1972, when a group of friends decided to do a fun ocean race from Cape Cod to Nantucket. As time passed, the Kennedys and other prominent families entered the race, resulting in increased popularity. Eventually, the crowd standing along the shore began to outnumber those racing the boats. An official "welcome home" celebration was added, and the result is a party that allows landlubbers the opportunity to join the fun without leaving the dock.

The race begins on Saturday morning in Hyannis, Cape Cod,

and ends in Nantucket during the late afternoon. Over 250 boats, bearing crews of 3,000 sailors and guests, pursue their course across the Atlantic Ocean to the Nantucket coastline. On the Nantucket shore the crowd anxiously awaits the first wave of maritime victors, who begin to arrive at around 4:00 P.M.

Thousands of J. Crew types take over downtown Nantucket. The town's only open-air bar on the harbor, Rope Walk (1 Straight Wharf), attracts a huge crowd of all ages, while Gazebo (1 Harbor Square) is an outdoor watering hole that pulls in a massive twenties crowd, less than a block away. The Club Car (1 Main St.) is an old train car that has been converted into a gathering place for all ages. A large crowd belts out popular tunes alongside the piano.

Saturday night's post-race tent party is the centerpiece of Figawi high jinks. It takes place underneath an enormous shoreline tent and begins at 6:00 P.M., after the majority of vessels have arrived. Tickets are only sold to the ships' captains, who in turn, distribute wristbands to their crew, and sometimes to attractive females.

Many a seafarer is tired by 1:00 A.M., while others are not quite ready to abandon ship. An option is to walk full steam ahead to the docks, where the parties continue for hours. A legion of boats, which range from multimillion-dollar yachts to multihundred-dollar pieces of driftwood, turn on the music and begin the late night Figawi fun. The parties are typically open to anyone who wants to climb aboard and make new friends.

TRANSPORTATION

You can get to Nantucket by plane, ferry, or private boat. The traffic will be unavoidable, so plan travel for Thursday if possible.

AIR: You can fly into Nantucket Memorial Airport (ACK / www.nantucketairport.com) on Cape Air for approximately $230 dollars in addition to your regular Boston airfare. US Air makes the flight from Philadelphia, Washington, and Boston. Jet Blue has recently added a Nantucket route, which leaves from JFK Airport in New York. Taxis are available at this small airport.

You can also fly into Logan International Airport (BOS / www.massport.com/logan), rent a car, and drive to the ferry in Hyannis, Cape Cod. Without traffic the drive takes ninety minutes, however Memorial Day traffic could delay your progress by two hours. After rental car, gas, and frustration, you may have been better off flying directly into Nantucket.

FERRY: The Memorial Day ferries from Hyannis to Nantucket fill up extremely fast. There are a few different choices in mode of ferry, but reservations should be made well in advance for them all. You can park a vehicle in Hyannis or take your car on the ferry with you. It's recommended that you park in Hyannis unless you absolutely need a car in Nantucket.

Steamship Authority: The "slow" ferry takes passengers for $15 each way, and passengers plus vehicle for $180 on a two-hour ride. The "fast" ferry takes passengers for $29.50 plus an additional $6 for bicycles, on a one-hour ride. Check the ferry schedule and make reservations by calling 508-495-3278 or by visiting *www.steamshipauthority.com.*

Hy-Line Cruises: The one-hour "fast" ferry takes passengers for $38 per way, and bicycles for an additional $6. The "slow" ferry takes two hours and costs $37 for a round trip. Make all reservations by calling 800-492-8082 or by visiting *www.hy-linecruises.com.*

Freedom Cruise Line: Hyannis can be a mob scene. Avoid congestion by making a reservation on Freedom Cruise Line, from Harwich Port, Cape Cod. Harwich Port is located three exits from Hyannis (exit 10 from Route 6). This ferry takes one-hour and fifteen minutes and is a passenger-only boat that makes only one or two trips a day to Nantucket for $38 per way. Visit *www.nantucketislandferry.com* or call 508-432-8999 for reservations.

P PARKING: Depending on your ferry line, parking ranges from $10 to $15 per day.

T TAXIS: Taxis are very reliable and are available at the ferry docks, the airport, and along Main St. Local cab companies are All Point Taxi and Tours (508-228-5779) and Betty's Tour and Taxi Service (508-228-5786).

BICYCLE: This is an excellent way to get around the island, especially during a busy weekend. Rental shops are available, but bring your own if possible.

ACCOMMODATIONS

The island of Nantucket is absolutely packed over Memorial Day weekend. People begin to make reservations up to one year in advance,

although you will be safe if you reserve a room in February. Nantucket's accommodations tend to be inns and bed-and-breakfasts as opposed to chain hotels.

INNS: Try the Nantucket Inn (1 Millers Way / 508-228-6900 / $180), the Veranda House (3 Step Lane / 508-228-0695 / $219), 76 Main St. Inn (76 Main St. / 800-876-6858 / $215), and Jared Coffin House (29 Broad St. / 508-228-2400 / starts at $155). All are beautiful historic mansions.

B&BS: Bed-and-breakfasts include Centre Street Inn (78 Centre Street / 508-228-0199 / $350) and the Anchor Inn (66 Centre St. / 508-228-0072), which has rooms with twin beds for $225. Brant Point Inn (6 North Beach St. / 508-228-5442) was voted best bed-and-breakfast by a local publication.

TICKETS

The general public typically sticks to the watering holes, while the boat crews hole up at the ticketed-only tent party.

What to Pack
- Sailor's cap
- Compass
- Deck knowledge (e.g., starboard is the right side of the ship; port is the left)
- Money—Nantucket is *not* a bargain-shopper's paradise

party tip

The regatta started with the dense New England fog, which rolls in along the sailboat's course early in the morning. Racers in the 1970s, speaking with a thick Bostonian accent, asked "where the f—k ahh we?" This phrase was shortened to "Figawi."

New Hampshire

LACONIA MOTORCYCLE WEEK

⭐ Laconia, New Hampshire
Nine days in mid-June
www.laconiamcweek.com

With its countless covered bridges and deep forests, abundance of waterfalls, and rich Colonial history, New Hampshire is the essence of East Coast tranquility. Combine a relatively small population with the fact that it's far removed from major metropolises, and the "Live Free or Die" state calls for one heck of a laid-back lifestyle. Laconia is a tiny 17,000-person town that lies in the center of New Hampshire on the shores of Lake Winnipesaukee. Each June, the waters of Winnipesaukee begin to vibrate, slowly at first but with increasing force, as thousands of choppers rumble toward Laconia.

The first Laconia Motorcycle Week was held in 1916, making it the oldest and certainly the most scenic of any major motorcycle rally. It has grown to the point where residents batten down the hatches, put their earplugs in, and watch as 300,000 hogs roll into town.

Bikers are kindred spirits with a brotherly bond, a similar sense of purpose, and a shared passion for the open road. The streets of Laconia are brimming with the sound of rock 'n' roll music and gearhead hysterics throughout the nine-day rally, although the final four days are typically the wildest. A very helpful event website (*www .laconiamcweek.com*) breaks down the day's events to the precise minute. Nearby Weirs Beach, a great spot on the lake, is an immensely popular hangout and the morning meeting place for many of the bike rides. The Lobster Pound (Route 3, Weirs Beach) is a huge bar that's converted into biker bliss and has live music. Broken Spoke Saloon

(1072 Watson Rd., Laconia) bills itself as the "biggest biker bar on the face of the planet." Headlining bands such as Foghat and Steppenwolf play at the Meadowbrook Musical Arts Center in Gilford throughout the week.

Laconia is located next to some of the largest mountains on the East Coast, and the rally's hill-climbing events are worth checking out. The Gunstock Hill Climb at nearby Gunstock ski resort is the most popular. Racers charge up a steep seventy-meter hill to the top of the ski jump landing area, performing some intense and muddy wipeouts in the process. A must-do is the Ride to the Sky, during which bikers ascend 6,288 foot Mt. Washington, the highest mountain in the Northeast. The winding road to the peak closes to car traffic on Monday and Thursday mornings, providing bikers ample opportunity to gaze at the amazing views without worrying about a tailgating Ford Taurus.

TRANSPORTATION

Many of the events, bars, and attractions are located in neighboring towns, which are spread out approximately ten miles from Laconia. Although a motorcycle is preferable, you do not need to be a hardened biker to attend. Cars are fine—you'll have just as much fun hanging out at the rally.

AIR: The closest airport is Manchester Boston Regional Airport (MHT / *www.flymanchester.com*), located fifty-two miles from Laconia, although you may find cheaper flights into Boston's Logan International Airport (BOS / *www.massport.com/logan*) located 100 miles away. Car rentals are available at both.

ACCOMMODATIONS

HOTELS: There are hotels in Laconia, Weirs Beach, Gilford, Lake Port, Winnisquam, Ashland, Meredith, and other neighboring towns. Spaces fill up fast, rates are raised during Bike Week, and making reservations a year in advance is not a bad idea. Many bikers make reservations for the next year's rally as they are leaving the current year's event. Most hotels have a five-night minimum during Motorcycle Week. In Laconia try the Landmark Inn (480 Main St. / 603-524-8000 / $134), the Margate on Winnipesaukee (76 Lake St. / 603-524-5210 / $119), or the Naswa Resort (1086 Weirs Blvd. / 603-366-4341 / $199). In Weirs Beach is Christmas Island Resort (630 Weirs Blvd. / 603-366-4378 / $99), Lazy E Motor Inn (808 Weirs Blvd. / 603-366-4003 / $178 or seven-day package for $1,250), Cottages at Tower Hill (Rt. 3 / 603-366-5525 / $90), and Cedar Lodge (Rt. 3 / 603-366-4316 / $69). Visit *www.laconiamcweek.com* for a further listing of hotels in neighboring towns.

CAMPING: Campgrounds are a popular choice among partygoers. Again, most campgrounds are making reservations for the next year's event as this one is ending. Campgrounds in Laconia will give priority to guests who've been staying with them for years, and oftentimes it's impossible to get in. Putting your name on a cancellation list is a good idea even if a specific area is full. However, by staying in a town five or ten miles outside of Laconia, you'll be guaranteed a much better night's sleep! Most sites charge between $50 and $100 per night, including full hookups for RVs and campers. Tent campsites are also available.

In Laconia is Paugus Bay Campground (96 Hillard Rd. / 603-366-4757), Hack-Ma-Tack Campground (Rt. 3 / 603-366-5877), and Gunstock (Rt. 11A / 603-293-4341). Four miles away in Meredith is Harbor Hill Camping Area (603-279-6910) and Clearwater Campground (26 Campground Rd. / 603-279-7761). Nearby Alton has Robert Knolls Campground (RR1 / 603-875-6388) and Green Tops Campground (96 Roberts Cove Rd. / 603-569-9878). For a further listing of area campsites visit *www.laconiabikeweek.net/camping*.

TICKETS

Many of the events during Motorcycle Week are free, although some of the contests require entrance fees for contestants. Tickets to the Loudon Classic bike races, held during the first three days of the celebration at the New Hampshire International Speedway, can be purchased at the gate for $13. The concerts at Meadowbrook Musical Arts Center tend to sell out, or come close. Visit *www.meadowbrook.net* to find out who's playing, and purchase tickets ahead of time.

What to Pack

- Camping equipment
- Ear plugs
- Dew rag
- Any T-shirt with a depiction of a skeleton on a motorcycle

party tip

Along with Illinois and Iowa, New Hampshire is one of three states with "no law" for motorcycle helmets. Many states require them for all riders, while others make them mandatory for motorcyclists under seventeen years of age. If you'd like to play a trick on a beefy, scary, biker dude, then just turn to him and say "Did ya hear that New Hampshire is going to start requiring helmets? Yep, this time next year we'll all get arrested if we show up to this thing without a helmet." Panic and anger are guaranteed to ensue. After that you're on your own.

New Jersey

A NIGHT IN VENICE

⊛ Ocean City, New Jersey
Second or third Saturday in July

One of the world's largest boat parades takes the Jersey shore by storm and lights up the Ocean City sky in the process. A Night in Venice is a magical evening for many East Coast vacationers who come to view this elaborate procession of boats in the bay. For many, the evening begins with oysters, champagne, and Italian opera—and ends with Jersey shore pizza and AC/DC.

The bridges into Ocean City are raised in the early evening, before the 6:30 P.M. parade start time. Be sure to get onto the island before this happens, or you will miss out. Starting at Longport Bridge and ending at Tennessee Avenue, 100 boats in all shapes and sizes parade in, each with a distinct theme. Some crews are dressed as the Beatles, while others suit up in the expected pirate garb. A variety of awards are given to boats with the best "flair." Over 300 bay-front houses participate as well, each being lit to the hilt, while hosting private soirées. It helps to know someone with bay-front property because crashing these parties is not an option.

More than 100,000 people of all ages infiltrate Ocean City during the Night in Venice. The Bayside Center (520 Bay Ave.) is the best place from which to view the parade, but a ticket must be purchased. Otherwise, head along the bay and join one of the gatherings of spectators that line the streets. Get somewhere early and stay, as traffic is pretty rough.

Any boat owner can register to sail. Another option is to board a party vessel that sails in the procession. Philadelphia Young Professional Singles group typically commandeers a barge and sells tickets. The Starfish boat always sails in the event; they boast the "best party on the water," broadcasting an FM classic rock radio show from the vessel, and selling tickets for $65 from 4:00 P.M. to 10:00 P.M. The Yacht Club (Bay and Battersea Rd.) throws a fun postparade dance party for all ages.

Ocean City is known for its mega-sized boardwalk, so leave some time to stroll down it. Hula Grill (940 Boardwalk) has the best eats along the 2.5 miles of pedestrian planks. Also, located just over the Ninth Street Bridge, Somers Point is where summertime lust comes to fruition for many of the enormous Night in Venice crowd. Crab Trap (2 Broadway) is an awesome joint with live music, and Charlie's (800 Shore Rd.) is a legendary local hot spot with the best wings at the shore. And it's always party time at Caroline's (450 Bay Ave.), with its huge deck and good-looking patrons.

TRANSPORTATION

✈ **AIR:** Fly into Philadelphia International Airport (PHL / *www.phl.org*) located an hour and ten minutes away or into Atlantic City International Airport (ACY / *www.acairport.com*) located forty

minutes away. Car-rental agencies are available at both airports.

ACCOMMODATIONS

◐ **MOTELS /** ◼ **HOTELS:** Motels and hotels include Coral Sands Motel (Ninth and Atlantic Ave. / 609-399-4540 / $189, 2 night min.), Bryn Mawr Hotel (724 Ocean Ave. / 609-399-8744 / $139), Bellevue Hotel (701 E. Eighth Ave. / 609-399-0110 / rate unavailable), Biscayne Suites (820 Ocean Ave. / 609-391-8800 / $289), Ocean Seven Motel (Seventh and Boardwalk / 609-398-2200 / rate unavailable), Watson's Regency Suites (901 Ocean Ave. / 609-398-4300 / $289), and Ocean Manor Hotel (Eleventh and Ocean Ave. / 609-399-1014 / $115). Visit *www.njoceancity.com* for further options.

🏠 **RENTAL HOMES:** While there are a fair share of motor lodges, motels, and hotels, houses are available to rent. One-bedroom units start at approximately $1,000 per week, two bedrooms go for $1,500, and three bedrooms start at $2,000. Visit *www.buyoceancitynj.com* or *www.vrbo.com* and book early in the summer.

TICKETS

If you wish to view the procession from the grandstands, then buy a $7 ticket for the Bayside Center. These seats sell out, so call the City Hall Annex (901 Asbury Ave.) at 609-525-9300 to purchase early. Gates open at 5:00 P.M., and a shuttle bus runs spectators from a free parking lot at twenty-sixth and Bay Ave. to the Bayside Center. The shuttle runs until midnight.

A ticket aboard the Starfish Party Boat costs $65. This six-hour cruise sails in the parade and leaves at 4:00 P.M., returning at 10:00 P.M. The boat sells out early—call 609-263-3800 or visit *www.starfishboats.com/night_in_venice.html* by May.

Those who want to enter their boat in the parade must fill out the entry form and submit it one week prior at the latest. Visit *www.njocean city.com* to download a form. You'll have a choice to enter over twenty categories of boat decoration, and a $500 prize is awarded to winners.

party tip

Shoobies is a term you will often hear during the summer months at the Southern New Jersey shore. This condescending regional slang refers to the weekend tourists who flock to the beach and cause major congestion from May to September. It was coined in the 1920s, when city folk packed their lunch in a shoebox for an oceanside picnic. These days, a shoobie is a pale weekend warrior who wears aqua socks and a colorful swim suit to the beach yet has no interest in surfing or swimming.

IRISH WEEKEND

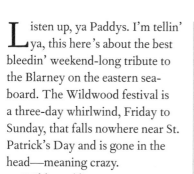

⊛ **Wildwood, New Jersey**
Third weekend in September
www.paddyswell.com/irishweekend

Listen up, ya Paddys. I'm tellin' ya, this here's about the best bleedin' weekend-long tribute to the Blarney on the eastern seaboard. The Wildwood festival is a three-day whirlwind, Friday to Sunday, that falls nowhere near St. Patrick's Day and is gone in the head—meaning crazy.

Wildwood lives up to its name as the wildest Jersey shore town, by throwing one last summer party before Old Man Winter drives beachgoers back to the city. As many as 250,000 Philadelphia-area residents, aged eighteen to sixty, descend upon the shore for an off-season Celtic bash that would knock the socks off St. Patrick himself.

The festival takes place in North Wildwood, specifically the Anglesea section, during the third weekend in September. Olde New Jersey Avenue, the city's main drag, is completely shut down to auto traffic for three days. Parades, dancing shows, and vendors line the streets from midday Friday until late

Sunday night. Head to the enormous party tent at the inlet, which hosts stellar Irish bands from 4:30 P.M. to 2:00 A.M. on Friday, 12:00 P.M. to 2:00 A.M. on Saturday, and 12:00 P.M. to 10:00 P.M. on Sunday. Black Thorn, considered by many to be the weekend's best band, is a fixture at Irish Weekend. Check the event website for times and location. The $10–$15 admission wristband includes food and drink.

Drinking and walking the streets is not considered a moving violation during this frolic. Beer stands are more common than fish 'n' chip vendors on Olde New Jersey Avenue. Each bar is filled with live music. Try the Anglesea Pub (First St. and Olde New Jersey Ave.), Keenan's Irish Pub (113 Olde New Jersey Ave.), or Westy's Irish Pub (101 E. Walnut), although you cannot lose anywhere.

TRANSPORTATION

AIR: Book flights into Philadelphia International Airport (PHL / *www.phl.org*) located an hour and a half away or into Atlantic City International Airport (ACY / *www.acairport.com*) located forty-five minutes away. Car-rental agencies are available at both airports.

TAXIS: Don't be surprised to see pink taxis, a Wildwood transportation staple. Local cab companies include Checker Cab (609-522-1431),

Costal Cab Co. (609-523-8900), Wildwood Cab (609-729-1911), and Yellow Cab (609-522-0555).

BUS: The New Jersey Transit Authority runs buses to Wildwood from various stops in New Jersey and Philadelphia. Visit *www.njtransit.com* for schedules and fares.

ACCOMMODATIONS

Wildwood has an enormous number of accommodations. Most are throwbacks to the 1950s, when L-shaped "doo-wop" architecture was the style of choice and room service was a hot dog on the boardwalk. You'll have a choice between motels (rather than newer hotels), bed-and-breakfasts, or rental homes. North Wildwood rooms fill fast, so book early.

MOTELS: Motels in North Wildwood include Florentine Family Motel (Nineteenth and Surf Ave. / 609-522-4075 / $125), Sand Castle Motel (7400 Ocean Ave. / 609-522-6946 / $125), Daytona Days Inn (4610 Ocean Ave. / 609-522-0331 / $135), and Sea Foam Motel (4110 Atlantic Ave. / 609-522-3765 / $72). Visit *www.wildwoodsnj.com/accommodations* for further options.

B&BS: Try Candlelight Inn (2310 Central Ave. / 609-522-6200 / $169), Sea Gypsy Bed & Breakfast (209 E. Magnolia Ave. / 609-522-0690 / $100), Enchantress Bed & Breakfast (2814 Atlantic Ave. / 609-523-1101 / $130), or the Cameo Rose (109 E. Twenty-fourth Ave. / 609-523-8464 / $125).

RENTAL HOMES: Renting a house with a group of friends is often the most affordable and most enjoyable way to go. Two-bedroom condos, which sleep five to seven people, average $1,100 for the week. Town homes are $1,500 and houses typically cost $2,000, although prices are all over the board. Most owners want to rent for the week; however this is not always the case. Check *www.vacationrentals.com* or *www.vrbo.com* for a range of options.

This is not a ticketed event; however you'll have to cough up $15 to enter the party tents. It's an experience well worth the money.

party tip

Be on the lookout for the infamous green fire truck, which is usually parked close by and can be rented by the hour. Fire hoses have been replaced with keg spouts and a hot tub is perched on top. Also be aware of an undercover partygoer disguised as a policeman. Armed with a billy club and dressed as a cop, "Officer Dan" roams the streets each year writing phony disorderly conduct citations to first-time partygoers.

THE HUNT

⊛ **Far Hills, New Jersey**
Third weekend in October
www.farhillsrace.org

Gluttons from the tri-state area head to the pastures of New Jersey for a steeplechase with a reputation. Commonly referred to as "The Hunt," the Far Hills Race Meeting is New Jersey's premier social calendar event of the fall. For over eighty years, the Garden State's marathon day of lawn socialization and utter buffoonery has been a favorite among city dwellers and suburbanites alike.

The race takes place in north-central Jersey at Moreland Farms, an area distinguished by wide-open, lush, green rolling hills. Far Hills has a population of just 859 people, but on race day the city expands to over 50,000. The majority of partygoers pour in from Hoboken, New York City, and surrounding suburbs. There are two main viewing spots at this informal race course, one being a hilltop corporate area and the other being the infield. As with many horse races, the infield is party central.

Tailgating begins at 8:00 A.M., although the races don't start until

1:00 P.M. This preppy crowd knows how to celebrate, so get some sleep the night before. The infield parking lot scene is comprised of loads of small canopies, where groups of ten to twenty friends create a home base from which they gallivant throughout the day. The Hunt is a BYOB party; don't expect beverage or food vendors. Bands play before the races, and unlike other steeplechases, spectators can wander from tent to tent without having to flash a tailgate-specific wristband. If you have a large group, then purchase at least four bales of hay when reserving your tailgating tent because the grounds get very muddy. The event website has a catering link—don't cart your supplies to the race.

The main event of the day is the single most famous steeplechase race in the country, the Breeder's Cup. Although most spectators watch the first five races halfheartedly, people tend to perk up for this event.

The race ends at dark, resulting in a mass exodus toward the train station and party buses. Far Hills has its own train stop, making this the transport of choice back to New York City and Hoboken,

New Jersey. It is recommended that you stay in one of these cities, because the train ride home is a party in and of itself. Get to the station as early as possible to grab a seat, or you'll be standing the entire way back. In Hoboken, Madison's Bar and Grill (1316 Washington St.), Liberty Bar (61 Fourteenth St.), Whiskey Bar (125 Washington St.), and City Bistro (56 Fourteenth St.) are the postrace hangouts.

TRANSPORTATION

✦ **AIR:** If staying in Hoboken or Manhattan, then book flights into Newark Airport (EWR / *www.newarkairport.com*), LaGuardia (LGA / *www.laguardiaairport.com*), or JFK Airport (JFK / *www.kennedyairport.com*). Occasionally fares will be much less at one of the three, and taxi fares are similar.

🚆 **TRAIN:** The absolute best way to avoid traffic, avoid driving, and get to and from the race quickly. Extra trains run during the Hunt, making the ninety-minute ride as smooth as possible.

From Hoboken: New Jersey Transit runs twelve trains between 8:05 A.M. and 12:05 P.M. from Hoboken Station to Far Hills Station.

From NYC: Six midtown trains run on the hour between 7:11 A.M. and 12:11 P.M. from Penn Station to Summit Station. You must transfer at Summit Station to continue to Far Hills.

To Hoboken: Twelve trains depart Far Hills Station every ten minutes between 4:30 P.M. and 7:00 P.M.

To NYC: Get on one of the New Jersey Transit trains and take to Summit Station. From Summit, six trains will depart between 4:42 P.M. to 7:42 P.M.

Ⓑ PARTY BUSES: You also have the option of reserving a party bus to run your group from New York City or Hoboken to Far Hills and back. These private charters can carry large groups, typically allow horseplay, and tend to be quite comfortable, plus you can carry your food and beverages aboard. The downside is dealing with traffic. A full day's rental typically costs at least $800. Try Fantasy Charter Bus (632-921-4835), Metropolitan Shuttle (866-556-3545), or On Time Limo (888-425-6878).

ACCOMMODATIONS

▇ **HOTELS:** There aren't hotels in Hoboken; however, they're just a couple of miles away in Jersey City and Weehawken. In Jersey City try Courtyard Marriott (540 Washington Blvd. / 201-626-6600 / $209), Hilton Doubletree (455 Washington Blvd. / 201-499-2400 / $229), and Candlewood Suites (21 –Second St. / 201-659-2500 / $180). In Weehawken are Sheraton Suites (500 Harbor Blvd. / 201-617-5600 / $324) and Park Avenue Hotel (60 Forty-eighth St. / 201-330-9494 / $75). Visit *www.orbitz.com* for further information.

From New York you can stay just about anywhere. Logistically it's best to stay in midtown, which is close to Penn Station. Midtown hotels include Holiday Inn (440 W. Fifty-seventh St. / 212-581-8100 / $331), Comfort Inn (129 W. Forty-sixth St. / 212-221-2600 / $300), and Best Western (234 W. Forty-eighth St. / 212-246-8800 / $350). Of course, the closer to Madison Square Garden, the better.

TICKETS

To reserve a tent space on the infield, which is recommended for ample fun, visit the event website and click on "reserved parking," or call 908-685-2929. These spaces cost $500, include one parking space and four admission badges, and are tax deductible. Purchase at least four bales of hay at $15 per bail. Reservations should be made by midsummer. You do not need a car to reserve an infield parking space.

General parking passes serve an off-infield lot, and can be purchased on the event website for $30. General admission, for those who purchased a general parking pass or who are too cheap to pony up for a tent, is $50. These tickets can be purchased at the gate on race day.

What to Pack
- Warm clothing
- Bocce balls
- Boots or shoes that won't get ruined in mud
- Tolerance for obnoxious Jersey guys

---

party tip

Betting on horses is prohibited at the Far Hills Race Meeting, although it is nearly impossible to put rowdy New Yorkers and horses together without some kind of illegal activity taking place. An under-the-table, low-stakes, off-track betting scene is very much alive, so bring cash. Be sure to pick up a program beforehand to give yourself the best shot.

New York

MERMAID PARADE

⭐ **Coney Island, New York**
First Saturday after summer solstice
www.coneyisland.com/mermaid.shtml

During Coney Island's heyday, in the 1930s through the 1950s, city dwellers went there to hit the beach, enjoy the amusement rides, and escape big-city life. From 1903 to 1954 Coney Island's Mardi Gras party was one of the hottest tickets in town. But like many great parties, attendance dwindled over time, until eventually the gathering ceased to exist. A resurrection of the forgotten Mardi Gras blowouts of yesteryear occurred in 1983, when a new twist was added: mermaids.

The Mermaid Parade pays tribute to the sand, the sea, the salt, and the air while attracting about 100,000 people and kicking off the beginning of summer in the Big Apple. Show up in street clothes and you'll end up feeling like a fish out of water during the nation's largest art parade and one of New York's most cherished celebrations.

Arrive on Saturday for the parade, which begins at 2:00 P.M. with a well-rested photo-taking finger. Expect to see the most elaborate sea-creature and underwater-god costumes that you can imagine. This gathering is all about self-expression, so paint your body, become your character, and don't act surprised when topless mermaids walk by. The parade, comprised of floats, marching bands, and characters on foot, starts on West Tenth Street, moves to West Sixteenth Street, heads north toward Surf Avenue, turns east on Surf, and ends on West Tenth. Feel free to hang out on the boardwalk, which offers very good views of the procession. If you'd like to march in the parade, then register on the event website or show up before 10:00 A.M. on Saturday, when registration ends.

The parade concludes at about 5:30 P.M., but you have many other options throughout the course of the day. If you've had your fill of floats and trumpets, then head to the beach and join the fun on the Coney Island sand. You can also stroll over to the amusement park and ride the legendary Cyclone roller coaster, perhaps the most famous ride in American amusement park history. Be sure to satisfy your appetite at world famous Nathan's Hot Dogs, home of the biggest annual hot dog eating contest in the world.

No matter how you occupy yourself during the day, be sure to get your tail to the Mermaid Parade Ball at 6:00 P.M. This whale of an aquatic dance party has recently been taking place at the Child's Restaurant Building on the boardwalk (at West Twenty-first St.) but it tends to move around each year—*www.mermaidparade ball.com* will post the exact location. An assortment of bands and DJs take the stage and burlesque dancers provide the backdrop as the partying reaches its peak. Officially the ball shuts down at midnight. Unofficially the mayhem continues in downtown Coney Island, on the boardwalk, as well as on the beach until the wee hours.

TRANSPORTATION

SUBWAY: Do not, under any circumstances, even dream of driving a car to this event. Stay the weekend in New York City and take the subway. Hop on the D, F, N, or Q trains and get off at Stillwell Avenue in south Brooklyn. A cab ride from midtown costs $50 and will take much longer.

AIR: Book flights into LaGuardia International Airport (LGA / *www.laguardiaairport.com*), John F. Kennedy Airport (JFK / *www.jfk-airport.net*), or Newark International Airport (EWR / *www.newark airport.com*). All are very close to downtown, and taxis are abundant.

ACCOMMODATIONS

If you stay in the city, then one place is really no better than another, as the subway system is extremely efficient. Visit *www.nyctourist.com* or *www.quikbook.com* to find a hotel in your price range.

HOTELS: Although Coney Island does not have any hotels, there are a few within a ten-minute cab ride; The Golden Gate Motor Inn (3867 Shore Parkway / 718-743-4000 / $100), Best Western Hotel Gregory (8315 Fourth Ave. / 800-329-7234 / $220) and the Comfort Inn (3218 Emmons Ave. / 718-368-3334 / $180) are all located in Brooklyn.

TICKETS

Entrance to the parade is free. There is a $10 fee to march as a participant and a $150 fee to be a judge. Visit *www.coneyisland.com/mermaid .shtml* to register.

Tickets for the Mermaid Parade Ball cost $10 in advance at *www.mermaidparadeball.com* or $15 at the door. You can also purchase a $50 VIP ticket that includes free champagne, appetizers, gift bag, and access to a VIP lounge.

- -
What to Pack
- Camera
- Touch-up paint
- Your costume—which you should wear on the subway
- -

party tip

Women are confronted with an interesting decision regarding the most important piece of their attire, the mermaid skirt. The general sentiment is that the two best options are the "two-part ruffle" and the "princess-seamed" styles. Most designers agree that taller, more slender women seem to benefit from the two-part ruffle, which accentuates their hips and long legs. The princess-seamed skirt is more flattering to a woman who's shorter in stature because of its lack of horizontal seams. Men can also utilize this information when trying to convince their female friends to attend. If a man is questioned beyond this basic information he should excuse himself to the restroom.

HALLOWEEN IN NEW YORK CITY

⭐ Manhattan, New York
October 31
www.halloween-nyc.com

The last day in October is eagerly anticipated by both candy-motivated schoolchildren and mischievous adults. Halloween for grownups is part "hall pass" and part "get-out-of-jail-free card," as wild behavior can be easily dismissed due to the spirit of the holiday. Many would argue that Halloween in their city deserves a place in this book, but only a New Yorker can claim residence for the best October 31 bash in the nation.

The frenzy in uptown, midtown, and downtown is off the charts, through the roof, and out of the park. The party is anywhere and everywhere, the costumes are outrageous, and the rules are few. Nothing is censored, nothing is sacred, and the only taboo is to not wear a costume.

Although the entire Big Apple bears festive fruit on Halloween, the sweetest bite is in Greenwich Village. New York's annual Village Halloween Parade is the largest Halloween celebration in the world—period. This mega-sized costumed procession on steroids was voted "Best Event in the World" for October 31 by "Festivals International." Over 50,000 participants—including dancing skeletons, puppets, statues of liberty, monsters, storybook characters, chess pieces, decks of cards, bare-bottomed men in drag, papier-mâché works of art, and live bands—march a mile down Avenue of the Americas, while 2 million spectators line the streets to watch. The floats are as intense as they are amazing.

Watching the parade is mandatory, and participation is encouraged. The parade begins at 7:00 P.M. and ends at 10:00 P.M., the route being Sixth Avenue, from Spring Street to Twenty-first Street. Anyone who wishes to march can line up on Sixth Avenue between Broome and Spring streets. It takes two to four hours to enter the procession, but organizers recommend arrival by 6:00 P.M. The waiting area explodes into one gigantic preparade party. Many spectators line up two hours early to claim a curb-side

spot, climb a tree, or hang from a street sign for maximum viewing pleasure.

After the parade you should go somewhere and stay. The number of bar and nightclub parties is staggering; they're all great, and most charge a $15–$40 cover for the costume party. Stay in Greenwich Village for action-packed entertainment, or go to Jekyll and Hyde Bar (91 Seventh Ave. S.), a haunted Halloween hot spot; the Slaughtered Lamb Pub (182 W. Fourth St.), appropriate with its dungeons and gothic décor; or Mars 2112 (1633 Broadway), a place that you've got to see to believe. Located in Times Square, Mars is a spaceship-themed, bi-level, 35,000-square-foot, multidimensional, intergalactic watering hole. Call 212-582-2112 for Halloween party ticket information.

TRANSPORTATION

The city is more of a madhouse than usual on Halloween, and driving is not recommended. If you can take a train from New Jersey, then do so.

AIR: Book flights into LaGuardia International Airport (LGA / *www.laguardiaairport.com*), John F. Kennedy Airport (JFK / *www.jfk-airport.net*), or Newark International Airport (EWR / *www.newarkairport.com*). All are very close to downtown and taxis are abundant.

TAXIS: Put your hand in the air and whistle.

SUBWAY: This is the fastest and most efficient way to move about NYC. Purchase a 1-Day Fun Pass for $7, good until 3:00 A.M., rather than stopping to pay $2 for each ride. Take the 1, 2, and 3 lines to Fourteenth Street and Seventh Avenue. Take the A, B, C, D, E, F, and Q lines to West Fourth and Sixth avenues.

ACCOMMODATIONS

HOTELS: New York boasts many downtown haunted hotels with bloodcurdling tales behind each one. Guests at Best Western (33 Peck Slip / 212-766-6600 / $410) claim that the hotel toilet paper eerily folds itself into a triangular shape at the end of the roll. The ghastly phone at Holiday Inn (138 Lafayette St. / 212-966-6600 / $299) knows what room you're calling from when you reach out to the front desk. Televisions at Sheraton (811 Seventh Ave. at Fifty-third St. / 212-581-1000 / $579) always reset themselves to the same pay-per-view movie channel. The Marriott (85 West St. / 212-385-4900 / $499) beds are mysteriously made up at the end of the day, and chocolate bedside wafers appear from thin air each evening at Embassy Suites (102 North End Ave. / 212-945-0100 / $439). For a complete list of hotels visit *www.nyctourist.com*.

This excellent website breaks down price, customer ratings, and location.

TICKETS

Buying a ticket for a specific costume nightclub party is a good idea. Many fill fast and have long waiting lines, whereas others are open to ticket holders only. Slipping the door attendant some extra cash never hurts either.

What to Pack
- Costume
- Train schedule
- Platform boots

party tip

If traveling with four or more friends, consider theme-based outfits. Examples include the Seven Dwarfs, a rock group, or *Scooby Doo* characters. While this is fun and draws attention, it also assists with late-night barhopping. When your group has a common motif, door attendants are much less likely to only let one member of your group in the bar and make the others stand outside in line.

THE WORLD'S LARGEST DISCO

⊛ Buffalo, New York
Saturday after Thanksgiving
www.worldslargestdisco.com

As the polyester curtain began to close on the disco era in 1979, Buffalo, New York, staged one final solid gold, platform-shoe-pumpin', bellbottom blowout that landed itself in the *Guinness Book of World Records* as "the largest disco event" ever. Soon afterward, a generation of Bee Gees fans and *Saturday Night Fever* buffs threw their arms up in surrender, finding solace in the dulcet tones of Lionel Richie and Flock of Seagulls.

However, in 1994, a local nonprofit called Conesus Fest for Charity decided to resurrect the music and fashion that many felt would be best left dead. Buffalo Convention Center employees spit-shined the disco ball that had been boxed up fifteen years earlier, wheeled out the old eight-track player, and told the world "I Will Survive." Although the 1994 event drew only 1,800, it's now one of the most sought-after tickets in the Northeast. In fact, general admission and VIP passes are sold out just minutes after going on sale. The World's Largest Disco raises over $1 million for children affected by cancer, allowing entrance to 8,000 lucky boogiemen and soul sisters.

The disco takes place on Saturday night from 9:00 P.M. to 1:00 A.M. Dressing up in leisure suits, gold chains, and afro wigs is mandatory for men, while hot pants and platinum blonde hair is a must for women. Each year an assortment of 1970s "Where Are They Now"–type celebrities do "The Hustle" alongside average Vinnies. Recent attendees have included Erik Estrada, Danny Bonaduce, Lucy from *Dallas*, Potsie from *Happy Days*, Leif Garrett, and the *Brady Bunch* brothers. The event is often recorded and aired on VH-1.

Chippewa Street is the place to be after the final ABBA song has been played. Soho (64 W. Chippewa St.) is a trendy bar that attracts a good-looking younger crowd, while 67 West (67 W. Chippewa

St.) is a good time with a mixed clientele and party atmosphere. To keep on dancing, head to Level (75 W. Chippewa St.), a multilevel dance bar that's always hopping.

And a visit to Buffalo isn't complete without a trip to Anchor Bar (1047 Main St.), the place that invented the original Buffalo Hot Wing, although locals tend to think that the wings at Duff's (3651 Sheridan Dr.) may have them beat.

TRANSPORTATION

AIR: Book flights into Buffalo Niagara International Airport (BUF / www.buffaloairport.com), located nine miles from the Buffalo Convention Center. Car rentals and taxis are available.

TAXIS: Buffalo taxi companies include Yellow Cab (716-877-5400), Liberty Cab (716-877-7111), Buffalo Taxicab (716-822-3030), and Cold Spring Taxi (716-866-4900).

LIMOUSINE: The official limo of the World's Largest Disco is the Esquire / Zoladz Limousine (866-937-4410), the state's longest and largest limo company. Mention the party for special pricing.

BUS / TRAIN: The Greyhound bus station is located in nearby Kenmore at 149 Keller Avenue. The Amtrak station is located at 75 Exchange Street in Buffalo.

ACCOMMODATIONS

HOTELS: Downtown hotels near the convention center include Holiday Inn (620 Delaware Ave. / 716-886-2121 / $124), Comfort Suites (601 Main St. / 716-854-5500 / $155), Best Western (510 Delaware Ave. / 716-886-8333 / $139), Adam's

Mark (120 Church St. / 716-845-5100 / $129), Hampton Inn (220 Delaware Ave. / 716-855-2223 / $139), and Hyatt Regency (2 Fountain Plaza / 716-856-1234 / $135). The most upscale hotel in the city is the Mansion on Delaware Avenue (414 Delaware Ave. / 716-886-3300 / $185).

TICKETS

Tickets go on sale in October and can be purchased through the event website or Ticketmaster—they have been selling out within twenty minutes. Check www.worldslargestdisco.com in September for specific dates. Six thousand general admission tickets are sold for approximately $50 apiece, although they can be found for as high as $200 on eBay. 1,000 VIP tickets go for $100 each. They include one-hour early admission, discounted drinks, complimentary hors d'oeuvres, access to a VIP dance party, and the opportunity to meet the celebrities from 8:30 P.M. to 9:30 P.M.

What to Pack
- Flowered shirt (unbuttoned to the navel)
- Humongous collar
- Tight baby-blue pants
- Gold platform shoes
- Gloria Gaynor's greatest hit(s?)

party tip

If there was ever an opportunity to stuff a sock down your pants, this is it. Just make sure that it's a striped tube sock, because that's what they wore in the '70s. A number of Buffalo-area clothing shops carry enough disco garb to convert the Buffalo Convention Center into Studio 54. Some great ones to stop in for last-minute costumes include DC Theatricks (747 Main St., Buffalo), Divine Finds (801 Elmwood Ave., Buffalo), Betsy Ross Costumes (9670 Main St., Clarence), and Arlene's Costumes (1225 Portland Ave., Rochester).

Pennsylvania

MUMMERS DAY PARADE

⭐ Philadelphia, Pennsylvania
January 1
www.mummers.com

The City of Brotherly Love does have its eccentricities, and the Mummers Day Parade ranks at the top of the list. This New Year's Day event is a long-standing, colorful tradition that has been woven deeply into the fabric of Philadelphia over the past 100 years. It's as much a part of the city as the Liberty Bell, Rocky movies, and cheesesteaks—combined.

This one-of-a-kind parade began in 1901, although its roots can be traced to a pagan ritual that crossed the Atlantic Ocean when the British settled in Philadelphia. Since its inception, the central figure of the parade, the "mummer," has evolved into a larger-than-life character in the greater Philadelphia area. The average mummer spends 364 days a year developing his musical routine, building sets, and rehearsing his appearance in the parade. However, for one day in January, the mummer captures all the fame and glory of a rock star in the Keystone State. His goal is not to win the prize money, but rather to win bragging rights for his "club," or cohort of area entertainers. Many of these clubs date back decades, and their fierce rivalries contribute to an extraordinarily high level of performance art.

The costumes are spectacles in and of themselves, some costing thousands of dollars and hundreds of hours to create. The results are massive, flamboyant getups that fall somewhere between circus clown suits and Liberace's stage attire. The Mummers Day Parade is an absolute must-see for the true-blue holiday season on the eastern seaboard. The parade begins at 9:00 A.M. at Broad Street and Washington Avenue, as the first wave of over 15,000 mummers begin to strut their stuff down the streets of Philadelphia in front of a million freezing spectators.

The mummers aren't the only ones who dress up. Showing up in jeans and a sweatshirt is an easy way to miss out. Don the most outrageous, colorful, shiny outfit you own; throw in a boa; and paint your face however you choose! There are no rules for this party. The parade lasts eight hours, as the different types of mummers (comics, fancy brigades, and string bands) move in their own unique style toward the end point, at City Hall. This is the best place from which to observe.

TRANSPORTATION

AIR: Fly into Philadelphia International Airport (PHL / www.phl.org) and grab a cab for the quick ride into Philly.

TRAIN: Philadelphia's Regional Rail system is an excellent means of maneuvering about the city, especially during the parade. The R1 through R8 trains radiate out from center city to the north, south, northwest, southwest, and west. The R1 comes into center city from the airport. The PATCO line comes in from New Jersey. Visit the Septa (Southeastern Pennsylvania Transportation Authority) website at www.septa.org to download complete train schedules. Customer service can be reached at 215-580-7800.

SUBWAY: There are two subway lines that stop at Center City / City Hall. The Market-Frankfort Line starts at Front Street, near the river, and goes west. The Broad Street Line begins at Patterson Avenue and travels north. Complete subway routes can be downloaded on the Septa website.

TAXIS: Taxis are in abundance at the airport and throughout the city. Stay away from car-rental agencies unless you plan on leaving the city.

ACCOMMODATIONS

HOTELS: Options within a short walk to the festivities include the Sofitel Philadelphia (120 S. Seventeenth St. / 215-569-8300 / $265), Doubletree Hotel Philadelphia (237 S. Broad St. / 215-893-1600 / $289), the Courtyard Marriott Downtown (21 N. Juniper St. / 215-496-3200 / $239), Loews Philadelphia Hotel (1200 Market St. / 215-231-7301 / $179), Rodeway Inn (1208 Walnut St. / 215-546-7000 / $179), and Alexander Inn (Twelfth and Spruce / 215-923-3535 / $109). The website www.orbitz.com has competitive rates for many Philadelphia hotels.

TICKETS

Sidewalk seating is best at the drill points, where the string brigades and fancy brigades stop to perform. These are typically located at the intersections of Broad Street and Locust, Pine, Washington, Tasker, Wolf / Ritner, Mifflin / McKean, and Shunk. The drill points tend to change each year. If there isn't room, then try Broad Street and Washington Avenue (comics, 9:00 A.M.), Broad Street and Snyder Avenue (fancies, 10:00 A.M.), or Broad Street and Oregon Avenue (string bands, 11:00 A.M.).

You can also purchase tickets to watch from bleachers at the judge's area in front of City Hall (Fifteenth and Market St.) or at the visitor center (215-965-7676) at Sixth and Market St. for $14.50. These are the best seats in town.

The fancy brigades hold two ticketed competitions, which take place at the Philadelphia Convention Center at 12:00 P.M. and 5:00 P.M. Purchase tickets on *www.ticketphiladelphia.org* or call 215-893-1999.

party tip

Philadelphians constantly argue over who makes the city's greatest cheesesteak. This debate has been raging for years and often ends in fisticuffs. Most do agree that the two genius creators of this steak and Cheez Wiz delicacy are Pat's and Geno's, located directly across the street from one another (where Ninth St. crosses Warton and Passyunk in South Philly). No matter which joint you end up at, there are a couple of important rules to follow when placing your order. Never say the word *cheesesteak* or you'll stick out like a sore thumb. Use *wit* or *witout* to convey your desire for onions (not *with* or *without*). A *wiz wit* is the most common order, meaning Cheez Wiz and onions. A *provolone witout* is a provolone cheesesteak without onions. Never say please or thank you. A simple *Gimme a wiz wit* will suffice. Order incorrectly and you will be banished to the end of the line.

GROUNDHOG DAY

⊛ Punxsutawney, Pennsylvania
February 2
www.groundhog.org

In the hierarchy of TV news personalities, weather forecasters are seldom afforded the respect reserved for their lead anchor counterparts. To add insult to injury, there's a weather-predicting woodchuck in Punxsutawney, Pennsylvania, who makes a college degree in meteorology look like a GED. Punxsutawney Phil, the only groundhog to ever draw a rock-concert-like audience, has been forecasting the length of winter with astonishing accuracy since 1887—and he doesn't need Doppler radar or a TelePrompTer to do so.

Scores of men, women, and children from all corners of the United States congregate at Gobbler's Knob on Groundhog Day, to watch as the most famous rodent in the land awakens from his winter slumber.

From the 1970s to the late 1990s, the second day of February was a rager at Gobbler's Knob. It seemed as though the entire Penn State campus, plus students from dozens of smaller Pennsylvania colleges, arrived in town on February 1 in RVs and campers. The tradition was to tap kegs, build bonfires, and party all night long until the 7:25 A.M. soothsaying time. The college crowd's antics eventually wore thin on the Punxsutawney Chamber of Commerce, as well as with innocent bystanders who hadn't been downing whiskey for nine consecutive hours. In order to re-establish a cleaner atmosphere, Gobbler's Knob now closes until 3:00 A.M. on February 2, and alcohol is prohibited.

While these restrictions may have curtailed the behavior of a few, the decision to make Groundhog Day more family-friendly has fostered a rebirth of this celebration and kept the Punxsutawney spirit intact. This event remains so unique and such a piece of Americana that simply witnessing it is more than just adding a check to the "I did that" column. Park at a series of Punxsutawney parking lots between 3:00 A.M. and 5:30

A.M. and catch the shuttle to Gobbler's Knob. Once at "the Knob," huddle around a bonfire and observe the mass of 20,000 eager spectators who've been collectively showing up for over 120 years.

At first light of the frosty Pennsylvania morning, the "Inner Circle" gathers upon the stage, surrounding Phil's famous tree stump. Sporting top hats, the keepers of the "prognosticator of prognosticators" knock three times upon the wooden door, and they pull the beast out from his lair. The crowd explodes with cheering and applause upon seeing the furry rock star. After a brief ceremony, the merry marmot makes his forecast. When Phil does not see his shadow it means the coming of an early spring, with the crowd responding favorably. When he sees his shadow, plan for six more weeks of winter, and a disappointed audience on Gobbler's Knob. Phil's prognostication has never been wrong—neither has a once-in-a-lifetime trip to Punxsutawney.

TRANSPORTATION

✈ **AIR:** Pittsburgh International Airport (PIT / *www.pitairport.com*) is the closest major airport, located an hour and a half away. You can also fly into smaller DuBois Jefferson County Regional Airport (DUJ / www.dujairport.com), located twenty minutes from Punxsutawney. U.S. Air is the lone carrier, and flights will cost an additional $150–$200.

P PARKING / SHUTTLES: You can walk one and a half miles to Gobbler's Knob from centrally located Barclay Square, or you can park and take a shuttle. Shuttles run from four separate locations between 3:00 A.M. and 6:30 A.M. To be safe, you should board a shuttle no later than 5:30 A.M. Shuttle pickup points are: The alley off West Mahoning Street downtown, the County Market in the Groundhog Plaza off 119 (from the north), the Wal-Mart along 119 (from the south), and the Punxsy Plaza off West Mahoning Street. Shuttles following the ceremony will run every fifteen minutes between 8:00 A.M. and 2:00 P.M. The ride costs $5 per person or $10 per family.

ACCOMMODATIONS

HOTELS: There are a number of interesting activities in town from February 1 to February 3, and spending the night and checking out the groundhog culture can be fun. People begin to make reservations for next year's event as soon as this year's event ends, and hotels always sell out. In Punxsutawney try Hotel Punxsutawney (108 N. Findley St. / 814-938-8182 / $75), Pantall Hotel (135 E. Mahoning St. / 814-938-6600 / e-mail jane@pantallhotel.com for rates), the Hunter's Lodge (20652 Rt. 119 / 814-939-7371 / $150), Jackson Run Bed & Breakfast (363 Jackson Run Rd. / 814-938-2315 / $75), and Plantation Bed & Breakfast (20652 Rt. 119 / 814-939-7371 / $85), which is part of the Hunter's Lodge. Neighboring towns like DuBois and Brookville have common chain hotels. Visit www.punxsutawney.com for a complete listing of area accommodations.

What to Pack
- Warm clothes
- Thermos
- "Phil for President" button

party tip

The average lifespan for groundhogs is six to eight years. Phil, on the other hand, has been alive and kicking since 1887. The secret to his longevity lies in the "elixir of life," from which the animal drinks each summer. The ingredients to this magical punch have never been divulged; but rumor has it that the concoction is comprised of Gatorade and Viagra.

Rhode Island

NEWPORT FOLK FESTIVAL

⊛ Newport, Rhode Island
First weekend in August
www.newportfolk.com

The Newport Folk Festival has as rich and interesting a history as any musical event in the country. As one of the nation's longest-running festivals, its stages have been graced by the greats of three generations worth of pop-culture icons. Although the event fell on hard times in the past, it has recently enjoyed a rebirth, and has become one of the top folk gatherings in the land.

Newport Folk attained instant popularity among the beatnik and folk crowds following its inception in 1959. Artists like Joan Baez and Bob Dylan headlined the early concerts, and famous performances by Johnny Cash and Howlin' Wolf provided exposure to fans of country and the blues. The festival's most notorious and well-known moment came in 1965, when crowd favorite Bob Dylan plugged in his guitar and played electric for the first time. This controversial decision was met with boos from a hostile audience who didn't approve of their hero abandoning his folk roots for rock 'n' roll. Of course, the transition proved to be a good one for Mr. Dylan, who has continually toured ever since.

The festival's unique warm-up show takes place on Friday night of the first weekend in August at the Newport Casino at the International Tennis Hall of Fame, a breathtaking mansion surrounded by lush grounds and an open-air concert area. A midsize headliner, which in 2007 was Linda Ronstadt, hits the stage while the audience mingles on the lawn.

Saturday's and Sunday's concerts are held at a venue of unparalleled beauty on the banks of Newport Harbor. Fort Adams

State Park gives concertgoers the opportunity to bask in the sunshine as sailboats cruise by, all the while listening to fabulous tunes. Although this is a folk festival, that term is loosely applied at Newport—recent performers have included the Dirty Dozen Brass Band, Grace Potter and the Nocturnals, and North Mississippi Allstars. Arts and crafts vendors line the outskirts of the grounds, and the crowd, which only numbers 10,000–15,000, provides for a pleasant midsized experience. The festival is sponsored by Dunkin' Donuts, and although the Newport Folk Festival of the 1960s would've gaped at the suggestion of displaying corporate logos, this sponsor has done a magnificent job of maintaining a connection to the past.

Board a water taxi after the shows and make a beeline to Newport's lively downtown scene. Thames Street, America's Cup Avenue, Memorial Boulevard, and Bellevue Avenue house the hot spots.

TRANSPORTATION

Newport is a charming coastal city with quaint cobblestone streets and ideal shopping, restaurant, and bar options. You don't need a car to attend the festival, but you may want to explore the area by car.

✈ **AIR:** The closest airport is TF Green International Airport (PVD / *www.pvdairport.com*), located forty minutes away in Warwick, Rhode Island. Boston's Logan International Airport (BOS / *www.massport.com/logan*) is an hour and a half away. Major car-rental agencies are available at both.

🚐 **AIRPORT SHUTTLE:** Cozy Cab offers excellent shuttle service between TF Green Airport and Newport for $20 per person each way. Buses run door to door every hour. Visit *www.cozytrans.com* or call 800-846-1502 for information and reservations.

🚕 **TAXIS:** Newport's cab companies include Cozy Cab (401-846-1500), Newport Pedicab (401-432-5498), Newport City Taxi (401-662-1407), and Moriarty's Taxi (401-841-0030).

🅑 **BUS / 🚆 TRAIN:** The closest Greyhound station is located thirty-three miles away in Providence at 1 Kennedy Plaza. The Amtrak station is eighteen miles away at 1 Railroad Avenue in West Kingston.

🅟 **PARKING:** Fort Adams lots charge $6 per car. A free shuttle carries concertgoers from the upper lots to the main gate.

🛥 **WATER TAXIS:** You can park a car at a downtown Newport lot and hitch a ride on a water taxi. Boats depart from the water taxi dock opposite from the Visitor's Center (23 America's Cup Ave.) regularly from 8:00 A.M.—they charge $5 each way.

ACCOMMODATIONS

🏨 **HOTELS:** Book hotel rooms well in advance as Newport summer weekends sell out fast. Hotels include Marriott (25 America's Cup Ave. / 401-849-1000 / $495), Best Western (151 Admiral Kalbfus

Rd. / 401-849-9880 / $209), Chanler Hotel (117 Memorial Blvd. / 401-847-1300 / $795), Harbor Base Pineapple Inn (372 Coddington Hwy. / 401-847-2600 / $130), Hyatt Regency (1 Goat Island / 401-851-1234 / $469), Newport Harbor Hotel and Marina (49 America's Cup Ave. / 401-847-9000 / $399), Motel 6 (249 J.T. Connell Hwy. / 401-848-0600 / $100), and Wyndham Inn on the Harbor (359 Thames St. / 401-849-6789 / $150).

📫 **INNS:** Beautiful inns and bed-and-breakfasts are abundant—visit *www.gonewport.com* for options.

🔥 **CAMPING:** The nearest campground is Melville Ponds Campground in Portsmouth, located ten minutes away. Tent camping is $25 per night and full RV hookup spaces cost $35. Call 401-682-2424 for reservations.

TICKETS

Tickets go on sale in late April. Three-day passes cost $135 and include a reserved lawn seat for Friday night and general admission passes for Saturday and Sunday at Fort Adams. Two-day passes for Fort Adams events sell out fast at $95.

Single-day general admissions at Fort Adams cost $55, and Friday night at the International Tennis Hall of Fame costs $50. Reserved seating, which gets you close to the stage, costs $75 per day at the Fort Adams shows. Call Ticketweb at 866-468-7619 to purchase, or download an order form from the event website.

What to Pack
- Low-backed chair
- Blanket
- Bob Dylan's *Blood on the Tracks*
- Affinity for the perfect bowl of clam chowder

party tip

Newport is home to the greatest clam chowder in the country, bar none. Many eateries display signs boasting the best in town, but locals head to the Chowder Bowl at Nye Beach (728 NW Beach Dr.) for an award-winning bowl of creamy chowda that has been known to render first-time tasters speechless.

Vermont

MAGIC HAT MARDI GRAS BLOCK PARTY

⭐ Burlington, Vermont
Mid- to late February
www.magichat.net

Georgia is known for its peaches, California has the country's top wine region, and the great state of Vermont is the front-running northeastern exporter of two American staples: ice cream and beer. Burlington is the Green Mountain State's Mecca for all things hip, and its Mardi Gras celebration is second to none in the North.

Much like another local favorite, Ben & Jerry's Homemade Ice Cream, Magic Hat Brewing Company is a Burlington business that was started by a pair of broad-minded entrepreneurs who believe in giving back to the community, and, well, partying. Since 1995, Magic Hat has been throwing a midwinter, snow-covered, block-party bonanza that raises funds for the Women's Rape Crisis Center as well as provides the town

with a celebration for all to rally around.

The exact dates tend to change depending on how hard it's snowing in February, so check the Magic Hat website for specifics. The action kicks off on Friday night with a Masquerade Ball at famed Burlington venue Higher Ground (1214 Williston Rd.), a movie theater turned ballroom that hosted some of the first Phish shows. Wear a mask to this New Orleans–style dance party with a seventeen-piece brass band, but get there early, as the ballroom has a capacity of 500. Downtown Burlington is also packed on Friday night, as the local contingent prepares for the following day.

Beginning at 3:00 P.M. on Saturday, the energetic parade starts on the corner of Main and Winooski streets. Over forty floats turn the corner onto Church Street, which is the place to be, no matter how frigid the weather. The party grows bigger each year with a crowd of over 30,000 who dress in colorful costumes. After an hour or so, a massive block party erupts in the Church Street Marketplace, and the gallivanting lasts until the wee hours. Anyone with some creativity can enter a float, and Magic Hat brews a specialty beer just for Mardi Gras—it's sold at all the local bars and restaurants.

Some bars and restaurants of note downtown include Red Square Bar and Grill (136 Church St.), a jazz / hip-hop club that attracts a college-age to thirties crowd. Check out Vermont Pub and Brewery (144 College St.), the state's first brewpub; Ri-Ra (123 Church St.), a popular Irish pub with green furniture; and Halvorson's (16 Church St.), an awesome place for beers and burgers. Nectar's (188 Main St.) is a Burlington institution with a student and locals crowd and live music nightly.

Magic Hat Brewing Company (5 Bartlett Bay Rd.) has free tours and tastings all weekend long.

TRANSPORTATION

AIR: Book flights into Burlington International Airport (BTV / *www.burlingtonintlairport.com*), located three miles east of Burlington. Car-rental agencies are available.

TAXIS: Local cab companies include Friendly Fare Taxi (802-310-8822) and Burlington Taxi (802-333-3333).

BUS / TRAIN: The CCTA or Chittenden County Transportation Authority runs buses all over town. Visit *www.cctaride.org* or call 802-864 CCTA for information. The Amtrak station is located at 29 Railroad Avenue, and Greyhound has a bus station at 345 Pine Street.

PARKING: There are three major downtown parking structures. Burlington Town Center Garage can be entered on Cherry, Bank, or Pine; Corporate Plaza Garage has its entrance on St. Paul; and Courthouse Plaza is accessible on Winooski Avenue.

ACCOMMODATIONS

HOTELS: Magic Hat has worked out special discounted rates at nearby Hilton (60 Battery St. / 802-658-6500 / $180)—just be sure to ask for the Mardi Gras room rates. Hawthorne Suites (401 Dorset St. / 802-860-1212 / $137) is within a couple of miles, as are the Sheraton (870 Williston Rd. / 802-865-6600 / $114), Doubletree (1117 Williston / 802-658-0250 / $129), Comfort Inn (1285 Williston Rd. / 802-865-3400 / $89), and Best Western (1076 Williston Rd. / 802-863-1125 / $100). The two closest bed-and-breakfasts are Willard Street Inn (349 S. Willard St. / 802-651-8710 / $135) and Lang House (360 Main St. / 802-652-2500 / $145).

TICKETS

Tickets to the Friday night Masquerade Ball at Higher Ground cost around $15 in advance and $18 at the door. You may be out of luck if you wait until Friday. Visit *www.highergroundmusic.com* or call the box office at 802-652-0777.

What to Pack
- Hat, gloves, warm coat
- Masquerade mask
- Phish's *A Live One*

party tip

It's never too cold for ice cream in Burlington, even in February. Although your mind may say "hot soup," your body should shuffle over to an ice cream parlor and pick up a triple scoop of Cherry Garcia. Ben & Jerry's website lists this fan favorite as its top-selling flavor, while its other musically named concoction, Phish Food, comes in at a respectable sixth. And Cherry Garcia amazingly re-enters the top ten with its low-fat frozen yogurt earning the ninth slot. That's what you call an encore!

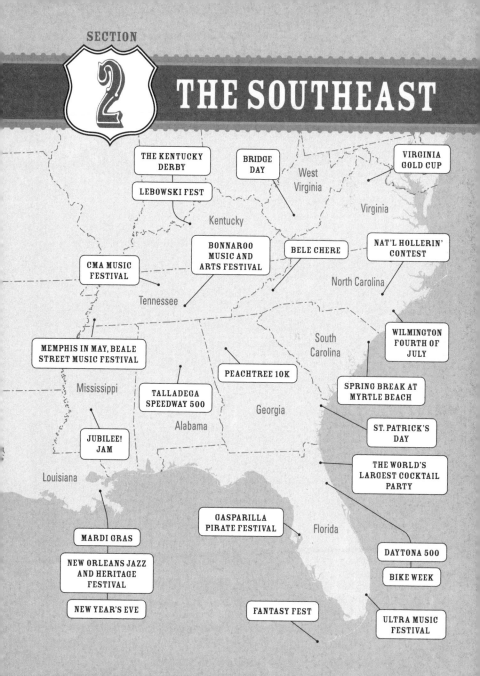

THE KENTUCKY DERBY

LEBOWSKI FEST

BRIDGE DAY

West Virginia

VIRGINIA GOLD CUP

Virginia

Kentucky

BONNAROO MUSIC AND ARTS FESTIVAL

BELE CHERE

NAT'L HOLLERIN' CONTEST

CMA MUSIC FESTIVAL

North Carolina

Tennessee

South Carolina

WILMINGTON FOURTH OF JULY

MEMPHIS IN MAY, BEALE STREET MUSIC FESTIVAL

PEACHTREE 10K

SPRING BREAK AT MYRTLE BEACH

Mississippi

TALLADEGA SPEEDWAY 500

Georgia

ST. PATRICK'S DAY

Alabama

THE WORLD'S LARGEST COCKTAIL PARTY

JUBILEE! JAM

Louisiana

GASPARILLA PIRATE FESTIVAL

Florida

MARDI GRAS

NEW ORLEANS JAZZ AND HERITAGE FESTIVAL

DAYTONA 500

BIKE WEEK

NEW YEAR'S EVE

FANTASY FEST

ULTRA MUSIC FESTIVAL

Alabama

TALLADEGA SPEEDWAY 500

⊛ Talladega, Alabama
First weekend of October
www.talladegasuperspeedway.com

There isn't a track in the world that exemplifies NASCAR's passionate and maniacal fan base like the Talladega Speedway. There are only two types of spectators who make the annual fall trek to this high-octane race—wild and rabid. Although this Nextel Cup Series Ford 500 does not attract the media hype bestowed upon the Indy 500 and Daytona 500, its infield scene is second to none.

Located forty miles east of Birmingham in rural Talladega, the Talladega 500 epitomizes Alabama pride like a Lynyrd Skynyrd song. The 2.6-mile tri-oval speedway is the fastest and most competitive and difficult track in NASCAR. Its abnormally wide lanes and steep embankments have resulted in world speed records, with stock cars frequently hitting 220 miles per hour. Massive fifteen- to twenty-car pileups have become commonplace due to the high speed and track design.

Ask anyone who's gone, and they will tell you that the infield is a superb spectacle. The 212-acre area inside the speedway becomes a scaled-down Mardi Gras–like microcosm of mayhem. Two main roads, Eastaboga Boulevard and Talladega Boulevard intersect near turns two and three, and become ground zero for Talladega's hysteria. Anything goes here, with major points awarded for creativity. Expect multicolored buses with gigantic stuffed animals riding on top, open-air dance floors, and everything in between. This is where NASCAR's most party-hungry fandom comes to play.

You'll have a choice of infield parking options. Most allow ticket holders to arrive on Thursday morning or evening and are valid until Monday, so plan to camp for at least three days. All types of food and beverages are permitted on the infield, and kegs are allowed. Pack plentifully, as a bottle of water costs $6, a hamburger costs $8, and a cup of beer runs just under $10. Don't skimp on grilling equipment. You'll see plenty of large welded barbecue pits, from which the scent of Southern culinary basics like crawfish, ribs, and fried green tomatoes fill the air. Over 143,000 people will fill the grandstands, while thousands of others camp on the infield. The most common postrace phrase among Talladega first-timers is "We've gotta come back next year!"

TRANSPORTATION

✈ **AIR:** Book flights into Birmingham International Airport (BHM / *www.bhamintlairport.com*). Car-rental agencies are available at the airport.

🚐 **RV:** Taking an RV to this event is optimal. You'll have a nice home base from which to spend the weekend on the infield. There are no electrical hookups; however, race personnel will dispose of all RV waste for a small charge. The Green and Red sections are designated for RVs, the Red being closest to turns two and three. Shower facilities are located in the green section, and are available to all RVs. RVs are allowed to enter the speedway

at 6:00 A.M. on Thursday, and your parking pass includes two admission tickets. You can view the infield map on the event website.

🚗 **CAR:** Driving a car onto the infield is another option. Bring a large, comfortable tent, as this will be your accommodation for the weekend. Cars are designated to the Blue and Yellow sections, Yellow being closest to turns two and three. Shower facilities are available in the Green section. Cars are allowed to enter the speedway at 6:00 P.M. Your parking pass includes two admission tickets. See the event website for an infield map.

ACCOMMODATIONS

🏨 **HOTELS:** If you prefer a hotel, book a room by February in Talladega. Local places to stay include Budget Inn (65600 N. Highway 77 / 256-362-0900 / $165), Somerset House Bed and Breakfast (701 N. Street / 256-761-1117 / $95), and Super 8 (220 Haynes St. / 256-315-9511 / $54).

TICKETS

All tickets should be purchased on *www.race tickets.com* early in the summer. For questions visit the event website or call 877-462-3342.

🚐 **RV:** Prices start at $330 for Thursday to Monday passes, which include two admission tickets. Spaces near the intersection of Eastaboga and Talladega Blvd. start at $425, which also include two admission tickets.

🚐 **FRONTRUNNER:** RVs can also park in the Frontrunner section, located on the far west side of the racetrack. These premium spots range from $425 to $525.

🚗 **CAR:** Spaces and campsites start at $285, which allows entrance at 6:00 P.M. on Thursday. For $245 you can arrive on Friday. These passes include two admission tickets.

ADMISSION TICKETS: You will have to pay $105 for each additional person in your party. For example, a RV / Car pass allows entrance for two people, but each person thereafter must buy a ticket.

What to Pack
- Tent (if you plan to camp)
- Grill/charcoal
- iPod with speakers to mount outside
- Mullet wig

party tip

The more inviting your parking space appears to the other fans, the greater the chances of a Talladega party coming to you. There will be competition, so pull out all the stops without cutting corners. Nothing spells Talladega nights like some dance-floor frills—a fog machine or foam machine are surefire ways to pull the masses in your direction, as is a disco ball.

Florida

GASPARILLA PIRATE FESTIVAL

⊛ Tampa, Florida
Last Saturday in January
www.gasparillapiratefest.com

Ye needn't be lookin' farther than this party if yer in the mood to walk the plank into a sea of a half million crazed lads n' lassies. Aye mateys, the Gasparilla Pirate Festival is Tampa's answer to the Carnival of Rio de Janeiro. Held each January for over 100 years, this four-mile-long conglomeration of humanity celebrates an invasion by legendary buccaneer Jose Gaspar, a swashbuckler who roamed the Florida waters in the eighteenth century.

On Saturday at 11:30 A.M. the *Jose Gaspirilla*, the largest fully functioning pirate ship in the world, will appear in Hillsboro Bay, where the Hillsboro River meets Tampa Bay. Flanked by countless pleasure vessels and operated by Ye Mystic Crew of Gasparilla, this three-story, 165-foot-long ship will make its way

toward the dock, firing countless cannonballs along the way. This invasion is considered a success when the mayor of Tampa begrudgingly surrenders the key to the city to the ship's crew.

Bayshore Boulevard, the most prestigious street in the area, is a 3.5-mile stretch of road that runs between the bay and downtown Tampa. Fans of useless trivia may appreciate the fact that the sidewalk along Bayshore Boulevard is the longest continuous sidewalk in the country. The street becomes a moving festival as the Parade of Pirates begins to snake its way toward the city. Over 100 floats, a dozen marching bands, and fifty crews of buccaneers make for the ultimate 500,000-person block party. Although bleacher tickets are for sale, a view from the street can be just as good. Stake your claim early on the Davis Island Bridge for a good view of the parade.

Downtown Tampa is home to the evening's festivities, namely the Pirate Street Festival, which takes place along Florida Avenue. Although this gathering begins before the ship has invaded the city, it gains steam once the parade has ended. You will find stages with live rock 'n' roll, food, and amusements, culminating in a city-wide celebration. By this point the atmosphere is pure entertainment, and beads are worth their weight in gold—pirate's gold that is.

Located in Ybor City, Seventh Avenue is the place to have a late night. This infamous street is a bar-hopper's heaven. Popular spots include the Rare Olive (1601 E. Seventh), a martini bar; Reservoir Bar (1518 E. Seventh); and Coyote Ugly (1722 E. Seventh). The Castle (2004 N. Sixteenth), the most eclectic club in Ybor, plays all the hits before they become mainstream, and the Amphitheater (1609 E. Seventh) is a dance club with a rotating dance floor.

TRANSPORTATION

✈ **AIR:** Fly into Tampa International Airport (TPA / *www.tampaairport.com*), located just a few miles from downtown Tampa. Car-rental agencies are located at the airport.

🚃 **STREETCAR:** A convenient way to get from Ybor City to downtown Tampa. Park at the Centro Ybor Parking Garage or the Palm Avenue Garage for only a few dollars and walk to the streetcar.

🚐 **SHUTTLE:** A shuttle is available to take partygoers to the parade (Hyde Park Ave. and DeLeon St.) from downtown (Raymond James Stadium, Lots 1 and 3) for $8.

🚕 **TAXIS:** Local cab companies include United Cab Company (813-251-6494), Cab Plus Inc. (813-250-0990), Tampa Taxi Incorporated (813-888-5008), ABC Taxi (813-872-8294), and Americab Taxi (813-837-4455).

ACCOMMODATIONS

🏨 **HOTELS:** Planning where to stay becomes an interesting decision. You can stay in action-packed Ybor City and take public transportation to the invasion at the Convention Center. Or you can stay close to the invasion and take public transportation back from the city at nighttime. Many regulars feel that reserving a room near the bay and taking a taxi home at nighttime is the best idea, as early day commuting becomes difficult. Hotels near the Convention Center include: Embassy Suites (513 S. Florida Ave. / 813-769-8300 / $319, two-night minimum), Marriott Tampa Waterside (700 S. Florida Ave. / 813-221-4900 / $200), Sheraton Tampa (200 N. Ashley St. / 813-223-2222 / $279), and Howard Johnson (111 W. Fortune St. / 813-223-1351 / $169). Hotels in Ybor City include: Hilton Garden Inn (1700 E. Ninth Ave. / 813-769-9267 / $249), Hampton Inn (1301 E. Seventh / 813-247-6700 / $249), Don Vicente De Ybor Historic Inn (1915 Republica de Cuba / 813-245-4545 / $209), and the low-priced Tampa 8 Inn (4530 E. Columbus Dr. / 813-621-4661 / $50). For a complete listing of hotels visit *www.tampaguide.com*.

TICKETS

This is a free event. Tickets are sold for reserved bleacher seating ($22), and to the Gasparilla Invasion Brunch ($46) on *www.gasparillapiratefest .com.* See the website for details.

What to Pack

- Plastic cups (glass is not permitted)
- Puffy shirt
- Buccaneer hat
- Eye patch

party tip

Many people bring their own alcohol, as the beer gardens tend to be spread out with long lines. For this reason it is very easy to make new friends via alcohol distribution, and some creativity in this area can really set you apart from the rest of the beer guzzlers. Superglue four shot glasses in a row to the fat end of a boat oar (pirates and oars go hand in hand). You can fill the shot glasses with rum (pirates and rum also go hand in hand), giving four people the opportunity to do a shot simultaneously when the oar is flipped over.

DAYTONA 500

⭐ Daytona, Florida
mid-February, but the date changes each year
www.daytona500.com

It's the Super Bowl of stock car racing, the Wimbledon of the NASCAR world, and the World Series of mullet hairdos.

In February of 1959 the Daytona International Speedway hosted the first ever Daytona 500. Fifty years and 2,000 tons of scorched rubber later this 500-mile adrenaline-pumping roller coaster ride has earned a simple nickname—"The Great Race."

The year 2008 marks the fiftieth anniversary of the highest-dollar-generating car race in the world. The Daytona 500 is a guaranteed sellout, as an estimated 100,000 people show up to the Daytona International Speedway for a ten-day celebration that culminates with the waving of the mighty checkered flag.

This gathering of die-hard NASCAR brethren makes for one of the best tailgate scenes known to planet Earth. If you are a fan, then grandstand tickets will give you the best views of the race. However, if you plan on showing up simply for the experience, then there is only one way to go—the infield parking lots. These lots are located inside the center of the race, and you needn't leave your parking area to watch the cars or to party NASCAR style.

There are a series of races that lead up to the Daytona 500. Your weeklong Infield Parking Pass will grant you access to a handful of preraces during the week before the main event. The scene during these contests is wild, and it's amazing to watch the speedway get more packed and rambunctious as the week progresses. Call 800-748-7467 or log onto the website for further information.

TRANSPORTATION

✈ **AIR:** You can book a flight into Daytona Beach International Airport (DBIA / *www.volusia.org/air port*). Car-rental agencies are at the airport.

🚐 **RV:** Renting an RV is essential to making this experience all that it can be. At the bare minimum your RV should contain a grill; tons of burgers, hot dogs, and brats; folding chairs; a kiddie swimming pool; and a dartboard. Alligator meat, a local delicacy, can add some local flavor to your RV cooking experience. Once you park you will be prohibited from leaving and returning, so plan for the week before you arrive. The one exception is the Lake Lloyd lot. Showers are available to all RVs. Vans and cars are also welcome in the infield.

🚌 **BUS / 🚆 TRAIN:** The Greyhound station is located at 138 South Ridgewood Avenue, and the Amtrak station is located at 100 North Atlantic Avenue.

ACCOMMODATIONS

🏨 **HOTELS:** There are a number of hotels within a couple of miles of the Daytona International Speedway; however, they are usually booked nine months in advance. It can even be difficult to find availability in hotels within sixty miles of the race. However, groups who plan ahead can get a room at the Ramada Inn Speedway, Suburban Extended Stay, Extended Stay Deluxe, Homewood Suites, Super 8, and La Quinta Inn. All are within one mile. Check out *www.priceline .com* for the most competitive rates. This scarce availability of hotel rooms is another reason to consider RV rental.

TICKETS

The racetrack is over 2.5 miles long, and different infield parking lots are available depending on your budget and vehicle.

Infield parking lot tickets for the Lake Lloyd lot cost $2,850 for seven nights. This is the only lot with full RV hookups for electricity, waste, and so on. Green, Red, Yellow, and West Horseshoe Grandstand lots are available for approximately $1,400 for seven nights for RVs. There are *no* hookups for these lots. Cars and vans will be designated to the Orange lot for $750 for the week.

Tickets for grandstand seating range from $100 to $200 for the Daytona 500, and approximately $55 for the earlier races. All tickets can be purchased online at *www.daytona500.com* or by calling 800-748-7467. Tickets go on sale in May.

Remember that you will not need grandstand tickets if you purchase space on the infield lots.

party tip

There is nothing more fun than getting into the spirit of an event, and the Daytona 500 is like shooting fish in a barrel in this regard. Pick the racer who has the lowest chances of winning the race and become his biggest supporter. Cover your RV in posters of his face and tell your neighbors that you have a feeling that this is his year. Talk about how much you love him while wearing a mullet wig and jawing on some chewing tobacco.

BIKE WEEK

⊛ **Daytona, Florida**
late February to early March
www.officialbikeweek.com

Thousands of hogs roll into Daytona, filling the coastal air with the sweet smell of exhaust and leather and signaling the start of the largest motorcycle rally in the country. Bike Week is an absolutely wild ten days of exotic rides, rockin' music, tasty food, races, shows, exhibits, and chrome galore. It's a pilgrimage, not only for the sacred brotherhood of roaring choppers, but for anyone who chooses to partake in one of the world's loudest social events.

Bike Week began in 1937, during the inaugural running of the Daytona 200. Over the past forty years the rally has expanded to encompass all of Volusia County, bringing with it 600,000 riders, a half billion dollars in revenue, and 900,000 square feet of black leather. The people-watching at this human safari is off the charts, the partying is not far behind, and the list of things to do is endless.

The Daytona 200 is a sixty-eight lap, 200-mile motorcycle race held at the beginning of Bike Week. Visit *www.daytonaintl speedway.com* for tickets and race information. Bike owners should hit the beach at Daytona, where you can ride in the sand for miles. A must-do ride is the popular twenty-two mile loop through some spectacular Florida scenery, which provides a nice break from the Daytona lunacy. Begin on John Anderson Drive at the Granada Bridge in Ormond Beach—visit *www.officialbikeweek.com* for the complete mapped-out route. Bruce Rossmeyer's Harley Davidson (1637 N. U.S. Route 1), the world's largest Harley Davidson dealer, has a twenty-acre parking lot that is hog heaven during the rally.

Main Street in Daytona Beach, from South Peninsula Drive to Ocean Avenue, is the hub throughout the ten-day event. This area is loaded with bars and restaurants, all of which are constantly packed, while the wildest-looking vehicles on two or three wheels parade down the strip. Check out expos from the biggest name motorcycle manufacturers, listen to live music, or just walk the streets and take in the scenery. The "Bike Week Pocket Guide" is a cheat sheet to the week's events, and you can pick it up anywhere along Main Street.

Bars and taverns beckon the male contingent hourly with wet T-shirt contests and scantily clad competitions. The most famous is "Cole Slaw Wrestling," taking place in Samsula at Cabbage Patch Bar (corner of Rt. 4118 and Rt. 415). While testosterone-fueled games are commonplace, there's plenty of fun for females as well. Popular Main Street biker bars include Dirty Harry's (701 Main St.), Froggy's Saloon (800 Main St.), Wiseguy's Watering Hole (415 Main St.), and Boot Hill Saloon (310 Main St.).

TRANSPORTATION

✈ **AIR:** You can book a flight into Daytona Beach International Airport (DBIA / *www./volusia.org/air port*) located ten minutes from downtown Daytona. Car-rental agencies are at the airport.

Ⓑ **BUS / 🚆 TRAIN:** The Greyhound station is located at 138 South Ridgewood Avenue, and the Amtrak station is located at 100 North Atlantic Avenue.

🚐 **RV:** RV campgrounds are in abundance. Many nonbiker partygoers drive an RV, while bikers trail their motorcycles in back of an RV.

ACCOMMODATIONS

Book a room or campground wherever you can. Accommodations fill extremely fast, so make your reservation now! Consider yourself lucky if you get a spot within ten miles of Daytona Beach sooner than a year in advance. The campgrounds are a nonstop party—hopefully you can sleep through the sound of roaring engines. If you can't find a room, then try the neighboring towns of New Smyrna Beach, Orange City, or Deland.

🏨 **HOTELS:** In Daytona Beach try Comfort Inn (730 N. Atlantic Ave. / 386-255-5491 / $159), Desert Inn Resort Hotel & Suites (900 N. Atlantic Ave. / 386-258-6555 / $230), Daytona Beach Oceanside Inn (1909 S. Atlantic Ave. / $139), Perry's Ocean Edge Motel (2209 S. Atlantic Ave. / 386-255-0581 / $165), and Best Western Mayan Inn (103 S. Ocean Ave. / 386-252-2378). More luxurious options include Hilton Ocean Walk Village (100 N. Atlantic Ave. / 386-254-8200 / $149), Hawaiian Inn (2301 S. Atlantic Ave. / 386-255-5411 / $179), Plaza Resort and Spa (600 N. Atlantic Ave. / 386-255-4471 / $229), and Shores Resort and Spa (2637 S. Atlantic Ave. / 386-767-7350 / $249). Visit *www.daytonahotels.com* for further choices.

🔥 **CAMPING:** Flea & Farmers Market Camping (2987 Bellevue Ave.) has tent and RV sites with hot showers and no hookups. Finish Line RV Park (217 Fentress Blvd. / 386-238-8221) has hot showers and twenty-four-hour security; it's walking distance to restaurants but doesn't allow tents. Cacklebery's Lot Next Door (560 CR 415, New Smyrna Beach / 386-428-5459) offers RV and tent camping, onsite entertainment, and beverage service. KOA Kampground (1440 E. Minnesota Ave., Orange City / 386-775-3996) has a breakfast restaurant, hot showers, and low rates. Thunder Gulch Campground (2129 N. U.S. Route 1 / 386-437-3135) has RV hookups and an onsite restaurant. Most campsites charge about $45 per night. Visit *www.discoverdaytona.com* or *www.officialbikeweek.com* for further choices.

TICKETS

A ten-day Daytona International Speedway super ticket grants you entrance to all the motorcycle events, including the Daytona 200. This ticket also includes overnight camping in turns three and four of the infield. Cost is $175. Visit *www.daytonainternationalspeedway* for tickets and information.

What to Pack
- Wallet Chain
- Earplugs
- Tattoos (fake or real)
- Earring (real)

party tip

Occasionally onsite is Biker Billy, the world's most outrageous television chef, slicing and dicing in his black leather jacket and dark sunglasses. This culinary master of hell is known for his hot and spicy dishes, often cooked on flame-throwing motorcycle exhausts. If you can't find Billy but want to try some fiery cuisine, enter one of the hot-wing eating contests that take place on Main Street.

ULTRA MUSIC FESTIVAL

⭐ Miami, Florida
Late March
www.ultramusicfestival.com

The Ultra Music Festival beckons the best DJs in the world to descend upon Miami every March for the largest and most intense rave in the United States. A pulsating crowd of 80,000 gyrates to breakneck rhythms in a trance of sensory overload. Laser light shows and monstrous three-dimensional screens enhance the euphoria, as club goers are pulled from one musical experience to another one. This is the reigning king of raves, and it occurs for two consecutive days in the clubbing capital of America.

The UMF is the grand finale of the Winter Music Conference, an annual industry gathering for DJs, promoters, and producers. The first UMF took place on Miami Beach in 1998, but its increasing popularity forced promoters to leave the sand dunes for a larger, more suitable venue. Bicentennial Park now serves as host, with the rave running Friday from 4:00 P.M.–12:00 P.M. and Saturday from 12:00 P.M.–12:00 A.M. The UMF plays host to over 100 bands, DJs, and producers, who perform throughout the course of the weekend. World-class fire-eaters and exotic dancers, imported from Ibiza and Amsterdam, add to the surreal landscape, while the music rarely stops. Float around from the main stages to ten enormous tents that host genres such as House, Techno, Breakbeats, Electro, and Drum and Bass. Recent performers have included the Chemical Brothers, Underworld, Fat Boy Slim, Carol Cox, Pete Tong, the Prodigy, and other industry megastars.

Arrive early, as the lines to enter in the evening are extremely long. Food is available onsite and blankets are permitted to relax on the lawn during the day. Be sure to designate a meeting area with your friends, as it is extremely easy to lose track of people. Bring cash, as a bottle of water costs about $7.

A limited number of VIP tickets are available for approximately three times the regular ticket price. These passes grant you access to two viewing decks above the stages, premium bar and food service, no-wait entrance lines, air-conditioned restrooms, and free coffee. Another perk is entrance into the VIP Village, which offers excellent views of the stage from hammocks, lawn chairs, and beanbag couches. Tickets are also available for the official after-party on Saturday evening in a nearby venue. This party is essentially a massive club that rocks well into Sunday morning.

If you plan on attending all weekend, save energy for Saturday night, when the after-party continues for hours. Raving on Friday and Saturday gives you the chance to take a well-deserved recuperation day at the beach on Sunday. Travel home on Monday if possible. Miami is known for its Cuban food, and "Puerto Sagua" is the best cheap Cuban eats in Miami Beach (700 Collins Ave.).

TRANSPORTATION

AIR: Fly into Miami International Airport (MIA / *www.miami-airport.com*). Many travel websites and airlines tend to have bargain sales on tickets into Miami. Try to shop around for the best rates.

CAR / TAXIS: It is recommended that you stay in Miami and take a taxi to Bicentennial Park at 1075 Biscayne Boulevard. Parking a car can be a major hassle. Renting a car for this party may not be the best idea, especially if you will be staying in Miami or near the beach without venturing too far away. Local cab companies include Coral Gables Taxi (305-889-9999), Metro Taxi (305-888-8888), and Super Yellow Cabs (305-888-7777).

BUS: The closest Greyhound station to South Beach is located at 1012 NW First Avenue in downtown Miami (305-374-6160).

ACCOMMODATIONS

HOTELS: Try to find a room within walking distance to the festival in the South Beach / Art Deco District near Collins Ave. The wait for a cab afterward can be long. Book early or you may get stuck with an expensive room. You can also stay at any hotel in Miami Beach or Miami proper while still keeping cab fare below five miles. There is an abundance of hotels; *www.miamihotels.com* is a nice website which is easy to navigate and offers competitive rates.

TICKETS

They go on sale two months prior, usually selling out fast. General Admission: Two-day passes—$120 / $30 in fees; Friday pass—$60 / $12 in fees; Saturday pass—$75 / $20 in fees; Saturday after-party—$40 / $8 in fees. VIP: Two-day pass—$350 / $55 in fees; Friday pass—$199 / $26 in fees; Saturday pass—$199 / $32 in fees.

There are sixty high-roller private tables for sale each day as well. Rates vary depending on group size. Call 786-312-0024 for details.

party tip

Tinnitus is the medical term for "ringing of the ears," a condition that you may very well suffer on Sunday and Monday. The best treatment is to retreat to a quiet place, remain calm, and take some ginkgo biloba and B-12 vitamins. Earplugs are another option if you aren't single.

FANTASY FEST

⊛ **Key West, Florida**
Mid- to late October
www.fantasyfest.net

There's never a dull moment at the ten-day hoopla of fantasy, fun, and exhibitionism that occurs during the brilliant Key West autumn. Fantasy Fest is all merriment and self-indulgence, mixed with some Florida sunshine and a crowd that throws societal norms out the window for one roaring week in October.

Started in the late 1970s, Fantasy Fest's original purpose was to bring people to Key West during the low tourism season. Mission complete—Fantasy Fest is now the highest revenue week of the year for the southernmost city in the entire United States. Over 100,000 revelers of all ages fill the city's concentrated downtown area for a glorious week of mischief, dancing, and uninhibited celebration.

The party begins on a Friday and ends nine days later. The first few days are merely a countdown to the utter lunacy that ensues on Wednesday. From this point on, masqueraders take over Duval Street for an unapologetic and unforgettable block party during which the word *conservative* holds no meaning. The Pet Parade signals the beginning of the hysteria, as four-legged furry friends in costumes walk their decked-out owners down the beachside area at the Schooner's wharf on Wednesday afternoon.

Thursday evening is the famed costume contest, otherwise known as "Pretenders in Paradise." Over $10,000 in cash is handed out to contestants whose outfits can cause many a Floridian's pacemaker to fail. For every stunningly perfect nude body covered in intricate body paint there's an elderly man wearing nothing but assless chaps. Key West resident Ryan Kempp commented, "Expect the sexiest costumes you've ever seen being worn by eighty-year-old women—they're totally shameless."

Friday night is the highlight, as the monstrous Masquerade March gets underway at 5:00 P.M. Beginning at the Key West Cemetery Francis Street entrance, anyone is welcome to join the two separate parades as they circle the block and eventually end up on Duval. An assortment of elaborate floats carrying live bands, and yes, more nude people, transform Key West into a scene that would leave Jimmy Buffett scratching his head. The Annual Street Fair follows at 10:00 P.M.—it's essentially a mile-long party comprised of artists, vendors, and gypsies.

Saturday is the most crowded day of the weekend; the streets are jam-packed with further unimaginable visions during the Duval Street Promenade.

Duval Street is blocked off throughout the week, and party people rarely come up for air. Drinking in the streets is allowed during Fantasy Fest, and the 4:00 A.M. bar time does little to coax people into their beds. Be sure to check out The Bull, the Whistle, and the Garden of Eden (224 Duval St.). These three bars in one location are among the most popular during the festival. The Bull is on the ground floor and has live music; the Whistle is the place to be seen, with large outdoor porches on the second story; the Garden of Eden, on the top floor, is a nonstop adult party with clothing optional.

TRANSPORTATION

AIR: Book flights into Key West International Airport (EYW / *www.keywestinternationalairport .com*), which is located just a few miles from downtown. Miami International Airport (MIA / *www.miami-airport.com*) is approximately 160 miles away and Ft. Lauderdale International Airport (FLL / *www.fortlauderdaleinternationalairport.com*) is 188 miles away. You may find better rates at one of these airports. Car rentals are available at all three.

SHUTTLE: Keys Shuttle (305-289-9997 / *www.keysshuttle.50megs.com*) runs buses into Key West from EYW, MIA, and FLL. Shuttles from Miami cost approximately $60 per way, and Ft. Lauderdale is a bit more expensive. Make reservations in advance.

TAXIS: Key West cab companies include Florida Keys Taxi (305-296-1800), Classic Cabs (305-294-2227), Maxi Taxi (305-296-2222), and Friendly Cab Co. (305-295-5555).

PARKING: City-run parking lots are available on weekends only and are within walking distance. They include Old Town Garage, Mallory Square, and Key West Bight. On Saturday you can also find parking at Key West High School (2100 Flagler Ave.).

BUS / TRAIN: The Greyhound station is located at 3535 South Roosevelt Boulevard. You can take the Amtrak as far south as Ft. Lauderdale, and then transfer to the Keys Shuttle (see above).

ACCOMMODATIONS

HOTELS: Some hotels are booked up to six months in advance for Fantasy Fest. Make your reservations early. Hotels include Fairfield Inn (2400 N. Roosevelt Blvd. / 305-296-5700 / $350), the Westin Key West Resort & Marina (245 Front St. / 305-294-4000 / $369), Sheraton (2001 S. Roosevelt Blvd. / 305-292-9800 / $277), Doubletree (3990 S. Roosevelt Blvd. / 305-293-1818 / $252), Hyatt (601 Front St. / 305-809-1234 / $480), Courtyard

Marriott (3031 N. Roosevelt Blvd. / 305-296-6595 / $389), and Best Western (3755 S. Roosevelt Blvd. / 305-296-3500 / $169). For further hotel listings visit *www.fla-keys.com/keywest*.

TICKETS

You must register to enter the Pretenders in Paradise costume contest on Thursday night. The deadline is typically on Tuesday. Registration fees are $10 for individuals or $20 for groups of four or more. Registration tickets can be purchased at the Pier House Resort and Caribbean Spa (1 Duval St.). Various bar costume contests have entrance fees from $10 to $20.

What to Pack
- Toga
- Body paint
- Black leather
- Your deepest fantasy

party tip

Body paint artists will give you free rein to design your evening's skin. During the trip down south, bring a pad and pen and sketch the funkiest or freakiest design that you can think of. Ideas include flames up your body, eyeballs on your eyelids, or a license plate on your rear. Hand them the paper and pray they get it right!

THE WORLD'S LARGEST
OUTDOOR COCKTAIL PARTY

⭐ Jacksonville, Florida
Last Saturday in October
www.georgiadogs.com / www.gatorzone.com

This is an event that has grown to mythic proportions and overshadows the football game that it celebrates. The World's Largest Outdoor Cocktail Party is the fiercest, most berserk, tailgate in the South and takes place before, during, and after the October meeting between the University of Florida Gators and the University of Georgia Bulldogs.

The game is held on neutral ground at Alltel Stadium, home of the Jacksonville Jaguars. This location is 340 miles from the Bulldogs' home in Athens, Georgia, and seventy miles from the Gators' field in Gainesville, Florida. Ticket sales are split down the middle, with the home team designation rotating each year. In 2006, the SEC (Southeastern Conference) asked the three major TV networks that televise the game not to refer to it as "The World's Largest Outdoor Cocktail Party," due to fears that the name encourages drinking. The contest is now officially called the Georgia-Florida or the Florida-Georgia game—but its reputation still lives.

Driving an RV to the event is an excellent idea. The RV parking lot across from the stadium, referred to as "RV City" opens at 6:00 A.M. on the Wednesday before the game. Florida fans park in "Gator Alley" while Georgians set up shop on "Bulldog Boulevard." Some set up kids' swimming pools filled with inflatable alligators, or strap on a dog collar for the week. A pleasantly unexpected aspect is the mingling of fans. Unlike other gridiron rivalries, the fans here socialize together. Georgia red and black and Florida orange and blue treat each other respectfully.

A few miles down the road is Jacksonville Landing. This pedestrian downtown area sits along the waterfront—and it's calamity during the game. Home to the city's nightlife, the Landing begins to rock on the Thursday before the game, and it doesn't stop until Sunday, or maybe Tuesday. An estimated 50,000 people fill the area, acting as though they are sitting on the fifty yard line. The best places to watch are Sneakers Sports Grille (111 Beach Blvd.), Bob Marlin's Sports Grill (798 S. Third St.), and the enormous Dave and Buster's (7025 Salisbury Rd.).

TRANSPORTATION

AIR: Book flights into Jacksonville International Airport (JAX / www.jaa.aero) located fifteen miles from downtown.

PARKING: Arrive early on Saturday to park at the stadium for $20. Additional parking can be found within walking distance around the Times-Union Center and at Jacksonville Equestrian Center.

SHUTTLE: JTA's Transportation Services runs shuttles from six downtown and suburban locations to the stadium for approximately $5 each way. The shuttle picks up at Jacksonville Landing on Hogan Street between Water and Bay streets two hours before kickoff to one hour after the final whistle. Visit www.jtaonthemove.com.

TAXIS: Jacksonville cab companies include Gator City Taxi & Shuttle (904-355-8294), Metro Cars (904-425-4444), Yellow Cab (904-260-1111), and City Cab (904-425-2222).

BUS / TRAIN: The Greyhound station is located at 10 North Pearl Street, and the Amtrak station is located at 3570 Clifford Lane.

ACCOMMODATIONS

HOTELS: Those near downtown include Crowne Plaza (1201 Riverplace Blvd. / 904-398-8800

/ $299), Wyndham (1515 Prudential Dr. / 904-396-5100 / $159), Hampton Inn (1331 Prudential Dr. / 904-396-7770 / $169), Hyatt Regency (225 E. Coastline Dr. / 904-633-9095 / $179), Embassy Suites (9300 Baymeadows Rd. / 904-731-3555 / $109), Super 8 (2228 Phillips Hwy. / 904-396-4090 / $125), and Days Inn (510 Lane Ave. South / 904-786-0500 / $72). The Omni (245 Water St. / 904-355-6664 / $149) is in the middle of the action. Visit www.priceline.com for hotel deals.

RV: RV city can hold close to 200 RVs, but spaces are on a first-come-first-serve basis. The lot opens at 6:00 A.M. Wednesday, and it fills quickly. Cost is $75 per night, paid at the gate.

TICKETS

You'll have to pick a side to root for before buying your tickets. Visit www.gatorzone.com or www.georgiadogs.com for $40 seats, when season ticket sales begin in April. Games typically sell out by early May. If it's already sold out, then you can purchase tickets via a ticket broker. They start at approximately $135 and go up to $500.

What to Pack
- Alligator meat for tailgate
- Bulldog mask
- Cool Toss cooler—a cooler and tailgating table in one

party tip

If you're coming in from out of town without tailgating supplies, pick up a few steaks, condiments, and charcoal. Put these supplies in a backpack and head for the parking lot. Wander the crowds until you find an age group and/or male-to-female tailgate ratio that piques your interest. Offer your goodies in exchange for access to a grill and keg.

Georgia

ST. PATRICK'S DAY

⊛ Savannah, Georgia
March 15–17
http://savannahsaintpatricksday.com

When one thinks of St. Patty's day extravaganzas, cities such as Chicago and Boston immediately spring to mind. However, deep in the South lies a place where this holiday has evolved into the most unique and outrageous week-long tribute to leprechauns in the country. The people of Savannah, Georgia, have had plenty of time to perfect their Irish festivities since the first celebration took place in 1812.

Savannah is the quintessential example of southern charm. Its legendary gardens, looming elm trees, and awe-inspiring architecture make it a worthwhile stop on any trip through the southeast. However, as any of the 400,000 people who pour in each St. Patty's Day will attest, this proud and proper city also knows how to trade in southern charm for merri-

ment. Year after year, March 17 in Savannah is the largest single-day gathering of people in the entire southeastern United States.

The party begins one week before March 17, when the town of Savannah awakens to find each of its distinguished fountains flowing green, indicating the arrival of leprechauns. The next few days are filled with events such as Irish music concerts, corned beef and cabbage eating contests, and artisan craft shows. These events tend to be geared toward families and are simply a warm-up to the seventy-two-hour party, which takes place starting on March 15.

The historic River Street district is home to the city's nightlife scene, and the chances are that you will spend the majority of your time on this strip along with 300,000 other green-decorated party animals. All the bars have takeout windows during St. Patty's week, so walking the streets and drinking green beer while looking for love is an option. Just be sure to get a wristband each day before imbibing outdoors! Start your day with the infamous "Kegs-n-Eggs" breakfast at the Rail Pub (405 W. Congress St.). This scene is an excellent mix of people, young and old, getting together and donning Irish pride.

The celebration culminates on March 17 with a huge parade through the streets. The entourage includes green goats, the world's tallest leprechaun, local beauty queens, and more Astroturf than you've seen in your life. The parade does not wind down River Street (it begins at Albercorn and Gwinnet and ends at Bull and Harris), and it's best to get to Calhoun Square early in the morning with lawn chairs, as this is a prime viewing spot.

TRANSPORTATION

AIR: Savannah is located approximately 250 miles southeast of Atlanta and is home to the second largest airport in Georgia, Savannah / Hilton Head International Airport (SAV). At times, flights into Savannah can be a little bit more expensive than flights into Atlanta; however this is not always true. Check online for fares. The drive from Atlanta to Savannah takes about four hours.

The Savannah / Hilton Head Airport (SAV / *www.savannahairport.com*) is serviced by most major carriers. Upon arrival ask a local cab company to take you the short distance to historic downtown Savannah or to your hotel.

BUS / TRAIN: Savannah is also easily accessible by Greyhound Bus, as thirty-two buses come in and out each day. The station is located at 610 Oglethorpe Ave. (912-232-2135), which is a five-minute walk to historic downtown and River Street. Visit *www.greyhound.com* for a complete bus schedule. The Amtrak station (2611 Seaboard Coastline Dr. / 912-234-2611) is located approximately four miles from River Street and the historic downtown. Taxi cabs are available at the station.

TAXIS: Local cab companies include Yellow Cab (912-604-9845), Discount Taxi (912-236-1133), and Magikal Taxi (912-897-8294).

ACCOMMODATIONS

HOTELS: It is wise to book your hotel at least eight weeks in advance. Savannah does have its share of hotel rooms; however, the best and most convenient area to stay is the riverfront district. This is ground zero for the major festivities, and real estate is nearly impossible to come by as Saint Patrick's Day approaches. Options include the Hyatt (2 W. Bay St. / 912-238-1234 / $169), Marriott (General McIntosh Blvd. / 912-233-7722 / $330), the Promenade (412 W. Bay St. / 912-233-1011 / $459), and Comfort Suites (630 W. Bay St. / 912-629-2001 / $199), as well as a wide selection of other chain and locally owned hotels that have locations in the riverfront historic district. For a complete list and availability visit *www.riverstreetsavannah.com*.

B&BS: To truly experience southern hospitality, see the bed-and-breakfast listings on *www* *party tip*

The absolute cornerstone meal of a Savannah St. Patrick's Day is green grits. It's a tradition that no visitor should leave town without having tried. Some salt and butter or honey goes well with this classic dish. Local legend has it that green grits makes you smart—and you may need to replace plenty of brain cells after this party!

What to Pack
- Green everything (underwear and lipstick included)
- Green food dye
- Pepto Bismol (green beer can be painful)

PEACHTREE 10K

⭐ Atlanta, Georgia
July 4
www.atlantatrackclub.org

Who would've thought that a 6.2-mile running race held in the Deep South during the dead of summer would be the largest and most illustrious 10K in the world? Fourth of July celebrations in Atlanta begin early in the morning as athletes gear up for an infamously challenging course, while the remainder of the city shows up to watch.

Known by locals as "The Race," the Atlanta Journal-Constitution Peachtree Road Race 10K is a long-standing tradition in Atlanta. This heart-pumping party has grown by leaps and bounds since its inception in 1970, attracting weekend trotters and champion-caliber runners from every corner of the globe. Signing up late is not an option, as the Peachtree grants entry to only the first 55,000 applicants, turning away thousands of hopeful runners in the process. If you can't or don't want to race, then join the 150,000 spectators who line the streets, and indulge in the social scene that's created by this run through the city.

Peachtree Road closes on July 4, before the first wave of runners is released at 7:30 A.M. from Lenox Square in Buckhead. Miles 1 and 2 are downhill and brimming with humanity, making this an apt time to absorb the jovial atmosphere. Thousands of "fans" line the streets, wrapped in flags, dressed in costumes, and blowing horns and trumpets—and some runner's attire isn't too different. Be sure to get splashed by the holy water being thrown by priests at "Jesus Junction," a three-church intersection at mile 2. The Heartbreak Hills begins at mile 3—this stretch sends at least a couple of victims into the intensive care ward each year—luckily, Piedmont Hospital is located across the street from the most difficult section. The remainder of the course has less dramatic peaks and valleys and ends at Piedmont Park.

Atlanta turns out in droves to witness the Peachtree 10K and to celebrate with its runners. There is a strong sense of city pride that even non-Georgians will experience. The establishments along the race offer early morning drink specials, mega-sized parties, live bands, and great views of the participants.

One of the most important race-day traditions is the T-shirt. Peachtree 10K shirts are given only to those who've run, and they hold an elevated status on July 4. If you completed the race, wear your shirt proudly for the remainder of the day. If you didn't run, there's always next year!

TRANSPORTATION

AIR: Book flights into William B. Hartsfield International Airport (ATL / www.atlanta-airport.com), located ten miles from downtown Atlanta. Trains run from the airport to downtown.

TAXIS: It's recommended that you do not rent a car. You should utilize taxis and the MARTA train system to travel within the city due to heavy traffic during the Peachtree 10K. Local cab companies include Atlanta Taxi Service (404-351-1111), Royal Cabbies (404-584-6655), Buckhead Safety Cab (404-875-3777), and Yellow Cab (404-521-0200).

MARTA: Spectators and racers can take the Metropolitan Atlanta Rapid Transit Authority trains, which begin running at 5:00 A.M. from all points in the city. The Orange Line runs to Lenox and the Red Line goes to Buckhead. Both lines run to and from the airport as well.

BUS / TRAIN: The Greyhound station is located at 232 Forsyth Street, and the Amtrak station is located at 1688 Peachtree Street.

ACCOMMODATIONS

HOTELS: Logistically it makes sense to stay close to Buckhead, as you'll spend a lot of time in that area whether you're racing or not. Nearby hotels include Embassy Suites (3285 Peachtree Rd. / 404-261-7733 / $139), Marriott (3300 Lenox Rd. / 404-262-3344 / $199), Comfort Inn (5793 Roswell Rd. / 404-252-6400 / $95), Doubletree (2061 N. Druid Hills Rd. / 404-231-4174 / $75),

Holiday Inn Express (505 Pharr Rd. / 404-262-7880 / $112), Hampton Inn (3398 Piedmont Rd. / 404-233-5656 / $149), and Ramada (2115 Piedmont Rd. / 404-876-4444 / $62).

TICKETS

The race entry form is printed in a mid-March edition of the *Atlanta Journal-Constitution* newspaper. The race fills extremely fast, and the first 45,000 entry forms received by mail are accepted. An additional 10,000 entries with postmarks through March 31 will be selected at random. Entry forms must be accompanied by a photocopy of your identification and a check for $28. Additionally, you must include documentation of a race greater than five miles that you've run for seeding purposes. Visit the event website for the specific date that the newspaper entry forms will become available and to find out if the $28 fee has increased. Complete everything properly or else you may not be accepted.

Out-of-state runners should send a number-ten-sized, self-addressed, stamped envelope to Peachtree (followed by the year), Atlanta Track Club, P.O. Box 12109, Atlanta, GA, 30355. The Track Club will mail you a copy of the entry form.

What to Pack
- Costume (optional)
- Running shoes (not optional)
- Endurance (optional if you want to lose)

party tip

The Peachtree 10K T-shirt does beckon a lot of high-fiving and hand-slapping throughout the day. An idea for the nonrunners is to visit eBay and purchase last year's T-shirt. Or better yet, play the role of the veteran and try to score a 1984 version.

Kentucky

THE KENTUCKY DERBY

⭐ Louisville, Kentucky
First Saturday in May
www.kentuckyderby.com

The first jewel in the Triple Crown of thoroughbred horse racing is Kentucky's most majestic social engagement. Louisville invites the world to its doorstep each May as millions tune in to the 134-year-old race on their television sets. What the TV cameras don't capture are the thousands of local house parties and the widespread galloping gala of enormous proportion in Louisville.

Every sports fan should experience the Derby once. This experience is not achieved by purchasing a sought-after ticket in Millionaire's Row, but instead by joining the ranks of the Derby's 70,000-person blue-collar crowd in the infield of Churchill Downs. The gates open at 8:00 A.M., but hordes of twenty- to forty-year-olds arrive as early as 3:00 A.M. to get in line for their corner of grass. Comradery is at

its peak, as is the chaos that lasts all day long in preparation for the greatest two minutes in sports.

The odds are 100-to-0 that the third turn on the infield is where you'll find the hub of hysteria. Shirtless young men dominate this portion, along with women who wear tight tops that read "Talk Derby to Me." It's amazing to look into the stands, particularly at Millionaire's Row, and observe the differences between fans wearing blazers and Sunday dresses and those in the trenches. Coolers full of food are allowed on the infield, and beer costs about $8 per cup.

Kentucky is the bourbon capital of the world, so it comes as no surprise that mint juleps are the drink of choice. Over 120,000 of these southern concoctions, which combine mint, bourbon, sugar, and water and cost about $10 each, are

consumed over the course of the day. The high rollers pay $1,000 for a mint julep served in a gold chalice with a silver straw. These $50-per-sip specials benefit retired horses and jockeys. The souvenir du jour is an official Kentucky Derby Mint Julep glass. Out-of-towners can be easily identified, as they carry a handful from the race.

Watching the race from the infield is close to impossible, so don't plan for a first-class view. Those who wish to bet should pick their horse the evening prior, place their bet upon entering the infield, and put the ticket somewhere safe. This move allows complete relaxation and enjoyment for the duration of the day. Louisville establishments stay open until 6:00 A.M. after Derby Day, providing spectators the chance to indulge in "après-race" for as long as they'd like. Head to Fourth Street Live, the city's main drag of restaurants, bars, and shopping. Mark's Feed Store (1514 Bardstown Rd.) has the best casual barbecue in town.

TRANSPORTATION

AIR: Fly into Louisville International Standiford Field Airport (SDF / *www.flylouisville.com*), located four miles from downtown and Churchill Downs. Taxis and rental cars are available.

PARKING: Driving to the race is a nightmare due to heavy traffic. Parking lots at Churchill Downs are typically reserved for VIP ticket holders and the media. There are a few lots next to the race; however, they sell out far in advance. Pay a resident to park on his lawn—the closer you get, the more expensive this becomes. $50 can buy a prime spot and $10 will get you within a mile.

SHUTTLE: A good option is to park for free at the Kentucky Fairgrounds and take a $10 shuttle to Churchill Downs. This shuttle runs back and forth from 7:30 A.M. to 8:30 P.M. Round-trip tickets can be purchased in front of Freedom Hall at the fairgrounds. Another shuttle services those staying at the downtown hotels for $5 each way.

WALKING: Downtown hotels are about four miles from Churchill Downs, but within walking distance to Fourth Street Live.

TAXIS: Take a taxi to Churchill Downs. Louisville cab companies include Ready Cab Co. (502-693-7334), Yellow Cab (502-636-5511), Day and Night Taxi (502-777-5516), Cross Town Taxi (502-625-7472), and Yellow & Blue Cab (502-939-5140).

ACCOMMODATIONS

HOTELS: Book a downtown Louisville hotel by February at the very latest. It is possible to find rooms up until one month before the race; however, the pickings are slim. Hotels typically raise rates by $100 and have three-night minimums during Derby weekend. Hotels as far as fifty miles away do the same thing. Downtown hotels include Holiday Inn (120 W. Broadway / 502-582-2241), Marriott (280 W. Jefferson / 502-627-5045 / $209), Hyatt Regency (320 W. Jefferson / 502-581-1234 / $990, three-night min.), the Brown Hotel (335 W. Broadway / 502-583-1234 / $189), Hampton Inn (101 E. Jefferson St. / 502-585-5657 / $589), and Courtyard Marriott (100 S. Second St. / 502-562-0200 / $417, three-night min.). Some hotels offer a free shuttle to Churchill Downs for guests. Visit *www.hotel-guides.us/kentucky/louisville-ky-hotels.html* for a complete listing of Louisville-area hotels.

TICKETS

Unlimited infield tickets are sold on race day only at the gates for $40 and are standing-room only. Visit the website for seated grandstand tickets.

What to Pack
- Raincoat
- Sunscreen
- Binoculars

---

party tip

Betting on the Derby is part art form and part crapshoot. You'll pick from twenty horses, most of which have never run in front of such a large crowd, are not on their hometown track, and are being ridden by new jockeys. This race is not a speed contest as much as it is an endurance test. Stick with horses with a Bayer Speed Figure of at least 100. Find out which popular jockeys have been riding one horse for at least six months. Take the dosage rating into account as well. This number will tell you whether the horse is bred from a strong line of equine royalty, and anything below 4.00 is optimum. When all else fails, write down the names of each animal and throw a dart.

LEBOWSKI FEST

⊛ **Louisville, Kentucky**
Usually mid-July, man
www.lebowskifest.com

L ouisville's annual Lebowski Fest is a bathrobe-cloaked, Caucasian-sipping bowlathon for fans of the Coen Brothers' 1998 cult classic *The Big Lebowski*. There are certain things that the Dude does for recreation—bowling, driving around, and the occasional acid flashback. And this party celebrates them all.

This two-day shindig, occurring annually since 2002, is all about the celebration of mediocrity and a great movie. The festival has received glowing reviews from the likes of *Rolling Stone* magazine, *Spin* magazine, and the *New York Times*. Attendance has grown from a few hundred to several thousand, spurring offshoot Lebowski Fests in cities such as Las Vegas, Los Angeles, Chicago, and New York. While these offshoot celebrations do attain a certain level of slackerdom, Louisville's festival achieves the ultimate state of dudeness.

In the film, the "Big" Lebowski character has an inner-city program called "Little Lebowski Urban Achievers." Therefore, those who make the pilgrimage call themselves "achievers." Beginning on Thursday or Friday, achievers check into the Executive West, the official hotel of the festival. At noon on Friday, saunter to the Brown Forman Waterfront Amphitheater as an array of musicians play the movie soundtrack while barbecue is served up—just take it easy and try not to spill your beverage, man. The headlining band, which has recently been My Morning Jacket, hits the stage at 6:00 P.M. After the concert, settle into your folding chair to watch an outdoor screening of *The Big Lebowski*, during which the crowd recites every line of the movie, roaring in laughter at the funniest ones. The Friday night after-party, from 1:00 A.M. to 4:00 A.M., is free with your concert ticket stub.

Saturday is dress-up day. Achievers, "amateurs," and "fascists" hit the Executive West Hotel pool for an 11:00 A.M. pool party, during which ample "Caucasians"

(White Russians) are consumed. At 1:00 P.M. the Lebowski Fest Carnival gets underway at the Executive Strike and Spare bowling alley parking lot, near the hotel. A series of carnival games keeps attendees occupied until the 8:00 P.M. bowling party. By this point, three-quarters of the crowd is dressed as a character from the movie—the two most popular costumes are the Dude and his purple-bowling-outfit-clad, hairnet-wearing nemesis, Jesus Quintana. Some achievers get extremely creative, dressing as characters that are mentioned but never seen (Cynthia and Marty Ackerman), or as the Dude's least favorite band, the Eagles. Grab some cocktails at the bowling alley bar, mingle among strangers who share your passion for *Lebowski*, and join the trivia and costume contests. The final pins are swept away at 1:00 A.M., and a late-night party at the hotel follows until the wee hours.

TRANSPORTATION

AIR: Book flights into Louisville International Airport (SDF / *www.flylouisville.com*), located one mile from the Executive West Hotel.

SHUTTLE: A Lebowski Fest shuttle will take you from the hotel to the Waterfront Amphitheater, located six miles away. Tickets are on sale in the hotel lobby for about $4 per way.

T TAXIS: Local cab companies include Yellow Cab (502-636-5511), Day & Night Taxi (502-777-5516), Towner Taxi (502-625-7472), Ready Cab Co. (502-693-7334), and Freedom Cab (502-964-2222).

B BUS / TRAIN: The Greyhound station is located at 720 West Muhammad Ali Boulevard, and the Amtrak station is at 500 Willinger Lane.

ACCOMMODATIONS

HOTELS: There's only one choice, man. The Executive West Hotel (830 Phillips Lane / 502-367-2251 / $94) has special rates for Lebowski Fest achievers, beginning at $94 per night. Due to increasing popularity, you should make reservations a few months in advance.

TICKETS

Tickets go on sale in the spring—visit *www.lebowskifest.org*. A weekend pass costs about forty clams and a Saturday pass is thirty bones.

What to Pack
- Bathrobe
- Sunglasses
- Flip-flops
- Personalized bowling ball
- Creedence Clearwater Revival tapes

party tip

The Dude knows that there's a right way and a wrong way to mix a Caucasian. To get into the spirit of the party here's the perfect recipe:

The Caucasian
2 parts Kahlua
1.5 parts cheap vodka

Mix in a highball glass and top with powdered nondairy creamer

There are certainly tastier versions, but this one captures the essence of "duderama."

Louisiana

MARDI GRAS

⊛ New Orleans, Louisiana
January 6 to the day before Ash Wednesday
www.mardigrasneworleans.com

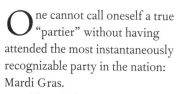

One cannot call oneself a true "partier" without having attended the most instantaneously recognizable party in the nation: Mardi Gras.

Although the Big Easy rages for an entire month, the final two weeks are the zenith of the celebration, with the last five days, from Friday to Fat Tuesday, the epitome of Mardi Gras madness.

Mardi Gras takes place throughout every corner of New Orleans and the surrounding suburbs, although the French Quarter has earned the reputation as the "epicenter of madness." The general attitude is "forget your worries and have fun," which is exactly what happens. Even in the wake of the devastation of Hurricane Katrina, Mardi Gras continues to be one of the top parties in the United States. In fact, the celebra-

tion has taken on a powerful "we will survive" attitude that fosters a sense of pride that radiates throughout the festivities. Bourbon Street, the famous setting of Mardi Gras hedonism, is absolutely packed full of tourists and locals who celebrate with sass during the country's most vibrant party.

Many tourists make the mistake of sticking only to the French Quarter—although this area is fun, it can also get claustrophobic. You can go anywhere in the city and find incredible merriment. The colorful Mardi Gras floats make their way though the streets over the event's final two weeks, amid waves of cheering and stumbling spectators. However, the crux of the procession occurs from Friday to Fat Tuesday.

The parade is made up of "krewes" that name themselves

after a Greek god or a mythological hero. Each krewe appoints a king or royal ruler, oftentimes a celebrity. The krewe's flamboyantly costumed members throw beads and trinkets from the floats to revelers clad in green, gold, and purple, who scramble to pick them up. Visit the event website for the krewe schedules and the routes they will take, and claim your spot early.

The effort undertaken to acquire beads is extraordinary. Historically, beads were meant to be given in exchange for a hug, a kiss, or a supreme celebratory deed. However, flashing a body part for beads is now a common practice that occurs mainly in the French Quarter, and it has become synonymous with Mardi Gras. Heed this warning if you're a woman. Many men on Bourbon Street after midnight are there just to see skin, and you should be aware of your surroundings at all times.

Be sure to munch on a King Cake, a traditional Mardi Gras pastry stuffed with cream cheese and fruit. Speaking of food, plan your meals early, and stash some sandwiches in your hotel room, as most restaurants are constantly packed. Live it up, blow off some steam, be safe, and enjoy the "Greatest Free Show on Earth."

TRANSPORTATION

AIR: Book flights into Louis Armstrong New Orleans International Airport (MSY / *www.flymsy.com*), located fifteen miles from downtown. Do not even dream of renting a car. A taxi into the city costs $28 for one to two people and $12 per person for three or more.

PUBLIC TRANSPORTATION: Shuttles, buses, and streetcars that run on normal schedules throughout the year do not even attempt to navigate Mardi Gras traffic. Consider this fact when you see a hotel advertisement that says "a quick streetcar ride to the French Quarter."

PARKING: If you drive into town and park illegally, you will regret it. Anyone who parks in front of a driveway, fire hydrant, or too close to the corner, within two blocks of the parade route, will receive an enormous fine and an impounded car.

TAXIS: Many locals cash in on the influx of people and shortages of cabs by turning their own car into a taxi—cardboard sign and all. Utilize these pseudo cabbies with discretion, or grab a ride with United Cabs (504-522-9771), American Taxi (504-299-0386), Yellow-Checker Cabs (504-525-3311), Coleman Cab Co. (504-586-0222), King Cab (504-491-1184), and Veterans Cab Co. (504-367-6767).

ACCOMMODATIONS

HOTELS: OK, you want to go to Mardi Gras. To be safe you should book a hotel room by August; however, it is possible to get a late room reservation. Procrastinators who make the decision around Christmas should call multiple hotels, which will undoubtedly be full, and put themselves on the cancellation list. Cancellations are commonplace. Do not go to New Orleans without a room reservation unless you relish the idea of being homeless.

A common misconception is that the parades come through the French Quarter—they do not. French Quarter hotel rooms are packed, expensive ($400 a night and often a five-night minimum), and lacking in the peace and quiet department. The hotels along the parade routes (Canal St. and St, Charles Ave.) are the most reasonably priced because they are not in the French Quarter, yet are within walking distance. The Marriott (555 Canal St. / 504-581-1000 / $199) and Sheraton (500 Canal St. / 504-595-5514 / $209) are excellent options just a short walk from Bourbon St. The Parc St. Charles (500 St. Charles Ave. / 504-522-9000 / $149) and the upscale Maison St. Charles (1319 St. Charles Ave. / 504-522-0187 / $185) are both located along the parade route. Visit www.neworleanscvb.com, or see the following section on Jazz Fest for further hotel recommendations.

What to Pack
- Jacket, raincoat, shorts, and T-shirts—unpredictable weather
- Masquerade mask
- Green, gold, and purple everything

party tip

The Hurricane is the official drink of Mardi Gras. Like any drink recipe, you'll find variations. But follow this one and you'll get your party started right.

The Hurricane
1 oz. white rum
1 oz. Jamaican dark rum
1 oz. Bacardi 151 rum
3 oz. orange juice
3 oz. pineapple juice
½ oz. grenadine syrup

Pour over crushed ice

NEW ORLEANS JAZZ AND HERITAGE FESTIVAL

⊛ New Orleans, Louisiana
Last weekend in April and first weekend in May
www.nojazzfest.com

Jazz Fest *is* New Orleans! This massive celebration represents everything that's wonderful and unique about the Big Easy: unmatched music and food, the mesmerizing architecture

and art, and a dynamic cultural smorgasbord.

Taking place over the final weekend in April and the first weekend in May, Jazz Fest draws upward of 600,000 music lovers for what many feel is the "best time to come to New Orleans." The Fair Grounds Race Course houses the events, which begin at around 11:00 A.M. and end at 7:30 P.M. each day. Elite musicians from around the world share time with local bands on multiple stages and inside musical tents, while artists display their creations throughout. The humongous size of the fairgrounds allows for acts to play simultaneously on different stages, with the headliners playing the final slot of the evening.

Jazz Fest not only pays tribute to the birthplace of jazz, but it ushers in all genres of music, keeping in line with the Big Easy's eclectic personality. Recent headliners have ranged from Ludacris to Norah Jones, and from Elvis Costello to Bruce Springsteen and Fats Domino. The lineup also features a rotation of Dixieland bands, accomplished Cajun and zydeco musicians, jazz virtuosos, and elderly Delta bluesmen, armed with sharp-cut suits and rings on each finger.

The main concerts end early in the evening, but the fun continues. Actually, it never stops. The Fair Grounds Race Course is a twenty-minute walk from the French Quarter, the city's hub. Buses run

back and forth; however, making the trek on foot is quicker and provides an opportunity to absorb unique New Orleans culture.

A slew of bars and clubs in and around the French Quarter host after-hours concerts by the headlining acts. Imagine going to see Lenny Kravitz, Sting, the Neville Brothers, or B.B. King in a dark bar—this is your chance. Venues typically include the Maple Leaf Bar (8316 Oak St.), Howlin' Wolf (907 S. St. Peters St.), Tipitina's (501 Napoleon Ave.), Twi-Ro-Pa (1544 Tchoupitoulas St.), and aboard the *Riverboat Cajun Queen*. The shows can take place from 1:00 A.M. to 5:00 P.M., and the schedule is announced just a few weeks before in "The Grid." Visit the website often until acts and venues are published. You may be able to walk into these intimate concerts, but tickets to popular shows are sold via Ticketmaster, Ticketweb, or at the club's box office. Often, tickets are sold for a show, but information about the time and venue are announced at the last minute.

TRANSPORTATION

AIR: Fly into Louis Armstrong New Orleans International Airport (MSY / *www.flymsy.com*), located fifteen miles from downtown. No need to rent a car—a taxi into the city costs $28 for one to two people and $12 per person for three or more.

🚌 **SHUTTLE:** An airport shuttle will take passengers into the business district for $13 per person. Call 866-596-2699 for reservations.

🚌 **JAZZ FEST EXPRESS:** This convenient air-conditioned bus takes concertgoers from the French Quarter and Central Business District right to the fairground gates. You must purchase a ticket at the bus station—a single-day round-trip fare from the French Quarter is $16. Bus stations are located at Steamboat Natchez Dock (600 Decatur St.) and at the Sheraton Hotel (500 Canal St.). The bus runs from 10:30 A.M. to 7:30 P.M.

ⓑ **BUS /** 🚂 **TRAIN:** Airport-Downtown Express will take passengers from the airport to downtown for $1 to $10 depending on destination. The Greyhound station is located at 101 Loyola Avenue, and the Amtrak station is at 1001 Loyola.

🅣 **TAXIS:** You'll use a taxi when going to the after-hours venues that are located on the north side of town, approximately five miles from the French Quarter. Local taxi companies include United Cabs (504-522-9771), American Taxi (504-299-0386), Yellow-Checker Cabs (504-525-3311), Coleman Cab Co. (504-586-0222), King Cab (504-491-1184), and Veterans Cab Co. (504-367-6767).

ACCOMMODATIONS

🏨 **HOTELS:** Jazz Fest is a cornerstone of New Orleans's tourism industry and every single room in town gets sold out. French Quarter hotel rates can be raised over twice their normal price on Friday and Saturday nights. However, staying in the French Quarter isn't as glamorous as it's made out to be. You'll be drinking by midday, up until all hours, and will probably want a good night's sleep at some point. This can be difficult in the noisy French Quarter. The downtown hotels on the other side of Canal St. (the dividing line into the

French Quarter) are quieter, better priced, and are only a five-minute walk or a short cab ride from action-packed Bourbon Street and the rest of the French Quarter. That being said, you should book any hotel room one year in advance!

Downtown hotels that offer special Jazz Fest rates include Courtyard by Marriott (124 St. Charles Ave. / 504-581-9005 / $189), Doubletree (300 Canal St. / 504-581-1300 / $199), Embassy Suites (315 Julia St. / 504-525-1993 / $144), Hampton Inn (1201 Convention Center Blvd. / 866-311-1200 / $209), Holiday Inn Express (221 Carondelet St. / 504-962-0800 / $179), La Quinta Inn (301 Camp St. / 800-531-5900 / $169), Pelham Hotel (444 Common St. / 888-856-4486 / $179), and Hotel Le Cirque (936 St. Charles Ave. / 800-684-9525 / $159).

French Quarter hotels with special Jazz Fest rates include Historic French Market Inn (501 Decatur St. / 888-766-3782 / $189), Holiday Inn French Quarter (124 Royal St. / 800-747-3279 / $195), Andrew Jackson Hotel (919 Royal St. / 800-654-0224 / $99), Astor Crowne Plaza (739 Canal St. / 866-750-4202 / $229), Bienville House (320 Decatur St. / 800-535-7836 / $225), Bourbon Orleans (717 Orleans St. / 800-999-3426 / $279), Chateau Dupre (131 Rue Decatur / 888-538-5666 / $185), and Chateau Sonesta (800 Iberville St. / 504-586-0800 / $279). For further listings of hotels visit *www.nojazzfest.com*.

TICKETS

Neither weekend is better than the other in terms of music—they're both great. Ticket sales and the lineup announcement usually become available in mid-February. Friday and Saturday tickets cost $35 per day via *www.nojazzfest.com* or Ticketmaster when purchased before the lineup is announced, $40 if purchased online after the lineup has been announced, or $45 at the gate. Thursday tickets cost $25–$30. If you plan to go on Friday and Saturday, then you must purchase two tickets! Visit the Jazz Fest ticket office at the Louisiana Superdome in person if you hate extra fees. Research ticket information for the late-night shows. The act you want may have tickets available through Ticketmaster or Ticketweb, or at the individual venue's box office. Some sell out and others don't.

party tip

The most famous of Louisianan dialects is Cajun French, and many visitors need a little bit of help to translate the fast pronunciation and unfamiliar phrases. A friendly Cajun greeting is "comment ca va (coam-on-sah-vawh)?" or "how are you doing?" "We got companie an I gona ax dem ta git down me" means "We've got guests and I'm going to ask them to come in." However, for Jazz Fest, the most important phrase is "laissez les bon temps rouler (less-say lay bon tohn roo-lay)!" meaning "let the good times roll!"

NEW YEAR'S EVE

⊛ **New Orleans, Louisiana**
December 31
www.neworleansonline.com

New Orleans's end-of-the-year celebration is a spectacle. Alongside Las Vegas, it easily ranks as the best in the nation. Between the tourists, the locals, and the thousands who come to town for the January 1 Sugar Bowl game, the city is a mob scene. Showing up without a plan for your evening is a surefire way to get bested by the mob, thus missing the fun that's to be had. There are necessary steps that will maximize the Bourbon Street New Year's experience.

First off, make the decision to attend this event early. Try to make hotel reservations by mid-October, if not sooner. The longer you wait, the farther outside of town, and farther away from the festivities, you'll end up staying. Expect to pay $225 a night for a room in the French Quarter, and about $150 a night for a room on the other side of Canal Street. Canal Street is only a five-minute walk from the action, and it's much quieter.

Secondly, do not arrive in town and then try to make New Year's Eve dinner reservations. New Orleans is home to the greatest restaurants and most exquisite cuisine in America, and dining in this city is an experience to savor. In fact, dining is a key element of the party, so spend some money and enjoy. Emeril's (800 Tchoupitoulas St. / 504-528-9393) is Emeril Lagasse's upscale Creole fusion restaurant—the Banana Crème Pie is off the charts. NOLA (534 St. Louis Ave. / 504-522-6652) is Emeril's other restaurant—it's a little less pricey but still affords the opportunity to enjoy Emeril's cooking. Andrea's (3100 Nineteenth St. / 504-834-9583) serves Creole-Italian cuisine—one of the city's best. Or check out Bayona (430 Dauphine St. / 504-525-4455), a critic favorite; Mandina's (3800 Canal St. / 504-482-9179), an affordable neighborhood restaurant; or K-Paul's Louisiana Kitchen (416 Chartres St. / 504-524-7394), which does blackened Cajun better than anyone else. Visit *www.neworleansrestaurants.com*

for further options and online reservations.

Many revelers mingle and move slowly among the Bourbon Street crowd to Jackson Square at midnight to watch the ball-drop along with the fireworks. Afterward they retreat back into the French Quarter.

If you feel the need to escape the Bourbon Street madness, then check out a variety of smaller events that capture the essence of New Orleans. "A NOLA New Year's Eve" is a free zydeco and Cajun-style music concert that starts at 8:30 P.M. along Decatur Street. Thousands of people gather alongside the mayor to ring in the New Year beneath a giant gumbo pot that is lowered from the roof of Jax Brewery. Mid-City's Annual Bonfire is technically an illegal event, but it occurs nonetheless. Gather with the locals at 10:00 P.M. along Orleans Avenue in mid-city. The ceremonial bonfire dance is worth seeing. The Galactic party at Tipitina's Uptown (501 Napoleon Ave.) is an always-packed high-energy musical extravaganza. Visit *www.tipitinas.com* to purchase tickets.

TRANSPORTATION / ACCOMMODATIONS

See transportation and accommodations sections in previous New Orleans events on pages 76–77 and 78–79.

What to Pack
- Multicolored masquerade mask
- Clothing that doubles as dinner attire and party gear
- American Express card for dinner—save your cash for the bars

party tip

A memorable stop during New Year's Eve is Mid-City Lanes Rock 'N Bowl (4133 S. Carrollton Ave.). Revelers of all ages fill the large wooden dance floor for Cajun, zydeco, swing, and rockabilly acts that play until the wee hours of the morning. If you need a break from two-stepping, rent a pair of multicolored bowling shoes and knock down some pins—old fashioned score sheets and pencils haven't given way to computerized scoring screens at this unique watering hole. The beer's real cheap too!

Mississippi

JUBILEE! JAM

⊛ Jackson, Mississippi
Mid-June
www.jubileejam.com

Years after June and Johnny Cash sung a little ditty about messin' around in Jackson, the capital of Mississippi obliged. Mississippi is the birthplace of American music, and Jackson is the center of its culture and arts scene. It's a city that cherishes old southern roots while looking ahead to its place in the "new South," and the annual Jubilee! Jam provides a quantum leap in the forward direction.

For over twenty years in downtown Jackson, the Jubilee! Jam has drawn an attendance of 50,000, making it the state's largest cultural and arts festival. It constantly ranks at the top of the South's most electrifying events, but exceptional community support offered during some unstable financial times has inspired the city of Jackson to rally around the jam, now more than ever.

This two-day southern street festival takes place on the second or third Friday and Saturday in June. Over fifty artists, thirty bands, ten DJs, and hordes of food vendors close down Commerce Street in the heart of downtown. Jackson's population is only 180,000, but the allure of this event is a huge party held within a midsize city full of soul. The action kicks off on Friday night around 6:00 P.M. and on Saturday at 3:00 P.M., lasting until midnight. Purchase tickets through Ticketmaster. Two huge stages and a number of smaller indoor venues host honky-tonk, funk, rock 'n' roll, and hip-hop acts like Bob Dylan, the Killers, Arctic Monkeys, North Mississippi Allstars, Black Crowes, Ludacris, and the Dirty Dozen Brass Band. The stages are set up in the streets so don't plan on sitting on a lawn. Wander back and forth from outdoor music to indoor lounges, check out the artist's village, and munch on Mississippi crayfish throughout the day. A carefree aura fills the streets, but the summer heat doesn't slow the crowd a bit. The whole weekend is priced reasonably.

The infamous triad of Jackson bars exude an outstanding danceable vibe throughout the weekend. The Red Room at Hal and Mal's (200 S. Commerce St.) bumps and grinds, hosting live music while packing in the crowd. W. C. Don's (218 S. State St.) and Martin's Restaurant and Lounge (214 S. State St.) are rhythm joints with drink specials and bands. These bars stay open well after the concerts have ended, and the lines form quickly.

TRANSPORTATION

✈ AIR: Book flights into Jackson International Airport (JAN / *www.jmaa.com*) located eleven miles from downtown Jackson. Car-rental agencies and taxis are available.

☎ TAXIS: Cab companies include Citi-Cab (601-355-8319), Deluxe Cab (601-948-4761), Yellow Cab (601-922-3782), and Jackson Taxi (601-354-1400).

🅑 BUS / 🚆 TRAIN: The Greyhound and Amtrak stations are located at 300 West Capitol St.

🅟 PARKING: Parking is available at lots surrounding Commerce Street as well as side streets.

ACCOMMODATIONS

🛏 **HOTELS:** You'll find reasonable prices in Jackson. Some of the nicer chain hotels have rooms in the low $100s, so you may be able to up your ante in this town. The closest downtown hotels include Marriott Downtown (200 Amite St. / 601-969-5100 / $170), Holiday Inn Express (310 Greymont Ave. / 888-400-9714 / $94), and Edison Walthall (225 E. Capitol St. / 601-948-6161 / $99). Other hotels that are within a few miles include Comfort Inn (2800 Greenway Dr. / 601-922-5600 / $60), Hilton (1001 E. County Line Rd. / 601-957-2800 / $139), Best Western (725 Larson St. / 601-969-6555 / $89), Courtyard Marriott (6280 Ridgewood Ct. Dr. / 601-956-9991 / $99), or Fairfield Inn (5723 I-55 N. / 601-957-8557 / $85).

TICKETS

Single-day tickets cost $20 in advance or $25 at the gate, and two-day passes are $40. Event organizers plan on selling VIP tickets—check the event website for details. Tickets can be purchased through *www.ticketmaster.com* or by calling 800-277-1700.

What to Pack
- Sunscreen
- Raincoat/umbrella
- Bug spray
- Johnny Cash's *Greatest Hits*

party tip

Do not miss out on the opportunity to gorge yourself on sweet Mississippi pecan pie, widely regarded as the best in the world. Many restaurants serve up healthy mouth watering slices, slow-baked with molasses, and delicious to the last crumb. A seasoned partier usually orders two slices, saving one for breakfast the following morning.

North Carolina

NATIONAL HOLLERIN' CONTEST

⊛ Spivey's Corner, North Carolina
Third Saturday in June
www.ibiblio.org/hollerin/hollerin.htm

We live in an age of cell phones, e-mail, text messaging, instant messaging, and electronic greeting cards. While these means of communication may be efficient, they also tend to be (*ssshhh!*) quiet. Do your true feelings ever get completely bottled up after interacting in such a soft and passive manner day after day? Do you ever get the primordial urge to stand on a platform, clench your fists, unbutton your shirt, and let out the loudest holler that your lungs can handle? If you've answered yes to either of these questions then the National Hollerin' Contest is definitely the place for you.

In 1969 the first National Hollerin' contest took place in sleepy little Spivey's Corner, North Carolina, to raise money for the volunteer fire department. This sprawling metropolis is home to over 440 people. No need for panic, because 3,000–5,000 visitors crash the Spivey's Corner high school football field each year for one of the most unique and bizarre festivals in the United States. This contest has gained national attention on late-night talk shows, in *Sports Illustrated* articles, and in numerous documentaries. Past invitees have included Ronald Reagan and the Shah of Iran. Although the contest's draw peaked in the mid-1990s, it is still going quite strong.

Try to arrive by 11:00 A.M. as the event begins early. The feel is very similar to a gigantic picnic, where delicious barbecue and watermelon are plentiful. Partygoers report feeling as though they've walked into an episode of *Dukes of Hazzard*. Events throughout the day include the Biggest Bell Pepper Contest, Watermelon Roll, Square Dancing Jamboree, and various pageants and games. Not to mention the Whistlin' Contest, the Fox Horn and Conch Shell Blowin' Contest, the Junior Hollerin' Contest, and the Ladies Callin' Contest. The final event of the day is the men's Hollerin' Contest. Anyone can compete, as long as they arrive and register at the event desk by 2:00 P.M. Musical entertainment includes country, gospel, and bluegrass acts.

Although this is one of the smaller parties featured, its charm is self-evident—make the trip just to say, "I did it."

TRANSPORTATION

✈ **AIR:** You can book a flight into Raleigh-Durham International Airport (RDU / *www.rdu.com*) for the hour-and-forty-minute drive.

ACCOMMODATIONS

🏨 **HOTELS:** If you plan on spending the night before or the night of, then book a room in Dunn, the closest town with accommodations. Hotels

include the Comfort Inn (131 Bud Hawkins Rd./ 910-891-2511 / $95), Econo Lodge (1952 Cedar Creek Rd. / 910-433-2100 / $60), and the Holiday Inn Express (900 E. Pearsall St. / 910-892-4400 / $81). Visit *www.dunntourism.org/Hotels.asp* for a complete listing of Dunn hotels.

TICKETS

No way. Just show up, write down your name, and give it your best holler.

What to Pack
- Sunscreen and a straw hat
- Your beverage of choice (keep those vocal cords lubricated)
- *Deliverance* soundtrack

---

party tip

A brief tutorial will benefit those who plan on entering the contest. First off, this is not a shouting match. Hollerin' is an art that takes many forms, but getting up there and screaming into the microphone is not one of them. Locals tend to cringe when tourists treat this as a volume contest. You don't want to embarrass yourself in front of all fifty locals, do you? You can holler like an animal, or as a duet with your friend. The point is to change the inflection and pitch of your voice—similar to yodeling. In recent years many winners have earned the gold ribbon by hollerin' a popular tune.

WILMINGTON FOURTH OF JULY

⭐ Wilmington, North Carolina
July 4

There are some exhilarating Fourth of July celebrations that occur between the Atlantic and the Pacific. Philadelphia, the birthplace of American freedom, throws a week-long kicker, and Houston is famous for the largest land-based fireworks show in the nation. But when you judge an Independence Day party on sheer energy and electricity, there is but one winner. Wilmington, North Carolina, is a 100,000-person city that steps up to the plate and knocks it out of the park on the most American of holidays.

Wilmington is nicknamed "Hollywood East" due to its charm and picturesque location on the Cape Fear River. It has served as the film site for TV shows like *Dawson's Creek* and *One Tree Hill*, and celebrity sightings are commonplace. An array of restaurants and bars fill the downtown area, and every single nook, cranny, and crevice is lined with proud Americans on July 4.

Over 60,000 people from across the country flock to the downtown to celebrate independence as if it were 1776.

Anyone who owns a boat or who has a friend with a boat begins their Fourth festivities on Wrightsville Beach, located five miles east of Wilmington. The beach itself and nearby Masonboro Island are very well worth the early day excursion from Wilmington. Water taxis will shuttle those without aquatic means from the beach to Masonboro Island, an undeveloped piece of land that explodes with midsummer antics and unrestrained revelry. A mass of boats, all tied together, surround the island and allow for partying Americans to hop from vessel to vessel. Bring what you need, as there are no services on the island—this includes restrooms. Although the fun will be difficult to leave, you should head back to downtown Wilmington in the mid-afternoon.

Once back downtown, enjoy watching the lunacy unfold. Front Street, the heart of Wilmington's nightlife, becomes packed beyond belief with sons and daughters of the revolution. Each establishment is bursting with humanity, and positive energy fills the air. Former area bartender Katie Cutter attests "Fourth of July on Front Street is so crazy that I used to make $800 in tips after just a few hours." The fireworks are launched from the river at 9:00 P.M. Water Street, along the bank, becomes a mass gathering—feel free to bring a blanket or lawn chair and perch on the cobblestone. Great places to watch the explosions from include Reel Café (100 S. Front St.), a tri-level building with multiple bars; Level 5 (21 N. Front St.), an old Masonic Temple with the best rooftop view in the city; and Firebelly Lounge (265 N. Front St.), a happening club with a nice outdoor patio.

Begin your morning on July 5 at Dixie Grill (116 Market St.), a funky country kitchen with the best breakfast in town. Afterwards, relax by walking along the river, taking a free trolley ride, or boarding one of the city's infamous

and quite inexpensive horse and buggies.

TRANSPORTATION

AIR: The closest airport is Wilmington International Airport (ILM / www.flyilm.com) located minutes from downtown, and serviced by Delta and US Airways. Taxis are available. Myrtle Beach Airport (MYR / www.myrtlebeachairport.com) is an hour and a half away with car rentals. The cheapest flights usually land in Raleigh-Durham International Airport (RDU / www.rdu.com), which is two and a half hours from Wilmington.

Ⓑ BUS / 🚂 TRAIN: The Greyhound and Amtrak stations are located at 201 Harnett St.

🚆 WAVE TRANSIT: Local transportation includes shuttles, buses, and trolleys, which run from downtown to neighboring suburbs and locations. Visit www.wavetransit.com for schedules and information.

Ⓟ PARKING: Parking along Front Street is nearly impossible after 3:00 P.M. You can find spaces about ten blocks from downtown; however, a walk through "rough" neighborhoods will be necessary. Parking garages are located at 130 N. Front and 116 N. Second Street. Residents will also allow you to park on their lawn for $5 for the day.

Ⓣ TAXIS: Trying to hail a cab after Fourth of July is difficult. You can call a taxi, but the chances are great that someone will steal it. Be prepared to fight for your ride. Cab companies include Costal Yellow Cab (910-762-3322), Village Taxi (910-538-4900), and Taxicabs Inc. (910-762-3322).

ACCOMMODATIONS

🏨 HOTELS: There are two hotels within walking distance to downtown—book a room by March or April. The Best Western (503 Nutt St. / 910-763-2800 / $189) and Hilton (301 N. Water St. /

910-763-5900 / $169) are both gorgeous properties located right on the water and are priced below $200 per night. You can also try Hampton Inn (2320 S. Seventeenth St. / 910-796-8881 / $159).

B&BS: Blue Heaven Bed & Breakfast (517 Orange St. / 910-772-9929 / $100 to $150) is among the nicest bed-and-breakfasts, and it's reasonably priced. Visit *www.discoverourtown .com/NC/Wilmington/Lodging* for a complete list of bed-and-breakfasts.

RENTAL HOMES: Many people rent condos or town homes as well—see *www.vrbo.com* for a list of vacation rentals by owner. Those who wish to beach camp can do so on the north end of Carolina Beach, located twenty miles from Wilmington.

What to Pack
- Swimsuit
- Uncle Sam hat
- Miniature American flags
- Twelve-packs—of sparklers

---

party tip

Wilmington is located thirty miles from the South Carolina border. South Carolina permits the sale of Class C Fireworks, which include Jumbo Moon Traveler Rockets, Mad Dogs, Titanium Rockets, Whistling Petes, Big Bomb Sky Crackers, and TNT Parachutes. It's illegal to cross the North Carolina border with this artillery, but then again, people drive all the way to Canada for prescription medicine.

BELE CHERE

⊛ **Asheville, North Carolina**
Last weekend in July
www.belecherefestival.com

The music and arts festivals that take place in nearly every midsize city across the country in June and July represent the essence of summertime Americana. Asheville, North Carolina, however, has the perfect combination of prosperity and bohemia, and it easily wins bragging rights as the largest and most celebrated free street festival in the Southeastern United States. Among a sea of competitors, Bele Chere is the unquestionable reigning king.

Surrounded by the mystic Blue Ridge Mountains, Asheville has a population of 75,000, making it the largest city in western North Carolina. The Arts and Crafts–style homes and Art Deco downtown buildings coupled with the beautiful location have helped to land Asheville on lists such as "The 50 Most Alive Places to Be," "Best Places to Reinvent Your Life," and "Happiest Cities for Women." Downtown is the funky center of the social scene and the location of Bele Chere, a three-day rockin' festival that brings a crowd of 350,000 good-timers into Asheville.

The streets are packed and the mood is purely festive. Eighty local and national music acts strut their stuff on six stages scattered throughout the Pack Square area. They play all day from Friday to Sunday, showcasing a range of genres. Recent performers include Rusted Root, Kenny Wayne Shepherd, Gin Blossoms, and Lovin' Spoonful. The biggest headliners hit either the Biltmore Avenue Stage or the Rock' n Kiss stage on Coxe Avenue, during the Festival Jam on Saturday night.

An array of artists showcase their talent in Art Park, located in the Asheville Savings Bank parking lot off Patton Avenue. You can escape the heat and the crowds by checking out paintings, photography, metalwork, woodwork, jewelry, and sculptures. Typical kitschy rides and games line the streets, many of which are inflatable. Be sure to sample microbrews from local brewers like French Broad Brewing Company and Pisgah Brewing Company—the Pisgah Solstice Tripel ale has recently won some major beer awards (be careful, it's 9.5 percent ABV).

Asheville boasts a huge selection of restaurants and bars (considering the city's size), and they are all packed during Bele Chere. The Orange Peel (101 Biltmore Ave.) is regarded as one of the best live music venues in the Southeast, and Barley's (42 Biltmore Ave.) is a pizza joint and bar with live music and the best pies in North Carolina. Hannah Flanagan's Irish Pub (27 Biltmore Ave.) has forty beers on tap and is a late-night hangout.

TRANSPORTATION

AIR: Asheville Regional Airport (AVL / *www .flyavl.com*) is located eleven miles from downtown and is serviced by Continental, Delta, Northwest, and US Airways. Flights into Asheville from many major U.S. cities are under $200, making this airport the logical choice. Taxis and car-rental agencies are available. Call 828-209-3660 for ground transportation information.

P PARKING: The downtown streets close during Bele Chere, and driving a car through the mass of people is not recommended. That being said, there are city parking decks located at the Civic Center, on Rankin Avenue, and on Wall Street. A number of temporary lots are scattered about downtown as well.

🚐 **SHUTTLE:** Two shuttle routes run partygoers back and forth from east and west sides of town. The East Shuttle picks up at the Asheville Mall on Tunnel Road. The West Shuttle runs from the K-Mart shopping center parking lot on Patton Avenue. These shuttles run every twenty minutes for a $2 round-trip fee.

🚲 **BIKE:** It's strongly recommended that you bring or rent a bicycle and use it as transportation to your hotel and back during the festival. You're guaranteed to maneuver about town much quicker on a bike than by any other means of transportation. Luckily Asheville is an outdoor enthusiast's town, and bike rentals are available. Try Hearn's Cycling and Fitness (34 Broadway St. / 828-253-4800) or Bio Wheels (76 Biltmore Ave. / 828-232-0300).

Ⓑ **BUS:** The Greyhound station is located at 2 Tunnel Rd.

ACCOMMODATIONS

Book a room within two months of the festival because accommodations will sell out. You can stay in chain hotels, inns, or bed-and-breakfasts.

🛏️ **HOTELS/INNS:** Those near downtown include Days Inn (120 Patton Ave. / 828-254-9661 / $185), Best Western (22 Woodfin St. / 828-253-1851 / $225), Renaissance Hotel (1 Thomas Wolfe Plaza / 828-252-8211 / $269), Baymont Inn & Suites (204 Hendersonville Rd. / 828-274-2022 / $159), Doubletree (115 Hendersonville Rd. / 828-274-1800 / $209), and Holiday Inn Express (234 Hendersonville Rd. / 800-465-4329 / $117). The Princess Anne Hotel (301 E. Chestnut St. / 828-258-0986 / $129) is a newly renovated historic inn close to downtown, and the Residences

at Biltmore (700 Biltmore Ave. / 866-433-5594 / $199) is a gorgeous all-suite hotel within walking distance to downtown.

☞ **B&BS:** Quaint bed-and-breakfasts line the downtown streets. Nearby ones include A Bed Of Roses (135 Cumberland Ave. / 888-290-2770 / $119), the Lion & the Rose (276 Montford Ave. / 828-255-7673 / $170), and Black Walnut Inn (288 Montford Ave. / 800-381-3878 / $175).

TICKETS

The Bele Chere Festival Jam is the only portion of the festival that costs money—and it's definitely worth it. Four or five high-energy bands hit the stages beginning on Saturday afternoon, playing well into the evening. Tickets cost $18 in advance by visiting the event website or by calling 800-594-8499. At the gate, tickets cost $23. You can also purchase tickets in town at Karmasonics Music Video (14 Haywood St.).

What to Pack
- Sunscreen
- Hiking shoes
- Bathing suit for hot springs
- Your prequalification letter from a mortgage lender—you may want to buy real estate

party tip

The lush green mountains surrounding Asheville contain some of the greatest hiking trails, waterfalls, and scenery in the eastern United States. Awaken each morning for a mountain bike ride or a jog in the Blue Ridge Mountains. Return from your activity, take a shower, and head to the party.

South Carolina

SPRING BREAK AT MYRTLE BEACH

★ Myrtle Beach, South Carolina
Mid-February to mid-March
www.springbreakmyrtlebeach.com

A tidal wave of 500,000 unin-hibited college students racing for the ocean can mean only one thing—spring break in Myrtle Beach. Upperclassmen, underclassmen, and random twenty-somethings reliving their youth come from all across the country in cars, buses, and airplanes, to a town that is built upon the concept of a sustained adolescence.

North Myrtle Beach transforms itself into coed central during mid-March, as locals flee, and rental owners pray that their abodes suffer only minimal damage during the storm. These neighborhoods will host more keg parties than you can count, as groups of twenty friends pack themselves into four-bedroom rental homes throughout North Myrtle.

If you're a student, avoid getting pigeonholed with the same old crowd from campus. It's perfectly acceptable to hop from one party to the next, making new friends and filling up your cup along the way. If you're a graduate looking to relive past college glories while hoping that nobody asks your age, then you are also welcome—just avoid referencing how dominating your football team was in the '89 Orange Bowl. Just remember, drinking on the front lawn is legal, but roaming the streets with an open container is not.

When the sun is shining, the Ocean Drive beach is the place to be. Jet Skis, parasailing, wakeboarding, and water skiing are available through Myrtle Beach Watersports (843-280-7777). Captain Smiley's Inshore Fishing charges $330 to take groups of three on a half-day fishing trip—book trips online at *www.captains*

mileysfishingcharters.com. Paintball U.S.A. (6602 Highway 707 / 843-650-1540) is located twenty-two miles from Ocean Drive, and is an excellent way to express pent-up frustration on close friends. You may need a reservation, so call in advance. NASCAR Speedpark (1820 Twenty-first Ave. / 843-918-8725) has seven tracks for miniature stock car racing excitement, as well as bumper boats and miniature golf.

Myrtle Beach has almost as many golf courses as it does grains of sand. Visit *www.golfdesk .com* (800-642-3108) to book tee times and find special discounts on a mind-boggling selection of courses.

The nightlife scene is fun, albeit the typical spring break, cheesy bar atmosphere. Broadway at the Beach is the center of Myrtle's nightlife scene, and one cover charge gets you into Jimmy Buffett's Margaritaville, the Hard Rock Café, Blarneystone's, and a host of others.

TRANSPORTATION

AIR: Delta, Continental, US Air, and Spirit fly regularly into Myrtle Beach Airport (MYR / *www* *.myrtlebeachairport.com*). Although it's a smaller airport, flights are very reasonable. Car-rental agencies are available. Cab rides to North Myrtle are approximately thirty-five minutes.

B BUS: There is a Greyhound station located just north of the airport.

T TAXIS: Cab companies are in abundance and rides show up quickly. Local taxis include Action Cab (843-361-2545), AAA Beach Connections Taxi (843-289-8600), Beach Checker Cab (843-272-6212), Friendly Taxi (843-488-0432), Tropical Taxi (843-268-7778), and Hillside Taxi (843-448-6652).

ACCOMMODATIONS

HOTELS: If you're going to stay in a hotel, the Ocean Drive Beach and Golf Resort (98 North Ocean Blvd. / 800-438-9590 / $68) is the optimal choice. This beautiful resort is located on the ocean, and the beach is just an elevator ride away. Rates start at $68 during the week and $100 on weekends. Nearby is the Avista Resort (300 North Ocean Blvd. / 800-968-8986 / $219). Other hotels are located closer to the Barefoot Landings area, outside of Spring Breaker's alley. For a complete listing visit *www.northmyrtlebeach.net.*

RENTAL HOMES: The ocean drive neighborhoods are the action hubs. Those who plan the trip will end up with houses, while everyone else claws for hotel rooms on the outskirts. The *www .springbreakmyrtlebeach.com* website contains student home rentals in North Myrtle. You even have the option of choosing a "party house." Each listing is complete with photos, home-specific information, prices, and ocean view availability. Prices range from $110 to $300 per person per week. Also included are listings with pools, pool tables, and other upgrades. Group size plays a role in price—the larger the group, the lower the price.

party tip

A town that practically beckons wild drunken behavior will naturally have its share of alcohol-induced arrests. Most of the charges fall into categories such as minor consumption of alcohol, marijuana possession, DUIs, and assaults. Should you find yourself in handcuffs, there *are* locals who can help to set your mind at ease and expedite your incarceration. A new breed of lawyer, the "spring break attorney" has surfaced as a very lucrative career option in town. These fearless champions of the frat boy will represent college students and even break the news to the parents back home. Although not cheap, they do typically reduce charges, reduce fines, and make it their personal goal to get their clients back on the beach by lunchtime.

Tennessee

MEMPHIS IN MAY, BEALE STREET MUSIC FESTIVAL

⭐ Memphis, Tennessee
First weekend in May
www.memphisinmay.org and *www.thebealestreettmusicfestival.com*

Welcome to the land of blues and barbecue. Memphis in May is a time for the capital of rhythm to host an array of weekend-long gatherings for its proud citizens. The whole month is chock-full of festivities, but the Beale Street Music Festival is the one not to be missed.

This three-day-long outdoor concert is held just a short distance from the downtown Beale Street area, in Tom Lee Park. The lineup contains blues, rock, gospel, and alternative music, and featured acts have included Bob Dylan, the Dave Matthews Band, the Offspring, Jerry Lee Lewis, and Little Richard. Over sixty performers take the stage throughout the course of the weekend, playing on four main stages, spread across thirty-three acres, while 300,000 people flock to the park. You can bounce back and forth from stage to stage, grabbing food and refreshments at a multitude of tents along the way. Shows begin at 1:00 P.M., giving concertgoers plenty of time to awaken for a leisurely breakfast of barbecued ribs before strolling down to the concerts. The stages are located on the banks of the mighty Mississippi, which provides the perfect local backdrop to this exciting weekend.

The shows end at 12:30 A.M., but the fun continues long after. Beale Street, nicknamed "the Bourbon Street of the Mid-South," is the epicenter of Memphis. This four-block-long drag of bars and restaurants is packed during the day and becomes complete mayhem once the concerts have ended. Nearly every establishment explodes with the sounds of the blues as venerable local guitar gods play to the dancing crowds inside. Bounce up and down the street's addresses from B. B. King's (#143) to Alfred's (#197) to the Rum Boogie Café (#182) for the best live music. Late night techno / house dance crowds flock to Club 152 (#152). After you've worked up an appetite, check out the Pig (#167), home of the best late-night eats on the strip. Drinking on Beale Street is legal, and many bars sell drinks through street-side take-out windows.

Don't leave town without having eaten a meal at Corky's, conspicuously located downstairs, in the alley behind 52 South Second Street. It has consistently been voted the number-one barbecue joint in town—ask them what types of beer they have and the answer will simply be "cold." Also, a trip to Memphis is not complete without a stop at Graceland, a short fifteen-minute cab ride from downtown.

TRANSPORTATION

If you'll be flying in, there is really no need for a car. The goal is to find a hotel within a few blocks of Beale Street and spend the weekend on foot.

AIR: Flights can be booked into Memphis International Airport (MEM / *www.mscaa.com*), located eight miles from Beale Street.

BUS: A Greyhound station is located at 203 Union Avenue, within walking distance to downtown.

TROLLEY: The Main Street and Riverfront Trolley Line runs north and south along the river. This trolley is a great way to get to the festival if your hotel is a couple of miles away.

TAXIS: Taxis are in abundance in Memphis. Try City-Wide Taxi (901-324-4202), Checker Cab (901-577-7777), Advantage Cab (901-844-9999), or Metro Cab (901-323-3333).

ACCOMMODATIONS

HOTELS: The absolute best hotel to stay in during the festival is the Peabody (149 Union Ave. / 901-529-4000 / $295). Rates are reasonable and the ambiance is unique. Twice a day, at 11:00 A.M. and 5:00 P.M., the red carpet is rolled out, the elevators open, and a squadron of ducks marches across the Grand Lobby after descending from their home on the top floor. Other nearby hotels include Doubletree (185 Union Ave. / 901-528-1800 / $299), Hampton Inn (175 Peabody Place / 901-260-4000 / $199), Artisan Hotel (1837 Union Ave. / 901-278-4100 / $132), Comfort Inn (100 N. Front St. / 901-526-0583 / $189, three-night min.), and Holiday Inn (160 Union Ave. / 901-525-5491 / $239). Visit *www.memphistravel.com* for a complete listing of nearby hotels.

Single-day tickets are $27.50 in advance or $33 at the gate. Three-day passes cost $63.50 if purchased before April 30th, otherwise they cost $82.50. Tickets can be purchased through Ticketmaster online, or by calling 901-525-1515.

What to Pack
- Beads
- B. B. King tunes
- Elvis sunglasses with *attached* sideburns

party tip

When in Memphis one must pay homage to The King, Elvis Aaron Presley. The best way to do this is to adopt Big E's favorite slang phrase "T.C.B. (takin' care of business)." When asked how he was doing, Elvis replied "T.C.B." When asked what he'd been up to, The Pelvis answered, "T.C.B." To truly embody the spirit of the city one must incorporate this acronym into one's vocabulary. Just remember, when at the Beale Street Music Festival it's all about T.C.B.

CMA MUSIC FESTIVAL

⊛ Nashville, Tennessee
First Thursday in June through Sunday
www.cmafest.com

Music City, Nashvegas, and America's Favorite City are all fitting nicknames for a town that's country to the core. Each June, the country music industry says "thank you" to its fans by hosting the biggest honky-tonk party in the country. The CMA Music Festival is a four-day gala of nonstop, Wrangler-jeans-splitting excitement, as the 191,000 fans who attended 2007's event will proudly attest.

CMA Music Fest begins the day after the TNN/CMT Country Music Awards Show, usually on the first Thursday in June. Unlike traditional festivals, CMA doesn't leave fans wishing that their favorite act had appeared on the bill. All of country's brightest stars are guaranteed to be in attendance because they're already in town for the awards show. One stadium-packing artist after another takes the stage in half-hourly slots; they play their best songs, and they perform with reverent swagger. Expect the likes of Trace Adkins,

Reba McEntire, Brad Paisley, Kenny Chesney, Shania Twain, and Toby Keith. A series of venues host the concerts and events, and all are located in downtown within walking distance of one another. The mission of CMA is best exemplified in the mornings, during Fan Fair. Beginning at 8:30 A.M. at the Nashville Convention Center, Fan Fair is an opportunity for fans to meet and greet their idols. Megastars say thank you to the diehards who have bought their disks and downloaded their music from the Internet by signing autographs and answering questions. Each artist will pass out time-specific tickets to those who'd like autographs, this way you don't have to stand in line all day—the tickets are dispersed according to the artist's schedule, so research when you get to town. Garth Brooks set the record in 1996, as he signed his name for twenty-three hours and ten minutes without a break.

Riverfront Park sits where First Avenue intersects with Broadway on the banks of the Cumberland River. It hosts the daytime events, from 10:00 A.M. to 6:30 P.M., Thursday to Sunday. Bring a blanket and a camera to this open-air venue, as there is a photo-taking area that allows for up-close and personal shots. Two stages are utilized, concessions are available, and whooping it up is encouraged.

Take the Shelby Street pedestrian bridge over the Cumberland River to LP Field, where sizzling headliners blow up the Nashville skyline each evening. The gates to the Tennessee Titans' football field open at 6:30 P.M., and the concerts start at around 8:00 P.M. Electrifying performances and sincere fan appreciation are the trademarks of the three-hour nightly concert sessions, which always sell out. Four-day ticket holders have access to the up-close photo area, which is located in sections 109 and 110.

Don't even dream about going to bed just yet—the late night scene starts once the LP Field concerts have ended, as downtown becomes crazier than a sprayed roach.

TRANSPORTATION

AIR: Book flights into Nashville International Airport (BNA / *www.flynashville.com*), located nine miles from downtown. Due to the influx of visitors, make car reservations early.

TAXIS: Nashville taxis include Allied Cab (615-885-2323), Yellow Cab (615-256-0101), Diamond Cab (615-254-6596), United Cab (615-228-6969), and Checker Cab (615-256-7000).

BUS: The Nashville MTA bus takes passengers from the airport to downtown Nashville for $1.25 each way. Pickup is on Level 1 at the ground transportation area. Return trips to the airport leave the Downtown Transit Mall, on Deaderick Street between Fourth and Fifth avenues. Call 615-862-5950 for further information. The Greyhound station is located at 200 Eighth Avenue.

FESTIVAL SHUTTLE: All venues and after-hours bars are located very close to one another; however, CMA does offer a shuttle that makes the loop to all major event sites. The shuttle runs every five to ten minutes, and is free for four-day ticket holders.

PARKING: If you'd like to purchase a four-day parking pass for LP Field call 800-CMA-FEST. Cars cost $30, vans are $62, and RVs are $122. Call early, as the number of passes is limited. Same-day paid parking for LP Field is available after 5:00 P.M. for $10 at Lots E and F. A number of surface lots and parking garages will be available in downtown Nashville within a short walk to the Shelby Street pedestrian bridge and LP Field.

ACCOMMODATIONS

HOTELS: Ideally you want to stay downtown; however, 20,000 hotel rooms versus 190,000 attendees does present a problem. Book a room six months in advance, if not more, to be safe. Downtown hotels include Sheraton (623 Union St. / 615-259-2000 / $219), Comfort Inn (1501 Demonbreun St. / 866-471-4467 / $249), Best Western (711 Union St. / 615-242-4311 / $254), Courtyard Marriott (170 Fourth Ave. N / 615-256-0900 / $209), Doubletree (315 Fourth Ave. N / 615-244-8200 / $259), Hilton (121 Fourth Ave. S / 615-620-1000 / $399), and Holiday Inn Express (920 Broadway / 800-315-2621 / $149).

RV: The closest RV parking area is the Tennessee State Fairgrounds, located five minutes from downtown at 625 Smith Street. They do not take reservations, however 200 spaces are available for $35 per night including hookups. Call 615-862-8980 or visit *www.tennesseestatefair.org.*

TICKETS

Tickets for next year's CMA Festival go on sale the Saturday of this year's event. Four-day tickets include entrance into all concerts, the autograph sessions, plus free shuttle rides. Four-day tickets are priced based upon the quality of seating for the evening concerts at LP Field. General Admission costs $110, Club Level is $125, Lower Level is $135, and Floor Level is $155. The highly sought-after Gold Circle tickets (directly in front of the stage) for next year's event can only be purchased at the LP Field Box Office (no phone or Internet sales) on the Saturday of this year's event. They will sell out on Saturday and cost $260. Single-day general admission tickets are $30 and Club Level seats are $40. Autograph sessions and shuttle rides are not included with single-day tickets.

What to Pack
- Comfortable shoes
- Pockets in which to keep your ticket on you at all times
- Camera and autograph book/pen
- Constraint on the urge to say, "Oh my god, yer my favorite!" while getting autographs

party tip

Music lovers cannot leave Nashville without having made a pilgrimage to the Grand Ole Opry. The best way to experience this legendary venue and museum is to book a tour, which includes fascinating stories of interesting behavior from the likes of Johnny Cash and Hank Williams. Opry tours during CMA Music Festival fill up quickly—call 615-871-OPRY or visit *www.opry.com.*

BONNAROO MUSIC AND ARTS FESTIVAL

⊛ Manchester, Tennessee
Second full weekend in June
www.bonnaroo.com

If rock 'n' roll was spawned from the marriage of country and the blues, then it seems perfectly fitting that Tennessee should host a rocking gala of this magnitude. After all, Nashville is the capital of country music, while Memphis is the birthplace of the blues. Bonnaroo, a musical Mecca in its own right, has become the emerald in the crown of premier U.S. rock festivals.

This four-day assault on the ears is held sixty miles southeast of Nashville, on a 700-acre farm in Manchester, beginning on the second Thursday in June. A sold-out crowd of 80,000 forms a very slow moving caravan that approaches the festival gates on Thursday afternoon. The parking lots and campgrounds open at 7:00 A.M. although the music does not begin until 7:30 Thursday evening. A wise idea is to arrive early in the morning and beat the masses. A series of checkpoints line the road, and all concertgoers must show their tickets or they'll be turned away.

Once inside, you can bounce back and forth between two main stages and four smaller venues, where acts are staggered throughout the day. Concerts on Friday and Saturday begin at 12:30 P.M. and go until 3:30 in the morning. On Sunday, the music ends a bit earlier. The final show of the evening (a.k.a. the "morning") is often an electronic act that churns out rhythmic rave and house music. Recent headliners have included the Police, Widespread Panic, White Stripes, Radiohead, Phil Lesh, Cypress Hill, the Dave Matthews Band, My Morning Jacket, David Byrne, Wilco, Gov't Mule, and the Flaming Lips.

Centeroo, the farm's main area, is where you'll be spending most of your time. It contains the stages, the arts and crafts tents, and just about everything else imaginable. Troo Music Lounge is a café that offers live music from up-and-coming artists, while the Arcade Discotheque is armed with video games galore, allowing addicts the opportunity to get their share of "Guitar Hero" while DJs spin in the background. The one-of-a-kind Silent Disco is a Bonnaroo staple—slip on a pair of wireless headphones and dance until 5:00 A.M. while DJs provide piped-in beats. An immensely popular hangout is the Broo'ers Festival, a gigantic microbrew tent that offers Magic Hat and Sierra Nevada to suds guzzlers who pull up a seat on a bale of hay. The Bonnaroo Cinema offers air-conditioning and the latest movies twenty-four hours a day, and the Salon can funkify your hair whenever you'd like. Oh yeah, there's a Jazz Club too. Centeroo is open twenty-four hours a day, beginning at 12:00 P.M. on Thursday. Be sure to bring enough green stuff—money that is. ATM lines are long and the machines frequently run out of cash.

TRANSPORTATION

AIR: Flights can be booked into Nashville International Airport (BNA / www.nashintl.com), located sixty-two miles away, or Chattanooga Metropolitan Airport (CHA / www.chattairport .com), located seventy-nine miles away. Car-rental agencies are available at both, although Bonnaroo

runs a shuttle service for ticket holders from BNA for $50. Visit www.bonnaroo.com for shuttle details and departure times.

BUS: There is a Greyhound station in Manchester at 617 Woodbury Highway, a one-mile walk from the festival grounds.

ACCOMMODATIONS

There are hotels in Manchester, and attendees can park in the day lots located off exit 111. The advantage is a better night's sleep. Most people camp.

CAR CAMPING: Four-day camping passes are included in the cost of your ticket. Car campgrounds open at 7:00 A.M. on Thursday and close at 3:00 P.M. on Monday. Cars will not be permitted to leave the campgrounds and return after 9:00 P.M. on Friday. You may bring a 1.5 kW or smaller portable generator. Family campgrounds are available, but only for those bringing sixteen-year-olds or younger. You must provide your own tents, and although food is for sale, bring your own to cut costs. Large pavilion canopies are not permitted.

TENT-ONLY CAMPING: Camping-only areas are available on a first-come-first-serve basis, and those who desire these spaces should arrive early with a large pack to carry their equipment. Check the map as you go through the tollbooths for the location of these sites. If they are full, just head back to the car camping lots.

RV: Taking an RV is a great idea. Designated lots are 20' × 50', and cost an additional $75 for the weekend. Tents can be set up beside your RV as long as they're within your allotted space. You may purchase one $25 "Companion Pass," which allows one car to be parked beside an RV. Cars should enter directly behind the RV because "holding spaces" is not allowed. RV passes must be purchased in advance, and everyone inside the vehicle must also have a weekend concert ticket.

Hookups are not provided, although an onsite service will charge to empty holding tanks and refill water. Gas is not provided, so fill up before you enter. You may run your generators at any hour of the day.

VIP CAMPING / RV: One vehicle pass is included with VIP tickets. VIP camping areas are generally quieter, with spacious lots (four times the GA campsite size), free catered meals, and discounted beverages. Luxurious air-conditioned bathrooms with showers are also available. RV owners must purchase an RV upgrade on top of their VIP tickets. The VIP lot RV amenities are similar to those at the VIP camping area.

TICKETS

You must purchase tickets early because Bonnaroo always sells out. Check the event website to find out when tickets go on sale—usually late February or early March. Tickets prices are tiered, depending on when you purchase. Early Bird weekend tickets cost $215–$220 including taxes and fees. Prices are raised in $15 increments as time goes on, and you have the option of splitting the cost into two payments. RV passes cost an additional $75. VIP tickets are sold in pairs for over $1,100.

This includes two VIP tickets to all performances, the VIP preparty on Thursday night, VIP lounge access at the concerts, special VIP entrance to all areas of Bonnaroo, and a host of other upgrades. Single-day tickets cost between $60 and $90. Visit *www.ticketmaster.com* to purchase.

What to Pack
- Camping supplies
- Raingear
- Trash bags
- Extra shoes
- Bug spray
- Cash

party tip

Avoid pitching your tent beside a young couple whom you do not know. The culmination of four days at a camping event where sleep is a luxury results in the possibility of late-night arguments. These couples may think that a tent's thin layer of nylon dulls the sounds of their relationship analysis, but your precious shut-eye will certainly suffer.

Virginia

VIRGINIA GOLD CUP

⊛ Great Meadow, Virginia
First Saturday in May
www.vagoldcup.com

The Virginia Gold Cup is the largest, most anticipated social gathering of the year in the greater Washington, D.C., area, and the epicenter of one gigantic thoroughbred affair.

The running of the Gold Cup has been taking place for over eighty years, and it draws a variety of fans, from yuppie professionals to families to party animals. Party buses headed from D.C. carry hordes of regulars, who know from experience to take public transportation to the massive 500-acre field. The viewing grounds are divided into three major areas: The North Rail (the party section) is located on the left side of the race course, the Members Hill (the networking and businessperson section) is in the center, and the South Rail (the family section) is on the right. While all sections typically turn into massive socials, the North Rail caters to the wildest stallions.

To partake in Gold Cup fandom you have a few choices. First, you can purchase a "rail space," allowing six people and one car into a North Rail tailgating spot, while two additional cars receive a general parking space. Or you can purchase a 15' × 15' tent for the day, which gives your group its own small North Rail chalet. You can bring your own food and drink or have your tent catered through vendors on the *www.vagold.com* website. The third choice is to pay approximately $70 to purchase a ticket through a group that already owns an enormous tent at the Gold Cup. These groups simply charge admission, and they provide round-trip transportation to the Great Meadow from Arlington, Virginia (near downtown D.C.).

The 50,000 spectators who descend upon this field always do so in proper Gold Cup attire. Don't come in jeans and flip-flops, as the best lawn parties strive to maintain a certain level of tradition. Women in particular have a chance to sprinkle some sass as sun hats are an absolute must—the bigger the better. Men, get out your ironing boards and press those pants, and complete the look with loafers, slicked-back hair, a polo shirt, and a pastel sweater tied around your neck—as you better milk this opportunity to showcase the preppy clothes that you never wear.

The gates open at 10:00 A.M., with prerace activities taking place from 11:00 A.M. to 1:00 P.M. The races, usually seven to nine of them, go from 1:00 P.M. to 7:00 P.M.

TRANSPORTATION

🅑 **BUS TOURS:** There are three types of organized bus tours that leave from and return to D.C. on the day of the race. These include:

D.C. Society of Young Professionals: This group has a huge tent reserved on the North Rail. Buses leave from Union Station at 10:00 A.M. and return at around 8:00 P.M. Your ticket includes a postrace party at the Capital City Brewing Company. Visit *www.dcyoungpro.com* by April to purchase a ticket. No, you do not have to be a young D.C. professional to get on the bus.

Party D.C.: Includes luxury buses to and from the Gold Cup and four North Rail chalet tents. Buses leave at 10:00 A.M. from Clarendon Ballroom in Arlington. The parties typically take place at the Clarendon Ballroom and another specified venue, featuring live music. A continental breakfast is available in the morning. Visit *www.partydc.com* by April to purchase a ticket.

University Row: This area has grown into a favorite among the twenty- to thirty-year-old groups, many of whom come with an alumni crowd from their alma mater. Groups from sixty-six different universities, ranging from the University of Michigan to USC and UVA, take over a huge fenced-in North Rail section, comprised of eleven tents. Despite the name, you do not have to be an alumnus / alumna from any of the specified schools. In fact, your education can be limited to a GED or Cosmetology Certificate and you'll still be fine. Buses leave from the Rock Bottom Brewery in Ballston between 10:30 A.M. and 11:30 A.M. and return at 6:00 P.M. Your ticket allows you to mingle at all University Row tents and includes entrance to the postrace party. Visit *www.universityrow.org* for information and to purchase tickets, which tend to sell out by late April.

✈ **AIR:** Book flights into Washington Dulles International Airport (IAD / *www.metwashair ports.com*). The airport is twenty-five minutes from the Plains.

ACCOMMODATIONS

You can either stay in D.C. / Arlington or a town closer to the races. Most organized North Rail tent parties offer prices with and without round-trip transportation from Arlington.

🛏 **HOTELS:** There are a few small towns with hotels within a fifteen-minute drive to the Plains. In Warrenton try the Howard Johnson Inn (6 Broadview Ave. / 540-347-4141 / $80), Holiday Inn Express (410 Holiday Court / 540-341-1070 /

$144), and Comfort Inn (7379 Comfort Inn Dr. / 540-349-8900 / $140).

The starting and ending points for the organized bus trips are in Arlington. Hotels in Arlington, near the Capital City Brewing Company (2700 S. Quincy St.), Clarendon Ballroom (3185 Wilson Blvd.), and Rock Bottom Brewery (4238 Wilson Blvd.) include the Hyatt (1325 Wilson Blvd. / 703-525-1234 / $169), Marriott (1700 Jefferson Davis Hwy. / 703-920-3230 / $119), and Hilton (950 N. Stafford St. / 703-528-6000 / $259). Arlington has an array of hotels, and you may want to book a location depending on which organized bus tour you'll be on. Visit *www.priceline.com* for competitive rates.

🖙 **B&BS:** The Red Fox Inn (2 E. Washington St. / 540-687-6301 / $170) and Welbourne Bed & Breakfast (22314 Red Farm Lane / 540-687-3201) are good options in Middleburg.

TICKETS

Tickets for organized bus tours start at $70 and go to around $105. Purchase tickets in March or April for the best rates. All transportation, food, alcohol, and party admittance is included—visit your organized bus tour preference to purchase. A North Rail or Oakwood Box parking space ranges from $275 to $550 and includes entrance for six people, and three vehicles. Tents, which start at $800 for a 15' × 15' space, are also available. Visit the event website by April for these tickets.

What to Pack
- Creased khakis
- Pressed collared shirt
- Dry-cleaned dress
- Iron, shoe shine, lint-removing brush
- Flask

party tip

The Gold Cup Steeplechase tends to draw a heap of young, aspiring professionals from Capitol Hill. Many of these blooming politicians and up-and-coming senators view this event as an opportunity to network and rub elbows with potential new allies. Avoid talking politics at this party or you may end up missing the horse race while a half-sauced intern rambles about American foreign policy.

West Virginia

BRIDGE DAY

⭐ Fayetteville, West Virginia
Third Saturday in October
www.officialbridgeday.com

The largest extreme sports event in the world is held each October in Fayetteville, West Virginia. Fayetteville is home to the highest vehicular bridge in the United States and the second-highest bridge in the world. This is not a party for the faint of heart or those afraid of heights, as an estimated 150,000 annual spectators will attest. This free-fall fiasco celebrates BASE jumping, a sport that gives new meaning to the word *courage*. Picture jumping off the highest bridge you've ever driven across with little more than a parachute in your hand. No ropes, no bungee, no fear.

The New River Gorge Bridge is a 3,030-foot-long steel-arch bridge that extends U.S. Route 19 over the New River, and is surrounded by lush green Appalachian Mountains. Its 876-foot height beckons adrenaline junkies. Over 450 BASE (an acronym that describes four objects from which to jump—bridge, antenna, span, and earth) jumpers descend upon Fayetteville to experience the four-second free-fall before deploying their parachute. The thrill of watching this spine-tingling event is second only to the rush experienced by the jumpers themselves.

Arrive in town on Friday for the "Taste of Bridge Day," a prejump celebration that takes place at many local restaurants from 5:00 P.M. to 9:00 P.M. The food is cheap and plentiful at most eateries, but the center of the action is Smokey's on the Gorge (310 Keller Ave.), an open-air joint with wonderful views overlooking the massive valley—just head one mile toward the bridge from downtown. BASE jumpers from around the world congregate at Smokey's to munch on the wild boar ribs.

Awaken on Saturday and get to the bridge as early as possible, as you will be joined by over 100,000 people vying for the best viewpoint. It's only a fifteen-minute walk from downtown, although shuttle buses constantly run back and forth, as the bridge is closed to traffic all day long. From 9:00 A.M. to 3:00 P.M., jumpers and repellers take turns making the plunge. Only one death has occurred in thirty years of Bridge Day.

You have a few unique options, other than simply watching. A number of rafting outfitters can take you down the New River rapids and underneath the bridge for some incredible views of the event—visit *www.newrivercvb.com* for a list of rafting companies. You can also take a "Down Under Tour," a $50 guided hike to the base of the gorge to watch the day's jumps—call 304-465-5617 for reservations. An idea for the bold is to slide, or "high-line," down a 700-foot rope attached to the bridge's catwalk after a safety and equipment lesson—call 800-634-3785 for information and reservations.

TRANSPORTATION

✈ **AIR:** Book flights into Yeager Airport (CRW / www.yeagerairport.com), located fifty-nine miles away in Charleston. Car-rental agencies are available.

🅿 **PARKING:** Free lots are available on the north and south sides of the gorge. On the south side, in Fayetteville, park at the high school, the courthouse, or the Board of Education. Nearby Oak Hill has a free lot at the K-Mart, and another at Wal-Mart along U.S. Route 19. On the north side, in Lansing, park at the visitor's center and walk across.

🚌 **SHUTTLES:** A shuttle leaves all parking lots on the south side for $2 for the day. On the north side shuttles leave from Crosier's (Rt. 19 and Milroy Grose Rd.) and the Lighthouse Worship Center (Rt. 19 and Smalls Branch Rd.).

ACCOMMODATIONS

🏨 **HOTELS:** The Comfort Inn (103 Elliotts Way / 304-574-3443 / $175) in Fayetteville and Holiday Inn (340 Oyler Ave. / 304-465-0571) in Oak Hill (ten minutes) are typically booked with BASE jumpers and vendors, but you're welcome to try. In between Fayetteville and Oak Hill is the New River Inn (9020 Fayette Landing / 304-465-0010 / $109), conveniently located near the shuttle bus pickup at the K-Mart. The White Horse Bed & Breakfast (120 Fayette Ave. / 304-574-1400 / $105) is a historic home in Fayetteville that sleeps thirty-five people.

⛺ **CAMPING/CABINS:** Fayetteville is an outdoor-sports Mecca, and as a result it offers an abundance of campgrounds for river rafters and mountain bikers. Rustic cabins, tent camping, and RV grounds are available. If hotels are booked, camping will be your best bet. Canyon Rim Ranch (RR 1, Fayetteville / 304-574-3111) offers tent camping for $10 per night, RV spaces for $20, and bunkhouses. Cooter's Cabins & Camping (RR 3, Fayetteville / 304-574-4002) has similar accommodations. Songer Whitewater (POB 300, Fayetteville / 800-356-7238) has tent camping for $10, rustic cabins for $60, and rustic bunkhouses for $120, and Rifrafters Campground (Rt. 19 and Laurel Creek Rd.) is similar to it. Ace Outdoor Center (888-223-7238) in Oak Hill has campsites, cabins, and bunkhouses. Call the Fayette County Chamber of Commerce at 304-465-5617 for further advice on campgrounds.

What to Pack
- Warm clothes if camping
- Camera if spectating
- Parachute if jumping

party tip

True extreme sports competitors are people of valor and might, but an event such as this one brings out a lot of big-talking wannabes. Be prepared for unavoidable conversation from kayakers about class-five rapids conquered this summer, climbers boasting about their latest six-pitch ascent, and mountain bikers yammering over the awesome suspension on their custom twenty-seven speed.

WE FEST

BLISSFEST

Minnesota

Wisconsin

Michigan

off the map

OPENING DAY AT
MILLER PARK

South
Dakota

BLACK HILLS
MOTORCYCLE
RALLY AT STURGIS

SUMMERFEST

FREAKFEST

HALLOWEEN
IN ATHENS

RAGBRAI*

OHIO STATE U
VS. U OF MICHIGAN
FOOTBALL GAME

Nebraska

off the map

COLLEGE
BASEBALL
WORLD
SERIES

Iowa

TASTE OF
CHICAGO

INDIANAPOLIS
500 CARB DAY

Missouri

CHICAGO JAZZ
FESTIVAL

Ohio

Kansas

THE LITTLE
500

PARTY COVE

WAKARUSA MUSIC
AND CAMPING
FESTIVAL

Illinois

Indiana

SOULARD
MARDI GRAS

RIVERFEST

COUNTRY STAMPEDE
MUSIC AND CAMPING
FESTIVAL

OKTOBERFEST-
ZINZINNATI

ROCKLAHOMA

Oklahoma

OKIE NOODLING
TOURNAMENT

off the map

Illinois

TASTE OF CHICAGO

⊛ **Chicago, Illinois**
Late June to early July
www.tasteofchicago.us

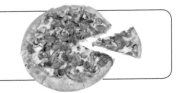

You'd be hard-pressed to find a town that embraces voracious carnivorous behavior like the Windy City. It's the land of steak and ribs, kielbasa and hot dogs, and the largest food festival from the Atlantic to the Pacific.

The Taste of Chicago is a two-week-long calorie-fest that begins in late June and goes through July 8. It's a no-holds-barred food free-for-all, where over 100 of the finest Chicago eateries offer samples of their famous dishes. Taking place in beautiful Grant Park, Chicago's "front yard," the Taste draws up to 3.5 million people per year. It's open from 11:00 A.M. to 9:00 P.M. daily. Entrance to this enormous outdoor food court is free; however you will need tickets to purchase drinks and to sample the food. Typically, food ranges from two to ten tickets per plate ($1.50

to $8). Be sure to try the local brew of choice, "Old Style." You can't leave without having indulged in some world-renowned deep-dish pizza, and Lou Malnati's is a true crowd pleaser. Go directly for the sausage and cheese pie, which, believe it or not, has fewer calories than its traditional all-cheese cousin. However, don't limit yourself to the deep dish—rookies are notorious for gorging themselves at the first few tents, thus losing their appetite. Choose sample portions over full plates to prevent premature withdrawal from this culinary extravaganza.

While the Taste of Chicago is based upon food, it is also a *huge* party. July 3 is the busiest night, as big-name musicians come to perform on two or three stages during the day and into the evening. These acts, which recently have included James Brown and Barenaked Ladies, will play until 8:00 P.M. They are followed by an orchestra that performs classic American music as a prelude to the most anticipated portion of the day. The closing piece, Tchaikovsky's *1812 Overture*, signals the beginning of a fireworks display that makes a KISS concert seem like child's play. The festival runs an additional half hour on the evenings of July 3 and 4. Stake out your corner of the lawn early.

After the Taste, head downtown to experience Chicago's nightlife. Lincoln Park, which attracts a young vibrant crowd, is home to countless bars, clubs, and restaurants. West Addison Street in Wrigleyville is a fun neighborhood close to Wrigley Field. Bucktown, on the northwest side of the city, has emerged as a hot spot over the past five years. For a listing of live music, shows, and nightlife events visit *www.chicagoreader.com*.

TRANSPORTATION

Use of public transportation is highly encouraged. Arrive early to avoid getting caught in gridlock.

AIR: Flights can be booked into O'Hare Airport (*www.ohare.com*) or Midway Airport (*www.chicago-mdw.com*). Bus, train, and taxis can be taken from here.

TRAIN: The El train is a very efficient means by which to move about the city. The Chicago Rapid-Transit system runs five major lines, which are labeled by color: The Red Line runs north–south, the Green line runs west–south, the Blue Line runs Wicker Park / Bucktown west-northwest to O'Hare Airport, the Brown Line runs the downtown loop to northern neighborhoods, and the Orange Line runs southwest to Midway Airport. Visit *www.transitchicago.com* to download and print all train and bus schedules. You can call 312-664-7200 for information over the phone. A "visitor pass" gives you unlimited access to train and bus rides for a day—it can be purchased at hotels, transportation hubs, at the airport, and online at *www.transitchicago.com* for $5. Multiple-day passes are also available.

BUS: A good option, especially for those staying near the lakefront, where trains are not available. Look for blue and white signs, spaced apart every couple of blocks. Buses are labeled according to the main streets they run along.

TAXIS: There are a host of taxi companies to choose from, including Checker Cab (312-Checker), Yellow Cab (312-taxicab), and Flash Cab (773-561-1444).

ACCOMMODATIONS

HOTELS: Many hotels are located just a short distance from Grant Park. Options include the Hilton Chicago (720 S. Michigan Ave. / 312-922-4400 / $229), the Chicago Essex Inn (800 S. Michigan Ave. / 312-939-2800 / $139), the Best Western Grant Park (1100 S. Michigan Ave. / 312-922-2800 / $200), Hard Rock Hotel Chicago (230 N. Michigan Ave. / 312-345-1000 / $259), Sheraton Chicago Hotel and Towers (301 East North Water St. / 312-464-1000 / $204), and Marriott Chicago Downtown (30 East Hubbard / 312-329-2500 / $199). Visit *www.hotels.com/chicago* for a complete listing.

TICKETS

Tickets are sold in sheets of eleven for $7. Buy a reasonable number up front to avoid multiple trips to the ticket line. Ticket sales end at 9:00 P.M. on July 3 and 4; otherwise the cutoff is 8:30 P.M.

What to Pack

- Wet naps
- Antacid
- A loose belt

CHICAGO JAZZ FESTIVAL

⊛ Chicago, Illinois
Labor Day weekend
www.chicagojazzfestival.org

The largest Jazz Festival in the United States is a gathering of 300,000 swingin' cats who invade Chicago to shim, sham, and shuffle over Labor Day weekend. This spectacular world-renowned event is the perfect reason to take a trip to the nation's third-largest city.

The Jazz Festival begins the Friday before Labor Day and goes through Sunday evening in Grant Park, Chicago's answer to New York City's Central Park, located between Michigan Avenue and Lake Michigan, with fantastic panoramas of both the city skyline and the enormous body of water. Much of the festival's lore comes from the fact that the event is free, yet the musical talent is world-class. Unlike many jazz festivals, which often feature rock 'n' roll and blues acts, this event is strictly high hat, saxophone, upright bass, and jazz guitar.

Jazz Fest opens each day at 11:00 A.M. and goes until 11:00 P.M. Internationally recognized and local musicians share three main stages—Jackson Stage, Heritage Stage, and Petrillo Music Shell. The music rotates from one stage to the next every four hours or so. Bring a lawn chair or blanket and sit on the grass while dulcet tones shiver and shake your soul. Past performances of note have included those of Miles Davis, Ella Fitzgerald, Anthony Braxton, Lionel Hampton, Johnny Frigo, Roy Haynes, and special dedications to the master, John Coltrane. The crowd is of all ages, a result of the creations of genius that transcend generational gaps.

The Rose Garden, just south of nearby Jackson Boulevard, hosts an art fair during the concerts. Check out the variety of creative and inspirational artwork and handmade crafts on display. Jackson Boulevard is also the food and beverage stop. Visit the wine and beer gardens, and chill underneath one of summer's final sunsets.

A ticketed event, oftentimes a Coltrane tribute, takes place at the Symphony Center (220 S. Michigan Ave.) on Thursday night before the Jazz Fest. This show has earned a fantastic reputation and typically features artists such as Joshua Redman and Ari Brown.

The Jazz Institute's famous Club Tour takes place the evening prior, on Wednesday. This tour kicks off the Jazz Festival, taking ticketed music lovers jazz-lounge hopping from 6:00 P.M. to midnight aboard a trolley.

TRANSPORTATION

AIR: Flights can be booked into O'Hare Airport (*www.ohare.com*) or Midway Airport (*www.chicago-mdw.com*). Bus, train, and taxis can be taken from here.

TRAIN: The El train is a very efficient means by which to move about the city. The Chicago Rapid-Transit system runs five major lines, which are labeled by color: The Red Line runs north–south, the Green line runs west–south, the Blue Line runs Wicker Park / Bucktown west-northwest to O'Hare Airport, the Brown Line runs the downtown loop to northern neighborhoods, and the Orange Line runs southwest to Midway Airport. Visit *www.transitchicago.com* to download and print all train and bus schedules. You can call 312-664-7200 for information over the phone. A "visitor pass" gives you unlimited access to train and bus rides for a day—it can be purchased at hotels, transportation hubs, at the airport, and online at *www.transitchicago.com* for $5. Multiple-day passes are also available.

BUS: A good option, especially for those staying near the lakefront, where trains are not available. Look for blue and white signs, spaced apart every couple of blocks. Buses are labeled according to the main streets they run along.

TAXIS: Cab companies include Checker Cab (312-Checker), Yellow Cab (312-taxicab), and Flash Cab (773-561-1444).

PARKING: This option is not encouraged because public transportation is so convenient. Parking is not possible on the festival grounds; however, there are garages nearby—arrive early because garages will be full. The Millennium Park Garage is located on Columbus between Randolph and Monroe. The Monroe Street Underground Garage is at Monroe and Columbus, and Grant Park Underground Garage can be entered at Michigan and Madison or Michigan and Randolph.

ACCOMMODATIONS

HOTELS: Many hotels are located just a short distance from Grant Park. Options include the Hilton Chicago (720 S. Michigan Ave. / 312-922-4400 / $269), the ritzy Chicago Essex Inn (800 S. Michigan Ave. / 312-939-2800 / $532), the Best Western Grant Park (1100 S. Michigan Ave. / 800-472-6875/ $170), Sheraton Chicago Hotel and Towers (301 East North Water St. / 312-464-1000 / $202), and Marriott Chicago Downtown (30 East Hubbard / 312-329-2500 / $259). Visit *www.hotels .com/chicago* for a complete listing.

TICKETS

The Jazz Institute Club Tour takes place on Wednesday before the festival. The tour usually kicks off at Andy's (11 E. Hubbard) at 6:00 P.M., and visits a number of jazz clubs until midnight. A tour trolley serves as transportation, adding to the rich feel of this tour. Tickets are $25 in advance and $30 on Wednesday. You can purchase tickets at any of the participating clubs, which are listed on *www .jazzinchicago.com*, or by calling 312-427-1676.

Tickets to the Thursday-night concert at the Symphony Center can be purchased by calling 312-294-3000 or by visiting *www.cso.org*. The show begins at 7:30 P.M., and tickets cost approximately $30. Purchase in advance.

What to Pack

- Lawn chair/blanket
- Picnic lunch
- Sunglasses
- Jacket for the evening
- Zoot suit

party tip

The best jazz bars in town are usually packed after the festival with fans who haven't heard their fill during the day. Try Andy's Jazz Club (11 E. Hubbard St.), known for constant music all day long. Green Mill (4802 N. Broadway Ave.) is a swanky joint with nightly jazz and character galore—it was once a hangout for both Al Capone and Charlie Chaplin. The Underground Wonder Bar (10 E. Walton St.) is a tiny place that's open every day of the year, with three nights of intimate blues and jazz performances weekly.

Indiana

THE LITTLE 500

⊛ **Bloomington, Indiana**
Mid- to late April
www.iusf.bloomington.com/little5frm2

This is a great reason to take a road trip to Indiana. "The World's Greatest College Weekend" is the undisputed king of campus keggers. For one week in April, students blow off classes and inhibition, and they unleash a truly monstrous bash. The sheer outrageous force of the Little 500 has even inspired MTV to forgo the beach and film its *Spring Break* series from Middle America.

This nonstop party celebrates the Little 500 bicycle race at Indiana University. Since 1951, this 200-lap, fifty-mile relay has been held at Bill Armstrong Stadium on the IU campus. The quarter-mile race features thirty-three teams, made up of four riders apiece, and claims Lance Armstrong as its most famous participant. The Little 500 inspired 1979's Oscar-winning movie *Breaking Away*, which depicted a townie team called the Cutters, who entered the race and beat the brash fraternity competition. The film put the event on the national map, and many of the teams who race today represent IU's Greek system—there are also nonfraternity teams who enter under the name Cutters. A stiff qualifying process determines entrance, so as a party participant you shouldn't plan on riding. Saturday is standing room only, as 14,000 people fill the stadium, but the entire week leading up to the event is when the rubber meets the road.

Indiana University's campus floods with students enjoying a mid-semester work stoppage and with alumni partaking in the perfect excuse to relive undergraduate escapades. All are welcome, although thirty-eight-year-olds should avoid discussing how difficult college was without the Internet. Parties are literally spilling out of houses everywhere. Fraternity and sorority houses explode with untamed antics 24/7. They host live music, including such notable bands as Guster, throughout the week. The "Student Ghetto" and off-campus houses also take the partying to epidemic proportions. Head south of campus to Third Street, or west of campus to Kirkwood Avenue. Typically you won't need a special invitation, nor is knowing the host a requirement.

The IU Auditorium often brings a headlining band to play Saturday evening after the race—recent acts have included the Roots, Wilco, and hometown favorite John Mellencamp. Many people on campus dress up, and biking is naturally the theme of choice. Wear some knee-high striped tube socks, short shorts, and a headband to fit in. It's recommended that you bring a bike rather than spend valuable partying time strolling about the campus.

TRANSPORTATION

✈ **AIR:** Book flights into Indianapolis International Airport (IND / *www.indianapolisairport.com*), located fifty-three miles from Bloomington. Car-rental agencies are available at the airport.

🚌 **SHUTTLE:** Bloomington Shuttle runs a bus every two hours from the airport to the Bloomington Courtyard Marriott and the Hampton Inn for $25 per way. Visit *www.bloomingtonshuttle .com* or call 800-589-6004 for schedules and to make reservations.

🅣 **TAXIS:** Use White Cab (812-334-8294) or Yellow Cab (812-336-4100).

ACCOMMODATIONS

🏨 **HOTELS:** Greek alumni can crash at the frat house, but don't expect to get any sleep, plus you may wake up covered in shaving cream. Make hotel reservations about four months in advance. Hotels include Courtyard Marriott (310 S. College Ave. / 812-335-8000 / $209), Hampton Inn (2100 N. Walnut St. / 812-334-2100 / $169), Holiday Inn Express (117 S. Franklin Rd. / 812-334-8800 / $179), Days Inn (200 E. Matlock Rd. / 812-336-0905 / $70), Comfort Inn (1700 N. Kinser Pike / 812-650-0010 / $130), Fairfield Inn (120 Fairfield Dr. / 812-331-1122 / $169), and Hilton Garden Inn (245 N. College Ave. / 812-331-1335 / $199). Visit *www.visitbloomington.com* for further hotel listings.

TICKETS

Tickets cost approx $27 for students and $35 for nonstudents. Visit *www.ticketmaster.com* or the Indiana University Auditorium at *www.iuautorium .com* for ticket purchases. Tickets do sell out, and the gates open at 5:30 P.M.

party tip

When party hopping along the swarms of raucous frat houses, be sure to stop in at the Phi Kappa Psi house. The actual trophy that the Cutters won in *Breaking Away* is boldly displayed in the fraternity dining room. If the bouncers try to steer you away from the shindig, simply tell them that you're a Phi Psi brother. The secret Phi Psi handshake is just like a normal shake, except you cross your pinkie finger through the frat guy's pinkie finger. He squeezes once, you squeeze twice, and he follows with three more. If they require more information, tell them that you graduated from Gettysburg College, home of the first Phi Kappa Psi chapter.

INDIANAPOLIS 500 CARB DAY

⊛ Indianapolis, Indiana
Memorial Day weekend
www.indy500.com

One of the oldest, most important, and widely viewed sporting events worldwide, it's the grandfather of open-wheel racing, with roots that are imbedded in Midwestern popular and sporting culture. Although race day attendance is estimated at 300,000 strong, it's safe to say that the entire state of Indiana welcomes Memorial Day weekend with open arms and a healthy all-American thirst for fast cars and cheap thrills.

The Indy 500, also known as "the Greatest Spectacle in Racing," has been held at the Indianapolis Motor Speedway in Speedway, Indiana, since 1911. More accurately tagged with the moniker "the Brickyard," a trip to this venue was somewhat of a pilgrimage for the Corn Belt youth of the 1960s through the 1980s. The infield, nicknamed "the Snakepit," was considered to be the largest party in America, as masses of maniacs guzzled beer, popped pills, smoked dope, and shed their clothing from morning till night on race day. Cars were allowed in the Snakepit back then, and they were frequently flipped over and set ablaze. Fights were commonplace, while turn four became the epicenter of all Indiana debauchery.

Realizing that this behavior could not be allowed to continue, organizers began to squash the party scene in the 1990s. Turn four was replaced by a large, grassy hill, parking passes on the infield became very limited, and police officers began to outnumber the pit crews. However, in similar fashion to a mutating virus, a good party can always find a way to survive.

Carb Day takes place on the Friday before the Sunday race; it's the drivers' last chance to practice the course. The ghost of "Indy 500 Past" thrives during this beautifully American combination of partying, racing, and rock 'n' roll. The event, hosted by Miller Lite, begins packing tens of thousands of fans into the speedway infield at 11:00 A.M. A concert kicks off in the late afternoon at 4:00 P.M.—Kid Rock played the 2007 event and whipped the crowd into a frenzy. Outside the speedway, Georgetown Road and Sixteenth Street are frequently shut down due to the festivities taking place in the street.

An option is to camp or park an RV outside of the race for the memorable tailgates, attend Carb Day, and hit the downtown Indianapolis bar scene during the race. Of course attending the race is great, but it lacks the energy of Talladega or the Daytona 500. You can either venture downtown or to nearby Broad Ripple Village, a hip town located ten miles north of downtown.

TRANSPORTATION

If you plan on staying downtown, drive your car to your destination and take buses or shuttles back and forth to the speedway. If you plan on camping, leave your car at your space and use the buses and shuttles to maneuver downtown and back to your lot.

AIR: Book flights into Indianapolis International Airport (IND / *www.indianapolisairport.com*), located six miles from Speedway and nine miles from downtown Indianapolis. Taxis are available, although you should book early. Shuttle buses also run from the airport to the Motor Speedway.

SHUTTLE / B BUS: The IndyGo bus runs from downtown to the Brickyard all day long each day leading up to race day. The bus line is Route 25–West Sixteenth Street, and tickets can be purchased in advance. Contact IndyGo at 317-635-3344 or by visiting *www.indygo.net* for downtown bus stop locations. On race day the buses begin running at 6:00 A.M. from the corner of Capital and Maryland, from Illinois and Market, from the Zoo, and from the airport to the Brickyard and back. One way costs $10, and round-trip is $15.

TAXIS: Cab companies include Ameritaxi (317-632-2222), Yellow (317-487-7777), Hoosier (317-534-0465), and Metro (317-247-8888).

Ⓟ PARKING: You can drive a car, not an RV, onto the infield for free. Parking is limited, and overnights are not allowed. The largest infield parking area is at turn three. There are many lots outside the speedway. "The North Forty" is a huge free lot to the north of the speedway that can be accessed via Thirtieth Street. The Coke Lot, off Georgetown Road and Thirtieth Street, charges approximately $15. You can also pay area residents $10 to park on their property within a mile of the track. Park quickly and do not waste a lot of time circling the speedway in heavy traffic—you'll cover twice as much ground on foot anyway.

ACCOMMODATIONS

🏨 **HOTELS:** There are hotels near the speedway as well as downtown. Depending on your love of auto racing, you'll have to make a choice. Those who have tickets to multiple events or want to spend time at the speedway should plan accordingly. If, however, you want to experience the downtown nightlife and social scene, then a downtown hotel may be best. Downtown hotels include Holiday Inn Express (410 S. Missouri St. / 317-631-9000 / $209), Courtyard (501 W. Washington St. / 317-635-4443 / $379), Days Inn (401 E. Washington St. / 317-637-6464 / $149), Embassy Suites (110 W. Washington St. / 317-236-1800 / $159), Hyatt Regency (1 S. Capitol Ave. / 317-632-1234 / $400), and Hampton Inn (105 S. Meridian St. / 317-261-1200 / $144). Less expensive options near the speedway include Ramada (5601 Fortune Circle / 317-244-1221 / $189), Super 8 (7202 E. Eighty-second St. / 317-841-8585 / $105), and Dollar Inn (9350 Michigan Rd. / 317-248-8500 / $110). Book a room as far in advance as possible—a year is not a bad idea.

🚐 **RV /** ⛺ **CAMPING:** Several four-day camping lots surround the Brickyard. Camping and RV parking begins on the Thursday before the race and goes through Sunday evening. You'll want to purchase a space in a north or south lot,

depending on where your seats are located (if you plan on attending the race). All camping is dry, no hookups are available. A four-day RV pass costs approximately $120, and tent camping is $50 per vehicle. Visit the event website or call 800-822-4639 to purchase passes. A private lot, the Wilcox Mobile Home Park, is located across the street with bathroom facilities, showers, and hookups. RV and tent campers are welcome—call 317-248-1311 for reservations and current rates. The American Legion has a five-acre field nearby that hosts RVs and tent campers. Call 317-244-9625 for availability and rates. Most lots fill up by March, so make your reservations early.

TICKETS

Carb Day tickets can be purchased through *www.indy500.com* or by calling 800-822-4639 for $10. Tickets are also available at the gate on Carb Day.

Bleacher tickets to the Indy 500 race run between $40 and $150 face value, but they always sell out. Purchase these tickets as far in advance as possible. Infield general admission tickets cost $20 and can be purchased at the gate.

What to Pack
- Cash—ATMs are few and far between
- Peyton Manning football jersey
- John Cougar Mellencamp CD

party tip

You shouldn't leave Indy without checking out the city's blues scene at the Slippery Noodle Inn. Make a point to stop by this bar and restaurant on the Saturday between Carb Day and the big race. Complete with two performance stages, this hopping joint is the oldest operating bar in Indiana and was used as a stop on the Underground Railroad.

Iowa

RAGBRAI®

⭐ **Across Iowa**
Last full week in July
www.ragbrai.org

The largest and longest-running bicycle ride on the planet is guaranteed to provide an extraordinarily wondrous week of memories to last a lifetime. For more than thirty-five years the RAGBRAI, or Register's Annual Great Bicycle Ride Across Iowa, has welcomed participants of all shapes and sizes, from all walks of life, and who hail from every corner of the globe. They come to Iowa to ride, to socialize, and to bask in the comradery and support that only an event of this magnitude and tradition can provide.

10,000 participants bike the length of Iowa over a seven-day stretch, during which a year's worth of sights will be seen. The ride begins in the western part of the state and ends in the east, at the Mississippi River. Although the route changes each year, the mileage is always 472, an average of 68 miles per day. RAGBRAI allows for 8,500 full-week cyclists and 1,500 one-, two-, or three-day riders. Each day affords an awesome glimpse of Americana, some good old-fashioned exercise, and a true sense of accomplishment. The nighttime is for reminiscing about the day's ride under the hot Iowa sun—and partying before it's time to get out there and do it again.

Bikers are treated like Olympians from the moment they arrive at the starting point. The route runs through countless one-stoplight towns, each one having petitioned to become a RAGBRAI pit stop. The townsfolk are grateful for the business that the event brings to their small community; they line the streets, holding banners, cheering, and offering food and water. Home-baked pies are sold in roadside church parking lots and community centers, old men blow horns, and children wave American flags at the never-ending sea of cycles. High school marching bands fill the air with their football fight song, while riders refuel with homemade lemonade. The tour is the spectacle of the year in these tiny towns, as 10,000 bikers plus a swarm of volunteers roll through their streets.

Sag Wagons will pick up those in need of a pedaling timeout, trucks carry riders' luggage, and the accommodations are provided by the town's residents. Anyone with a piece of property sponsors riders, who camp on their lawns or stay in their homes. You'll shower in their bathroom, or you may end up showering in the middle school locker room. Three-time RAG-BRAI veteran Brett Kemp stated, "It's the most relaxed I've ever been after any vacation. There's no business calls, no e-mail, no news—it's just the road and the towns. RAGBRAI is the ultimate decompression. . . . I've been to Mardi Gras and a lot of other great parties, but I've never seen such a blend of great times and great people."

TRANSPORTATION

There are a number of travel options to get to the starting town. Out-of-towners typically fly into Des Moines or Omaha, Nebraska. Pack your bike in a box, and label it clearly—airlines usually charge about $80 to ship a cycle. You may also ship your bike directly to the starting town, and ship it again from the ending town. Private charter bus companies run shuttles that carry riders, their equipment, and bicycles to the starting town, and back from the end point. These charter buses leave from several Iowa locations as well as from Nebraska, Minnesota, and Wisconsin cities. Services vary from year to year, so visit the event website for bus service for the upcoming event. Book flights for the day before bus departure, and use the following day to travel to the pickup point.

You can also arrange for a group to travel to the starting point via van or RV. One person in your group can act as the driver while everyone else rides their bikes. Rotating drivers each day is a popular option. Register your support vehicle online.

Sag Wagons patrol the routes to pick up those who are in need of assistance. If you're too tired or your bike breaks down, you can board one of these vehicles.

Ride in a straight line, keep to the right, and be conscious of your surroundings. Pass on the left and stop at lights and stop signs. RAGBRAI does an excellent job of keeping the roads clear of motor vehicles; however they will occasionally pass you. Event organizers allow one piece of luggage and a tent per rider, which will be carried aboard a truck. Have your bag on the truck no later than 8:00 A.M. each morning. A series of bike shops are located along the route.

ACCOMMODATIONS

RAGBRAI is mainly a camping event. When you register online, you'll receive a registrant packet that will outline your options. Camps are set up at community centers, at schools, and in the backyards of private residences. You may also opt to stay in a resident's home by enclosing $3 per night in your mail-in packet. If your group has an RV, naturally you can sleep in it. Hookups are not available; however, dumping is.

Food and drink are plentiful along the course. Bring enough cash to purchase food ($35 per day is recommended), but carrying energy bars and water is necessary. A shuttle bus runs riders from the campsites to shower facilities—sun-heated portable showers are also popular among riders.

TICKETS

You may register on the event website as early as November 15 or as late as April 1. The ride is only open to 8,500 riders, with a random lottery determining who can and cannot ride. Most applicants are allowed entry, but an unlucky few hundred are not. Visit the website on May 1 to find out if you've made the cut.

A week-long rider fee costs $125, a week-long nonrider fee is $35, and a vehicle permit is $35. Those who wish to ride from one to three days can pay $25 per day.

Individuals can join a team by visiting the event website's message board and making contact with teams who are looking for members. Groups who enter as a team must have a "group contact." This person is responsible for making one payment for the entire group.

Keep your wristband on throughout the race and place your bike plate on your bike.

What to Pack
- Tent and camping equipment
- Tire repair kit and spare tubes
- Helmet, riding gloves, and bike shorts
- Chamois cream

party tip

Chamois cream will become your best friend. If you're not already familiar with this fabulous product, you soon will be. Find a tree or building each day after breakfast and lunch and disappear behind it. Grab a handful of chamois cream and do not apply sparingly. After all, your bike isn't the only thing that needs lubricant!

Kansas

WAKARUSA MUSIC AND CAMPING FESTIVAL

⊛ Lawrence, Kansas
First weekend in June
www.wakarusa.com

Pack your tie-dyes, shine up those Birkenstocks, and head to Kansas for one of the premier jam-band shindigs in the land. The Native Americans who once roamed these Midwestern plains had a word for the shallow river that snakes through the heart of the Sunflower State. *Wakarusa* means "ass-deep," although the fun that's to be had at this festival runs much higher than the river. What really sets Wakarusa apart from the slew of alternative-music summer shows is its dedication to one specific genre. While many festivals cast a wide net, attempting to reel in varied artists, Wakarusa is proud to celebrate hippie culture alone, in all its mellow and unkempt glory.

Wakarusa, a considerably young celebration, only dates back to 2004. Popularity has spread like wildfire since its inception, as over 60,000 concertgoers from all fifty states, and 100 big-name musical acts make their annual trek toward Middle America.

The shows take place on five major stages over four days, and recent headliners have included Ben Harper, Yonder Mountain String Band, Gov't Mule, the Flaming Lips, and the String Cheese Incident. An excellent event website provides a printable breakdown of the stages and set times. The guitarists strum their opening chords at about 11:00 A.M. and play until 3:30 A.M. or 4:00 A.M., with the headlining acts staggered throughout. The festival grounds are located just outside of Lawrence, a charming little city, which is home to the locally beloved University of Kansas Jayhawks.

Camping from Thursday to Monday is recommended on this beautiful 400-acre sprawl of land. The grounds, which are a short walk from the stages, have restroom facilities and a store for all essentials. Bag your trash each evening and leave it on the road for morning pickup. Wakarusa has an array of daytime events outside of the music scene, including a drum circle (usually led by a rock star), morning yoga, hoop dance lessons, and a fantastic disc golf course (the deadhead sport of choice). You can also venture out to Clinton Lake, located four miles east of Clinton, for swimming, boating, fishing, and picnicking. If you've had too much sun, too many microbrews, or have overexhilarated yourself, then look for a "St. Bernard." This friendly group of volunteers can assist with any type of situation. The event organizers go above and beyond the call to make this as pleasant an experience as possible.

TRANSPORTATION

✈ **AIR:** Flights should be booked into Kansas City International Airport (MCI / *www.kansas-city-mci.com*), located forty-five miles from Lawrence.

Ⓑ **BUS / 🚂 TRAIN:** A Greyhound station is located at 2447 West Sixth Street in Lawrence,

and an Amtrak station is located at 413 East Seventh Street.

ACCOMMODATIONS

🔥 **CAMPING:**

General Camping Pass: This is included in four-day ticket prices. Each ticket is good for one vehicle and one tent. Arrival begins on Thursday at 8:00 A.M. No early arrival is allowed. You will camp next to your car and have access to restrooms, hand-wash stations, potable water, a general store, and ATMs.

Upgraded Camping Pass: You will have the option of upgrading your campsite to an area that contains a grill, fire pit, and picnic table. These upgrades cost approximately $80 and sell out very quickly. Check the website in April for details. Upgraded campers can arrive at 4:00 P.M. on Wednesday.

Premium Camping Pass: Campers with RVs must purchase these types of passes, which include your four-day concert tickets. You will have access to a grill, fire pit, picnic table, and water and electrical hookups. Purchase early as the hookups are available to a limited number of campsites. Arrival begins at 4:00 P.M. on Wednesday.

VIP Camping Pass: VIP passes are available and many people feel that this deal is well worth it. These tickets include front-row seating at all stages, round-the-clock free food and beers at the concert fields, two catered meals a day in the VIP pavilion, ultraclose camping with twenty-four-hour security, premium restroom and shower facilities, and access to the campfire ring. Purchase your VIP pass far in advance, as they do sell out quickly. Arrival begins at 4:00 P.M. Wednesday.

TICKETS

Tickets go on sale in April via *www.wakarusa.com*. Ticket prices have been climbing steadily each year, but at the time of writing they are as follows:

Single-day passes: $50–$60; four-day passes; early bird (in April) for $110, regular (before mid-May) for $125, and gate for $159; upgraded/premium passes: $260; VIP passes: $395.

What to Pack

- Small, portable grill with charcoal
- Rain coat
- Lawn chairs and lawn games
- Insect repellent with DEET—use on you and your campsite at least twice a day!
- Toilet paper

party tip

You will see an abundance of Caucasian males with dreadlocks, donning colorful Jamaican caps and Bob Marley T-shirts. Perhaps their dreadlocks are unequally weighted. Maybe they have a rock in their Birkenstock. Whatever the reason, these good-natured, well-meaning lads at shows like Wakarusa are disproportionately uncoordinated, compared to the general population. They can rarely throw a Frisbee, and pose little threat during a game of horseshoes.

COUNTRY STAMPEDE MUSIC AND CAMPING FESTIVAL

⊛ Manhattan, Kansas
Last weekend in June
www.countrystampede.com

One of the nation's most massive multiday music festivals takes place in Manhattan . . . Kansas that is. "The Little Apple" becomes overrun with mechanical bulls, party campgrounds, carnival games, and thunderous guitar riffs for four glorious days in late June. Hold onto your hat because the Country Stampede has evolved into the wild western equivalent to Woodstock, minus the mud fights.

Tuttle Creek Park, located just north of Manhattan, is an enormous, lush green patch of land that has served as the festival grounds since 1996. Attendance has increased by more than a third over the past few years, and it now draws 150,000 cowpokes of all ages.

The festival takes place from Thursday to Sunday, and the four-day camping permit begins on Wednesday. Wednesday and

Thursday are both heavy traffic days, so an option is to arrive at Tuttle Creek Park anytime between Sunday and Tuesday. You can pay $10 a day to arrive early, and this $10 is worth the avoidance of hours spent sitting in your car while waiting for a campsite. Primitive campsites, meaning no hookups, are available on a first-come-first-serve basis. Preferred campsites with power are very limited, go on sale in December, must be purchased over the phone, and sell out within an hour. Call 785-539-2222 to find the exact time and date that these preferred sites go on sale. The camping areas are within walking distance to the concert stages and are a round-the-clock party, some with later curfews than others.

Acts such as Trace Adkins, Alan Jackson, ZZ Top, Gary Allan, Toby Keith, and Gretchen Wilson have played in the past. A main stage and a couple of side stages are set up. The gates open at 4:00 P.M. on Thursday and at 11:00 A.M. from Friday to Sunday. Plenty of onsite food is available, but bring your own for the campsites.

In 2007 a new addition was added, Tuttleville. Located in the far southwest corner of the concert area, Tuttleville is a party of its own. Smaller, less-known acts play rap, bluegrass, and cutting-edge country. McGraw's Saloon, a temporary bar, is set up underneath an enormous tent. On Saturday the infamous "Hick Chick" competition rewards women with the greatest display of redneck abilities. Categories include tobacco chewing, pie eating, belly dancing, and watermelon seed spitting.

TRANSPORTATION

It's best to make this hoedown a camping trip, although you can certainly fly in and rent a car. If you do fly, make a special stop to load up on camping supplies.

✈ **AIR:** Manhattan Regional Airport (MHK / *www.ci.manhattan.ks.us/Airport.asp*) is a small airport located just a few miles outside of town. Several flights per day connect through Kansas City to this airport. Car-rental agencies are available. Kansas City International Airport (MCI / *www.flykci.com*) is the closest major airport, about two hours away.

🚌 **SHUTTLE:** KCI Roadrunner Express runs a shuttle from the Manhattan Airport and from KCI into Manhattan. Call 785-537-2086 for schedules and tickets.

ACCOMMODATIONS

🏨 **HOTELS:** Manhattan has a nice selection of hotels for those who aren't camping. Hotels sell out months in advance, so plan accordingly. Options include Holiday Inn (Seventeenth and Anderson /

785-539-7531 / $137), Super 8 Motel (200 Tuttle Creek Rd. / 785-537-8468 / $107), Fairfield Inn (300 Colorado St. / 785-539-2400 / $160, three-night min.), Hampton Inn (501 E. Poyntz Ave. / 785-539-5000 / $140), and Comfort Inn (150 E. Poyntz Ave. / 785-770-8000 / $140). Those who want to do some gambling can book a room at Harrah's Prairie Band Casino (12305 150th Rd. / 785-966-7777 / $169).

CAMPING: Campgrounds open the Sunday before the festival to the Monday after. A camping pass must be purchased separately from concert tickets. This camping pass covers your site costs from Wednesday to Monday, and a $10-per-day charge is applicable from the Sunday before to the Tuesday before. You will purchase a four-day camping pass along with your tickets, but the sites themselves are first-come-first-serve. In other words, you are guaranteed a spot somewhere. Many people arrive weeks prior to stake their claim, but flagging or roping off a site is not allowed. Showers are available.

The Horseshoe Bend Campground, located west of the festival grounds, has a 2:00 A.M. curfew. Primitive and preferred sites are available. The Branding Iron Campground has a 12:00 A.M. curfew and primitive sites only. Passes to both sites include one tent and one vehicle, one camper and one vehicle, or one motor home. If you have additional vehicles, purchase an additional vehicles pass. Fire pits, grills, trees, and picnic tables are available at the 20' × 30' sites. Preferred sites at Horseshoe Bend sell out the day they go on sale.

TICKETS

Ticket prices depend on when you purchase. They are arranged as early bird (before April 30), advanced (May 1 to June 20), or gate pricing. Single-day tickets are $52, $62, or $67, and four-day tickets are $92, $112, or $122. Primitive campsites are $117, $142, or $170, and preferred sites with RV hookups are $215 (there's no way you'll get one at the gate). A four-day car parking pass without camping costs $30, and an additional car pass is $50. A VIP section includes access to a hospitality tent, private restrooms, two catered meals per day, free beverages, and premium concert seating. This package costs $427, $477, or $502.

Tickets can be purchased through *www .countrystampede.com* or by calling 800-795-8091. Call early to guarantee a camping space.

What to Pack
- Sunblock—lots of it
- Extra flip-flops
- Food/beer for your campsite
- Campsite decorations
- Slip 'n Slide

party tip

An easy way to make friends is to construct a lasso game outside of your campsite. Pound a post into the ground and challenge passersby to secure a rope around said post from a given distance.

Michigan

BLISSFEST

⭐ Bliss, Michigan
Second weekend in July
www.blissfest.org

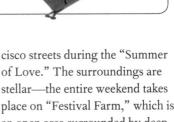

There's obviously something other than football, fishing, and cold weather that residents of the Great Lakes State do well. They throw one heck of a peaceful hippie party, man. Blissfest is Michigan's annual Folk, Blues, Bluegrass, and World Music camping festival, where the only thing that rivals the sense of harmony with nature is the scent of patchouli oil in the air.

Since 1981, Blissfest has summoned jam-band lovers, spastic dancers, and those who have a deep respect for Mother Earth to the rural northern Michigan woods for three days of music, dancing, and bliss. The age range runs the gamut, from three-year-olds in tie-dyed garb, to twenty-one-year-olds who discovered the Grateful Dead last semester, to aging hippies who roamed the San Fran-

cisco streets during the "Summer of Love." The surroundings are stellar—the entire weekend takes place on "Festival Farm," which is an open area surrounded by deep woods. The parallels between Blissfest and the Ewoks' Endor Forest are many.

The festival begins in the late afternoon on Friday and goes on until late Sunday night. Three stages are set up in an area that does not offer much shade, so prepare appropriately. Entertainment is comprised of all-day musical acts, drum circles, juggling contests, African dance classes, guitar lessons, magic acts, and open mic sessions. A host of miniature workshops are available, including kite-making, Hula Hooping, and Chinese meditation. Healing arts booths offer massage, acupuncture, and herbal treatments. Unofficial herbal treatments of the inhaled persuasion take place in the woods throughout. There is something happening at all hours to satisfy the inner love child in everyone.

Blissfest can accommodate 4,500 people per day. Camping for the weekend lends added enjoyment, as approximately 6,000 people per year will attest. A series of ten campgrounds line the north and west sides of the farm, and they are divided into underage, or family, camps and over-twenty-one areas. Keep in mind that the youngest person in your group determines the area in which you stay. Campsites are large enough to accommodate two cars, one RV, and a tent, or three tents—no more than eight people are allowed per site. Campgrounds are designated as "quiet zones" between the hours of 1:00 A.M. and 8:00 A.M. Acoustic guitar sing-alongs are acceptable at all hours (unless the guitar player is terrible). Food vendors are available. A bus runs between Blissfest and nearby Sturgeon Bay, the location of one of the best beaches on Lake Michigan. Bell's Brewery is the local microbrewer of choice. Have a great Blissfest, dude.

TRANSPORTATION

Blissfest is located seven miles southwest of Bliss, Michigan, in the northwesternmost part of the state. The closest large town is Harbor Springs, located twenty-two miles from Bliss. The address for Festival Farm is 3695 Division Road, Harbor Springs, MI 49740.

AIR: Two small regional airports service the Harbor Springs area, and car-rental agencies are available at both. Pellston Regional Airport (PLN / www.pellstonairport.com) is located twenty miles from Harbor Springs and has a couple of Northwest flights per day that connect through Detroit. Cherry Capital Airport (TVC / www.tvcairport.com) is located seventy-seven miles away in Traverse City and is serviced by Northwest, American, and United. The closest major airport is Gerald Ford International Airport (GRR / www.grr.org) located 210 miles from Bliss.

ACCOMMODATIONS

CAMPING: Camping is recommended, although Blissfest campsites are rustic and do not have RV hookups. Campsites are 25' × 50' and include solar showers, water, PortaJons, and sinks. Fires are not permitted. The over-twenty-one areas are Blissville Camp North, Blissville Camp South, and Back 40 Camp. An abundance of forest camping is also available. Camping check-in time is 10:00 A.M. on Friday and checkout is 12:00 P.M. on Monday. There are private campgrounds within fifteen miles that do have RV hookups. Visit www.blissfest.org for listings and contact information.

HOTELS: Two hotels offer Blissfest Packages. They are Holiday Inn Express (1600 U.S. 31 North / 231-539-7000 / $112) in Pellston and Birchwood Inn (7077 South Lake Shore Dr. / 231-526-2151 / $69) in Harbor Springs. Keep in mind that they are not exactly close by.

TICKETS

Internet ticket sales end on July 11—all tickets purchased after July 6 must be picked up at the gate. Camping passes are sold separately from tickets, and should be purchased prior to arrival, as spaces tend to fill up. Advanced weekend tickets cost $70, and weekend tickets at the gate cost $80. Weekend camping passes cost $18 if purchased online, and are $20 at the gate. Single-day tickets cost $30 on Friday, $45 on Saturday, and $25 on Sunday. All are sold on *www.blissfest.org*.

What to Pack
- Sundress or overalls
- Tofu burgers
- Hemp everything
- Grateful Dead's *American Beauty*

party tip

Seasoned blissful attendee Dr. Brett McClintock eloquently summed up his experience over the years. "If you enjoy folk music, herbal supplements, and periodic nudity (both male and female), then Blissfest is for you, brother." Dr. McClintock's whole life is seemingly a blissfest.

Minnesota

WE FEST

⭑ **Detroit Lakes, Minnesota**
Thursday through Saturday of first full weekend in August
www.wefest.com

A boisterous country music festival is Minnesota's largest annual camping gathering and a vital artery in the "Heart of America's" social calendar. We Fest is reason enough for anyone who's in need of a multiple-day raging hoedown to head north to the Land of 10,000 Lakes. Whether you're a country music fanatic, or someone who just loves a party, this event makes for an unforgettable summertime experience.

Over the past twenty-five years, We Fest has become a bright beacon of good times for country music fans. The acts are always top-notch, as ten-gallon superstars hit the stage over the event's three-day stretch in early August. What truly provides the spark, however, are the festival's intangible qualities—excitement and positive energy. Its reputation as a nonstop party, an adrenaline-packed gathering of no-holds-barred merriment, and the hottest honky-tonk scene around, is what attracts a crowd of 50,000.

The Soo Pass Ranch is the ideal location for a festival like this. A long wooden corral with a centrally located amphitheater, it suspiciously resembles a John Wayne movie set, and concertgoers' outfits seem to confirm this observation. Actual saloons, rather than beer tents or stands, have been constructed inside the corral—just tie your horse out front. Large grassy hills rising above the rest of the area serve as the general admission section, while seated areas are down below. Get to the entrance early each day if you want to stake your claim on a proper piece of the prairie. An excellent impersonation of running with the bulls (minus the bulls) takes place as soon as those corral gates swing open. Thousands of people and their party-hungry mentalities make a mad dash to prime viewing spots, marking their territory with a folding chair.

The We Fest caters to both types of music—country and western. Recent performers have included Toby Keith, Big and Rich, Brooks and Dunn, Tim McGraw, Willie Nelson, Keith Urban, Lee Ann Womack, Trick Pony, and Kenny Chesney.

The camping scene defines the true personality of We Fest. A series of campsites surround the Soo Pass Ranch, each serving a specific demographic. There are RV and tent sites for everyone from hard-partying twenty-somethings to vacationing families to Nicaraguan transvestites with prosthetic legs. Most people feel that the campsites are the backbone of the fun in Detroit Lakes. A different theme is applied to each year's festival, and many people dress their vehicles and sites in the appropriate décor with hopes of winning a prize for the most unique campsite.

TRANSPORTATION

The Soo Pass Ranch is four miles south of Detroit Lakes, Minnesota, on U.S. Route 59. From Minneapolis take Interstate 94 west to exit 50 and go north on U.S. Route 59. The Ranch is 225 miles from Minneapolis. Expect heavy traffic on Wednesday on your way in, but many people put the car in park and socialize on the road.

AIR: Book flights into Hector International Airport (FAR / www.fargoairport.com) in Fargo, North Dakota, located one hour away.

SHUTTLE BBUS: You can purchase a three-day shuttle bus ticket for $12 that gives you unlimited rides from your campsite to the concert and back. Single-day passes cost $5.

ACCOMMODATIONS

CAMPING: When camping at We Fest, you must purchase an assortment of tickets. Each person in your group needs a per-person camping pass ($50) or a VIP camping pass ($100), good from Wednesday to Saturday. Each car needs a vehicle permit ($60); each RV needs a large-vehicle permit ($120), or a VIP camping vehicle permit ($150). The VIP site is a bit tamer than the general campgrounds, but it sells out quickly. A limited supply of electrical permits can be purchased for RVs as well ($100). Electricity is available at VIP, Lake Satellite, Northwoods, Blue Ox, and Accessible campsites. All permits can be purchased on www.wefest.com.

Bathrooms, hand-wash stations, potable water, and showers are available at all sites. Vehicles are parked as they come in—there are no reserved spaces. Therefore, if traveling with friends in separate cars, drive in together. You can bring your own food and beverages, but kegs are not allowed. The curfew is 2:00 A.M. at all sites; however, some sites obey this loosely enforced rule better than others. See below for details.

Under twenty-five: These wild sites include Viking and Eagle / Hilltop. Both are late-night hot spots, with Viking being the wilder of the two.

Twenty-five to thirty: Blue Ox is a mature party spot that sells out quickly, and Oatfield attracts those who like to cut loose and then go to bed. WoodChuck and Valley are two newer options for this age group.

Thirty and over / Family: Lake Satellite and Northwoods are family atmospheres with a strict noise curfew. The VIP site falls in this category.

All ages: Accessible campground is open to campers who don't like to give away their age. Strict noise curfews apply.

TICKETS

Nine different levels of tickets are available. They are based upon proximity to the stage. Tickets go on sale prior to the announcement of performers, but they always sell out. Purchase through the event website by March or April. General admission three-day tickets sell for $100, with reserved lawn seats going for $120. VIP seating, which includes complimentary meals and beverages, starts at $525 and goes to $650. The fastest-selling are reserved seating in sections 1, 2, 9, and 10, costing approximately $150, and including easy access to a cash bar. Purchase these hot tickets a year in advance. Skybox grandstand tickets provide a bird's-eye view for $300. All concert tickets must be purchased separately from camping tickets.

What to Pack
- Camping supplies
- Folding chair
- Assortment of games/campsite decorations
- Lasso and bandana

party tip

We Fest is the original home of the "Midwest breast enlargement." Knowing that this is the last place they'll get frisked, certain daring cowgirls make it a point to smuggle bottles of booze in their brassieres. Keep this in mind when someone offers you a swig.

Missouri

SOULARD MARDI GRAS

⊛ St. Louis, Missouri
Saturday before Fat Tuesday through Fat Tuesday
www.mardigrasinc.com

For close to thirty years St. Louis has been hosting a Mardi Gras blowout that gives those feisty folks in New Orleans a run for their money—and their beads. The six-week-long party in the Gateway to the West is the region's largest and longest celebration. It's also a glamorous glutton's hog heaven!

Taking place in Soulard, the second largest Mardi Gras celebration in the country attracts 500,000 of the area's most extreme festivalgoers. Soulard, a French neighborhood located just south of downtown St. Louis, is loaded with restaurants, shops, and watering holes. This residential area, one of the oldest sections of the city, is a total mob scene throughout the weekend. The festival officially begins on the "Twelfth Night," twelve days after Christmas, and ends six weeks later, when a hun-dred thousand livers simultaneously fail on Fat Tuesday.

Events leading up to the final week include wine tasting, a Cajun cookoff, children's fairs, and the world's largest pet parade. Sure these events are fun, but the party-wise and true Mardi Gras revelers begin to invade St. Louis on the final Saturday of the event.

The Pyramid Grand Parade begins at 11:00 A.M. in downtown St. Louis on Saturday, winding its way into Soulard. The parade is comprised of over 100 elaborate floats manned by costumed Cajuns, waving to hundreds of thousands of onlookers along the streets. Families and children are welcome to observe, but when the parade ends at 2:00 P.M., Mardi Gras becomes an "adults-only" party.

In similar fashion to a caged lion being set free, festivalgoers storm the streets as soon as the final float has zipped by. With necklaces in tow and beers in hand, the die-hard Mardi Gras contingent begins a flesh-for-beads free-for-all. The often chilly costume party encompasses the entire neighborhood of Soulard. Head for the party tents if it's cold—they charge a cover fee, but have food and drink specials galore, along with live music and indoor plumbing. Two headlining bands, which in the past have included They Might Be Giants and Dr. John, play the outdoor stages near Broadway Street. Do not bring outside beverages into the party.

The revelry continues on through Fat Tuesday when a "Light Up the Night" parade showcases Saturday's best floats. The beads make their final appearance during the postparade street debauchery, which includes a Miss Soulard Mardi Gras contest.

TRANSPORTATION

✈ AIR: Flights should be booked into Lambert-St. Louis International Airport (STL / www.lambert-stlouis.com) located sixteen miles from downtown St. Louis. Car-rental agencies are available.

🚌 SHUTTLE: If driving, park at a downtown lot and take the free shuttle to Soulard. Take the Green Shuttle from lots at Tenth and Spruce, Ninth and Clark, or Clark and Tucker. The Purple Shuttle leaves from Clark and in-between Broadway and Fourth. Gold Shuttles serve lots at Sixth and Chestnut, Fourth and Pine, Seventh and Pine, and Eleventh and Pine.

🚇 METRO: The Metro operates a $5-per-way shuttle from the Civic Center at Fourteenth and Clark to a convenient pedestrian walkway at Tenth and Marion, from 9:00 A.M. to midnight.

🚂 TRAIN: The Amtrak station is located at 550 South Sixteenth Street. Visit www.mardigrasinc.com to learn about discounted Soulard Mardi Gras rates.

🚕 TAXIS: Cab companies include Auto Livery Cab Co. (314-241-5022), St. Louis County Cab Co. (314-991-5300), American Cab Co. (314-531-8766), Gateway Taxi (314-652-3456), Midwest Cab Co. (314-776-7400), and Yellow Cab (314-361-2345).

ACCOMMODATIONS

🏨 HOTELS: Soulard is a residential neighborhood, so you will have to stay in downtown St. Louis, just a mile away. Downtown hotels sell out fast, so call a couple of months in advance. Many will have special Mardi Gras rates, offering shuttle rides to the event and a much-needed late checkout. Hotels include Hilton (1 S. Broadway / 314-421-1776 / $139), Crown Plaza Riverfront at the Arch (200 N. Fourth St. / 314-621-8200 / $95), Sheraton (400 S. Fourteenth St. / 314-231-5007 / $163), Holiday Inn (811 N. Ninth St. / 314-421-4000 / $109), Hampton Inn (333 Washington Ave. / 314-621-7900 / $114), and Courtyard (2340 Market St. / 314-241-9111 / $129). Visit the event website for a listing of hotels offering special packages.

TICKETS

Soulard Mardi Gras is a free event, but tickets are needed for the VIP Bud Light Tent, open 8:00 A.M.

to 9:00 P.M. You'll be in the lap of beaded luxury, but only 1,000 tickets are sold at a cost of $100 per. Check *www.mardigrasinc.com* months in advance to purchase tickets.

party tip

Street meat is out in full force. St. Louis-style barbecue sauce is a sweet and spicy vinegar-and-tomato-based mix. You can sample this local delicacy at "Sweet Meat Stix," where the slogan is "The Best 12 Inches in the Midwest." If you don't like barbecue then try a hot dog from "Big Balls Little Weenies."

PARTY COVE

⊛ Lake of the Ozarks, Missouri
Memorial Day weekend

The wettest and most outlandish party in the country can be simply described as "floating hedonism." Thousands of tethered boats form maritime mayhem for three summer days of excess and exhibitionism. Party Cove is not for the meek, the timid, or those who prefer clothing. In fact, as any Missourian will attest, it's not for the amateur partygoer either.

Lake of the Ozarks is a gigantic man-made body of water in the center of Missouri with a 1,150 mile shoreline—longer than the California coast! Its beauty and countless secluded coves make it the premier weekend destination for many families and those seeking relaxation or solitude. At the nineteen-mile marker, however, is a place where solitude is utterly rejected. Located in the Grand Glaize Arm of the lake is Anderson Hollow Cove, commonly dubbed "Party Cove." Any summer weekend is a free-for-all at Party Cove, but hot and sunny Memorial Day weekend is typically the busiest.

This Redneck Riviera is located off Osage Beach, just over the Grand Glaize Bridge. Every type of boat imaginable, from multimillion-dollar yachts to wave runners, goes slowly through the "no wake zone" between the entrance of the Glaize Arm and the bridge. After the bridge you can crank it up a notch before rounding the peninsula and arriving at the cove. Boat owners and party lovers from across the country pour into Osage Beach each summer to get their fill of Mardi Gras on water. It's estimated that up to 3,000 boats carrying 8,000 people occupy the cove during the three-day holiday weekend. Over time, the location of Party Cove has changed due to real estate growth, although it looks like it's found a permanent home at mile marker nineteen.

Party Cove etiquette is to approach a group of boats that are tied together and ask permission to tie on with them. Permission is rarely declined, so be sure to ask people in your demographic or those whom you'd like to meet. Groups of boats become their own party microcosm, with people hopping back and forth from one boat to another. One portion of the cove, known as the Gauntlet, contains two enormous rows of vessels facing each other. The strip of water in between is known as Bourbon Street. Music blares from the speakers, and the scene is utter silliness. If you want to meet someone across the water, just jump in and swim up to their boat. The age ranges are wide, and making new friends is easy.

A slew of multistory lakeside establishments surround Lake of the Ozarks; they contain rooftop dance parties, volleyball courts, easy dock access, and all-around spring break atmosphere for twenty-five- to forty-year-olds.

TRANSPORTATION

AIR: The closest airport is Springfield-Branson National Airport (SGF / *www.sgf-branson-airport. com*), located two hours away. St. Louis International Airport (STL / *www.lambert-stlouis.com*) and Kansas City International (MCI / *www.flykci.com*) are both approximately a three-hour drive. Car-rental agencies are available at all three.

BOATS: The lake is extremely crowded over Memorial Day weekend, and the water is very choppy as a result. It is not recommended that you take anything smaller than a thirty-foot vessel out on the water. Drinking and boating can also be a major problem, so be sure to have a sober driver. You can rent a boat from any marina on the lake for multiple days over Memorial Day weekend—the farther your marina is from mile marker nineteen, the longer it will take to get to Party Cove. Lake of the Ozarks Marina rents fifty-six-foot houseboats for three days over Memorial Day weekend for $2,900. This souped-up barge sleeps twelve, comes complete with a kitchen, living room, barbecue, two refrigerators, shower, and one and a half bathrooms. They also have fifty-nine- and sixty-five-foot houseboats available. Visit *www.lakeoftheozarksmarina.com* or call 800-255-5561. For a complete listing of lakeside rental shops visit *www.lakelinks.com/boating/rentals.htm.* Make your reservations by March.

ACCOMMODATIONS

RENTAL HOMES: You can easily rent a house or condo on the lake. If you plan on renting a boat for the week (or weekend), and do not want to sleep onboard, it may be best to rent a lakeside property. Prices range depending on size and type of property, but you can spend $1,000 for the week for a house that sleeps eight people. Visit *www.lakerentals.com/lakes/lake-ozarks* or *www.vrbo.com.*

HOTELS: There are hotels available; however, many are older and do not have access to private docks. Inn at Grand Glaize (5142 Highway 54 / 800-348-4731 / $119) is right on the water with boat rentals, for $169 per night.

What to Pack
- Bathing suit (optional)
- Waterproof camera
- Water guns and balloon launchers
- Blow-up toys
- Binoculars

party tip

A Party Cove tradition you must try is the ceremonial water gun volley—especially if you're trying to meet people. Gigantic Super Soakers, water cannons, and water balloon launchers line ships' decks. Commence firing when you spot a boat with an interesting crew. This is the Party Cove way of saying, "Are you from around here?" If they return fire, then you have clearance to board their ship. The second part of this tradition is that the guns must be filled with alcohol. Rum and Coke usually make for good ammunition, but a sticky margarita concoction can really disable your enemy.

Nebraska

COLLEGE BASEBALL WORLD SERIES

⊛ Omaha, Nebraska

The two middle weeks in June

www.cwsomaha.com/stadium/omahas-johnny-rosenblatt-stadium.html

Baseball's intimate relationship with the American Corn Belt was eloquently captured in the 1989 blockbuster *Field of Dreams*. Baseball fans relished the image of wholesome farm boys of yesteryear who traveled from one Midwestern minor league town to the next and played for the love of the game during a simpler time. A lot has changed—but at least one purity has remained. For the past fifty years, the eight best unpaid teams in the nation assemble in Omaha, Nebraska, to try and slug their way to the Division I National Championship.

A trip to this event is a pilgrimage of sorts for the 290,000 people who descend upon the heartland of America each summer. The College World Series is the largest baseball event in the world, bringing in over 130,000 folks from out of state. It's a dream come true for the players, who battle in front of 23,000 people at Rosenblatt Stadium, not to mention a national ESPN audience.

Any resident of Omaha will attest that the first weekend of the tournament, Thursday night through Saturday night, is the city's most hopping weekend of the year—the result of an influx of fans and students who root for teams that have not yet been eliminated. The Cornhusker State becomes a melting pot of Southerners, Midwesterners, and Californians who come to town to celebrate and watch baseball.

Tickets for the games go on sale in April through Ticketmaster and cost around $20. Seats are fairly difficult to come by, as only a small portion are sold to the public. Scalpers are plentiful outside of the stadium—expect to pay twice the face value. Bleacher seats, which are the college crowd's haven of choice, go on sale about an hour before each game. The line, which forms three hours early, wraps around the stadium. Whether you have a game ticket or not, Zesto's is the hub outside of the stadium. This historic burger and ice cream joint has an enormous beer garden and has become an Omaha institution.

Located five miles west of Rosenblatt Stadium, Pauli's has become a College World Series party institution. It's normally a hole-in-the-wall dive bar, but each June they fence off a couple of parking lots, drawing over 3,000 baseball fans nightly. ESPN announcers frequently mention this unlikely hot spot, and nine-time World Series attendee Chris Olson proudly proclaimed, "I've been to Mardi Gras, Vegas, you name it. But the most beautiful women I've ever seen are at Pauli's. It pretty weird, considering the place is in Nebraska."

TRANSPORTATION

The stadium is a few miles from the hotels, so do not plan to walk to games. Read below for transportation options.

AIR: Book flights into Omaha's Eppley Airfield (OMA / www.eppleyairfield.com), which services eastern Nebraska, western Iowa, and northern Kansas. Make a car reservation well in advance—the airport is six miles from downtown.

CITY SHUTTLE: The Metro Area Transit runs shuttle service to Rosenblatt Stadium from six Omaha and Council Bluffs locations for $3 per way. They only run thirty minutes prior to and the thirty minutes after the conclusion of each game. Visit the event website for pickup locations.

HOTEL SHUTTLE: Renting a car is not necessary if you're staying in a hotel with a courtesy shuttle. In fact, having a car can be somewhat bothersome—check with your hotel when making reservations.

PARKING: Stadium parking is very limited and is usually reserved for season ticket holders. The stadium is located in a residential neighborhood, and most residents charge $20–$30 to park on their property for the day. This is your best bet.

TAXIS: There is a taxi stand near Zesto's. Local cab companies include Checker / Yellow Cabs (402-339-8294) and Safeway Taxi (402-342-7474).

BUS / TRAIN: The Greyhound station is located at 1601 Jackson Street, and the Amtrak station is at 1003 South Ninth Street.

ACCOMMODATIONS

HOTELS: Book a hotel nine months in advance to guarantee a room in either west Omaha or in Council Bluffs, Iowa—the World Series gets so crowded that waiting to reserve a room is not an option. Party people usually prefer Council Bluffs, due to the casino / bar scene. Casinos include Harrah's (2701 Twenty-third Ave. / 712-329-6000 /

$89) and Ameristar Casino (2200 River Rd. / 712-328-8888 / $259). Also in Council Bluffs is Holiday Inn (2202 River Rd. 712-329-1987 / $143), Days Inn (3208 S. Seventh St. / 712-366-9699 / $91), Country Inn & Suites (17 Arena Way / 712-322-8282 / $170), Comfort Suites (1801 S. Thirty-fifth St. / 712-323-9760 / $170), and Fairfield Inn (520 Thirtieth Ave. / 712-366-1330 / $179). In west Omaha try Hilton Garden Inn (17879 Chicago St. / 402-289-9696 / $209), Holiday Inn Express (17677 Wright St. / 402-333-5566 / $132), and Country Inn & Suites (11818 Miami St. / 402-445-4445 / $199). For further listings visit *www.visitomaha.com* or *www.councilbluffsiowa.com*.

TICKETS

For reserved seating and box seating visit the event website often and find out exactly when tickets will go on sale—a limited number are available and they sell out in sixty minutes! Box seats cost $24–$32, and reserved seats are $19 per game. Unlike these tickets, general admission tickets are good for the entire World Series. They are sold in a booklet of ten for $60 in April. Otherwise single GA tickets cost $9 at the gate, and unused seats are resold. GA tickets can also be upgraded, if upgrades are available, at the stadium box office. Tickets are mailed in early May. Tickets are available on *www.ticketmaster.com*.

What to Pack
- Baseball mitt
- Cornhuskers baseball hat
- Knowledge of college baseball basics (yes, they are allowed to use metal bats)

party tip

Former president George H. W. Bush is the College World Series' most famous player. He played first base for Yale in the inaugural C.W.S. in 1947, when they lost the championship game to California. Bush went 0 for 7 but returned the following year in 1948 for a memorable moment against USC. The future president waited in the on-deck circle, with the bases loaded and his team down in the bottom of the ninth of the final game. He would have certainly come up for a crucial at-bat, but the man before him hit into a triple play.

Ohio

RIVERFEST

⊛ Cincinnati, Ohio

Sunday of Labor Day weekend

Labor Day weekend signals the end of days by the pool, midday barbecues, and flip-flopped fun all across the United States, but Cincy does not let go so easily. It saves the best for last by launching its biggest single-day celebration of the year, Riverfest. Whereas many people hope for a nice long summer, the season can't go fast enough for Cincinnatians.

Riverfest is an opportunity to say goodbye to summer with a bang. Half a million people invade downtown Cincinnati for a day of merriment, sun, and awe-inspiring explosions. The day begins at noon; however, dedicated enthusiasts begin to arrive as early as 7:00 A.M., claiming pieces of lawn around Sawyer Point, or Yeatman's Cove, on the banks of the Ohio River. Boats arrive up to one week

early to stake their claim on the river. From noon to 9:00 P.M. there is an assortment of clean entertainment that includes live music on two stages, carnival games, skydiving, river races, and food galore.

The highlight of Riverfest is a 9:15 P.M. nuclear fireworks show that is easily one of the best in the country. Lasting for a half hour, this dazzling display is guaranteed to delight people of all ages who congregate along the river, on rooftops, in the streets, in restaurants, and on boats in the river. Six barges fire over 6,000 rounds of colorful bombs from the river, lighting up the entire city skyline.

Another notable event takes place earlier in the afternoon at 3:00 P.M. The Rubber Duck Regatta is a quarter-mile quack of a river race, during which 100,000 bath-time buddies float their way down the Ohio. For $5 you can sponsor a duck—proceeds go to the local food bank.

Expect gridlock traffic after the fireworks display. Many of the streets surrounding the river-front area will be closed, lending literal meaning to "Labor Day." People have to find parking and walk for miles, then return to their cars afterward only to sit in more traffic. Taking a taxi is not much easier. If you're staying in the city, use a bike to maneuver through this mess.

TRANSPORTATION

✈ **AIR:** Fly into Cincinnati International Airport (CVG / *www.cvgairport.com*) located thirteen miles south of downtown Cincinnati. Rental cars are available.

🚌 **SHUTTLE:** Airport Executive Shuttle can take you downtown for $15 one way, $25 round trip. Call 800-990-8841 for information.

🚌 **FESTIVAL TRANSPORTATION:** The Cincinnati Metro runs buses from a number of local park-and-ride to Riverfest. Stops are located in Evandale, Blue Ash, Union Township Civic Center, and Western Hills Plaza. Fares are $5 round trip. Visit *www.sorta.com* or call 513-621-4455 for information.

Ⓓ **DRIVING** / Ⓟ **PARKING:** Brave souls who want to park at the festival should exit onto Second Street from Interstate 71 or Interstate 75. Or exit on Pete Rose Way, make a left, and try to find a space along the street.

🚕 **TAXIS:** Cab companies include Yellow Cab (513-241-2100), Skyline Cab (513-251-7733), Suburban Cab (513-471-2222), and Veterans Cab (513-531-9300).

🚲 **BIKE RENTAL:** Don's Hobby and Bike Shop (4915 Glenway Ave. / 513-921-5366) and City of Cincinnati (4740 Playfield Ln. / 513-321-7333) rent bicycles.

ACCOMMODATIONS

🏨 **HOTELS:** Downtown Cincinnati hotels include Days Inn (2880 Central Parkway / 513-559-0400 / $45), Garfield Suites (2 Garfield Pl. / 513-421-3355 / $94), Ramada (800 W. Eighth St. / 513-241-8660 / $79), Cincinnati Hotel (601 Vine St. / 513-381-3000 / $175), and Hyatt Regency (151 W. Fifth St. / 513-579-1234 / $360 package deal from Sat. to Mon.). Visit *www.cincinnatiusa.com* for further listings. The closest hotels to the riverfront are located on the Kentucky side of the river in Newport; however, the bridges close at around 5:00 P.M. Try Comfort Suites (420 Riverboat Row / 859-291-6700 / $180) or Travelodge (222 York St. / 859-291-4434 / $65, no cancellations).

TICKETS

BB River Boats sells tickets to its bash, which includes dinner and drinks. The boat stays docked on the Kentucky side of the river and tickets cost $90 per person. It's an upscale way to enjoy Riverfest and see the fireworks, and it can be quite fun. Tickets sell out by June, but you can reserve spots up to a year in advance. Visit *www .bbriverboats.com* for more information, schedules, and tickets.

party tip

The greatest contribution that Cincinnati has ever made to the party scene is undoubtedly the game cornhole, a game that has players trying to toss a bean bag in a hole in a raised wooden platform. This action-packed contest is fun for all ages, and a perfect way to make friends at Riverfest. Large items are not allowed in, but portable cornhole games and rules can be found online. It's such a Cincinnati staple, that you'll have folks lining up to challenge the winner.

OKTOBERFEST-ZINZINNATI

⭐ Cincinnati, Ohio
Third weekend in September
www.oktoberfest-zinzinnati.com

Experience a world-class Bavarian beast of a beer fest without having to board a plane to Munich. Cincinnati plays host to America's best and largest version of the historic German celebration. In fact, many Germans feel that one word truly captures Cincinnati's Oktoberfest—*unwiderstehlich*!

A multitude of Midwestern cities pay homage to their strong German heritage in the months of September and October, but Cincy has taken the Oktoberfest celebration to another level. 600,000 people infiltrate its streets for two gluttonous days of dancing, eating, and *andeine ganze nacht durch machen* (all-night partying). This massive block party began meekly in 1976, but its *bier* gardens, gourmet food vendors, and German-style picnic tables, now engulf six full city blocks.

The mayhem takes place along Fifth Street, from Race Street to Broadway, on Saturday from 11:00 A.M. to midnight, and Sunday from 11:00 A.M. to 10:00 P.M. The opening ceremonies begin on Saturday at 10:30 A.M. with a parade of men in short shorts, dark socks, and loud shoes, who tap the first keg at all tents along their march. The crowd responds to this initial tap with great enthusiasm, for a weekend of Bavarian excess is now underway.

Although the festival officially takes place on Saturday and Sunday, the Gemuetlichkeit Games kick off the celebration at noon on Thursday. These three contests, designed to build momentum for the weekend, are an Olympiad of classic German feats of strength. The first event, "Hammering Nails" is a highly complicated match during which contestants must hammer as many nails as possible into a tree stump within the allotted amount of time. "Beer Barrel Roll," a game of mental prowess, awards players who can quickly roll a wooden barrel around the course. The grand finale is the "Bier Stein Race." Madchens, or German beer girls, must run around a course with full steins of beer, without spilling.

The Chicken Dance Song is a DJ's surefire way to liven up a rigid wedding, but Cincy has given a whole new meaning to this German ditty. The Crown Prince of Bavaria assisted the city in setting a Guinness World Record at the 1994 Oktoberfest, as over 48,000 people participated in the dance. Each year since, Oktoberfest tries to break this World's Largest Chicken Dance record. Weird Al Yankovic led the 1999 festivities on his kazoo, and Verne Troyer—Austin Powers's "Mini Me"—shook his little booty chicken-style in 2002. Vince Neil, lead singer of Motley Crue, led the crowd in the 2004 World's Largest Chicken Dance. Incidentally, this spectacle was voted VH1's "least metal moment" in the entire history of rock 'n' roll.

TRANSPORTATION

AIR: Book flights into Cincinnati / Northern Kentucky International Airport (CVG / *www.cvgairport.com*) which is located thirteen miles from downtown. Car-rental agencies and taxis are available.

OKTOBERFEST EXPRESS: This shuttle runs from four park-and-ride locations around the Cincinnati area. The Western Hills Plaza and Forest Park park-and-ride stops are dropped off at Sixth and Race streets. The UC Raymond Walters College in Blue Ash and Union Township park-and-ride stops are dropped off at Fourth and Sycamore streets. Fares are $3 one way and $5 round trip.

SOUTHBANK SHUTTLE: This shuttle runs from designated stops along the riverfront cities of

Covington, Newport, and Cincinnati every fifteen minutes until thirty minutes after the festival has ended. Fares are $1 per way.

TAXIS: Local cab companies include AAA Yellow Cab (513-821-8294), Eastside Yellow Cab (513-528-6400), Community Cab (513-721-2100), and United Cab (513-251-1155).

BUS / TRAIN: The Greyhound station is located at 1005 Gilbert Avenue. The Amtrak station is located at 1301 Western Avenue.

ACCOMMODATIONS

HOTELS: Downtown hotels within a short distance to the festival include Hilton (35 W. Fifth St. / 513-421-9100 / $199), Hyatt Regency (151 W. Fifth St. / 513-579-1234 / $169), Ramada (800 W. Eighth St. / 513-241-8660 / $79), and Garfield Suites (2 Garfield Pl. / 513-421-3355 / $94). For further listings visit *www.downtowncincinnatihotels .com*. Book a hotel room by June, if not earlier.

TICKETS

Entrance to the Oktoberfest is free. Food is reasonably priced at $2 to $6 for à la carte items. Beer is reasonably priced, depending on the brand.

What to Pack
- Dirndl/lederhosen and wooden shoes
- Suspenders
- Hat with a feather
- The largest beer stein you can find

party tip

The Germans have a word that refers to those partygoers who overestimate their ability to handle the large quantities of beer that are available during Oktoberfest. *Bierleichen*, meaning "beer corpses," is a term you should commit to memory before this party. The real Germans will love you for it.

HALLOWEEN IN ATHENS

⭐ Athens, Ohio
Saturday before or after October 31

Halloween is to Athens, Ohio, what Christmas is to the North Pole. It's the maximum in monstrous mischief, the pinnacle of witchlike wickedness, and the most phantasmagorically fantastic day of the year in this southwestern Ohio community.

Over 60,000 students and out-of-towners take to the streets in celebration of pagan pride for what has been dubbed "Ohio's largest outdoor cocktail party." Costumes are a must, so get out the afro wig, bell-bottoms, platform boots, baby bottle, or hillbilly teeth, and head to Athens, where Halloween has evolved from a seasonal gathering into the social event of the year.

Athens is home to Ohio University, a midsize 20,000-student school that is dwarfed under the looming shadow of its prominent athletic superior, Ohio State University. When looking at a map, Athens appears as nothing more than a small dot between the Appalachian Mountains and miles of open fields. However, the bustling cobblestone streets, abundance of nightlife, and all-around bohemian atmosphere are a direct contrast to the seemingly endless acreages of farmland that surround the city. Socially, Athens is an oasis in the middle of a desert.

Ohio University recently received a prestigious award from the Princeton Review as the number-two party school in the nation. The main drag, Court Street, houses eighteen bars within just a two-block radius. That translates into one watering hole per seven paces, about three times better than the student-to-faculty ratio at OU. Factor in 60,000 costumed crazies and you have one ghastly bar crawl.

The Court Street drag turns into a full-fledged block party quite early in the day on October 31. Halloween is actually a city-sponsored event, drawing in tens of thousands of people from all across the East and Midwest. Although college students are in abundance, this scene knows no age limits, especially when some face paint or a mask can easily turn back the clock. Decked-out bands play in the streets while the Halloween spirit works its wonders in removing inhibitions. The Union is the hottest dance spot in town, where you can boogie within a sea of pirates and princesses under the mesmerizing flashing of a disco ball. Live music is a nightly occurrence at the Blue Gator and O'Hooley's. Wander from place to place, enjoying the outdoor scene along the way.

If Halloween is your favorite holiday, then Athens should be a high-priority destination.

TRANSPORTATION

AIR: Flights should be booked into Port Columbus International Airport (CMH / *www .port-columbus.com*). A car should be rented at the airport for the ninety-minute drive to Athens.

PARKING: Parking is extremely limited and highly regulated during Halloween weekend. Do not park on campus, as these spaces are reserved for students and faculty with permits. Your best bet is to leave your car at your hotel or park in the Athens County Fairgrounds for the weekend. Shuttles run from the fairgrounds to the downtown area.

AIRPORT SHUTTLE: A shuttle is also available from the airport. They charge approximately $130 per person for one-way service, with a $20 charge per additional person. Visit *www .athensshuttle.com* for additional information and reservations.

BUS: Lakefront Lines is the only bus company that makes daily stops in Athens from several Ohio cities. Buses leave Cleveland daily at 9:35 A.M. arriving at 2:05 P.M. Buses leaving Columbus at 12:40 P.M. arrive at 2:05 P.M. Rates start around $50 for one-way service.

ACCOMMODATIONS

HOTELS: Several hotels are available in town. These include AmeriHost Inn (20 Home St. / 740-594-3000 / $94), Hampton Inn (986 East State St. / 740-593-5600 / $169), Ohio University Inn (331 Richland Ave. / 740-589-3704 / $117), and Super 8 (2091 East State St. / 740-594-4900 / $65). Book a hotel room by late August.

What to Pack

- A money belt to keep essentials should you be without pockets for the evening
- A spectacular costume ("I'm dressed as myself" need not attend.)
- Your entire costume (a lack of horns quickly transforms a devil into Little Red Riding Hood)

party tip

Be on the lookout for Halloween's most common last-minute offender, "Clown Wig Guy." This sorry excuse for a festive participant waited until the very last second before deciding on his extraordinarily creative ensemble, a clown wig. "Clown Wig Guy" usually borrows the wig from a friend, although occasionally he'll run down to the drug store and pick up the cheapest thing they have. He is easily distinguished by his everyday jeans, button-down shirt, and boring shoes. Show him no respect, as he deserves even less.

OHIO STATE UNIVERSITY VS. UNIVERSITY OF MICHIGAN FOOTBALL GAME

⭐ **Columbus, Ohio**
Final game of the regular season, late November
www.ohiostatebuckeyes.com

Having earned ESPN's title of "the greatest North American sports rivalry," this collegiate football slugfest has been the highlight of the schedule for even the most casual fan since 1897. Calling the annual November engagement between the University of Michigan Wolverines and the OSU Buckeyes a "rivalry" is a major understatement—"blood sport" is more like it. These two teams face each other on the final day of the season for sixty brutal minutes, in a game that's transcended sports to become a social phenomenon.

As if the rivalry alone were not enough of an incentive, the outcome of this contest typically determines the winner of the Big Ten Conference, the Rose Bowl game, and often, the National Championship. The most famous meeting occurred in 1950, when one of the worst blizzards on record blew through Ohio. The "Snow Bowl" was played in unthinkable conditions, but Michigan escaped with a 9–3 victory after a game total of forty-five punts. From 1969 to 1978 OSU's head coach, Woody Hayes, and Michigan skipper (and a former OSU assistant), Bo Schembechler, led their teams in "The Ten-Year War," during which one of the two teams won the Big Ten title six times. In 2006 both teams entered the game with 11-0 records, and Ohio State came away with a 42–39 win.

The game's location rotates back and forth each year between Ann Arbor and Columbus. As a prelude to the contest, the energy is electrifying at both Michigan's "Big House" and OSU's "The Horseshoe," but when forced to choose between the sites, OSU wins. Michigan's parking lot lacks a formal tailgating area and is not in close proximity to most watering holes. Many students are forced to preparty at home or in fraternity houses, which detracts from the onsite intensity. Add the fact that the stadium is fairly quiet (supposedly due to its layout) and fans jingle their keys rather than yell and scream. Sorry, Michigan.

With over 50,000 total students, Ohio State is the largest university in the country. Any football Saturday in Columbus means that a massive 7:00 A.M. tailgate commences in the lots surrounding the Horseshoe (Ohio Stadium), a mammoth stadium that holds over 100,000 Buckeyes. When Michigan is in town the scene reaches its zenith, and the crowds begin to gather as soon as the sun makes its first appearance in the cold Ohio sky. Corporate-sponsored tents are set up around the stadium, with the rowdier tailgates located farther away.

Parking your car off campus, and walking down Lane Avenue over the Olentangy River is a memorable experience. Hineygate is an enormous outdoor party located just across the street from the football stadium. If you don't have tickets, watch the game on Hineygate's big screen TVs and eat hot wings for breakfast, lunch, and dinner.

TRANSPORTATION

AIR: Book your flight into Port Columbus International Airport (CMH / *www.port-columbus.com*) located seven miles from downtown and ten miles from campus. Car rental and taxis are available.

SHUTTLE: A number of shuttles run from the airport to downtown every twenty minutes. Reservations are not necessary. Carriers are Arch Transportation (614-252-2277), Super Shuttle (614-252-5555), and Urban Express Transportation (614-856-1000).

BUS: You can ride the COTA, or Central Ohio Transit Authority, to all points in and around Columbus. The COTA has a special game-day shuttle that takes fans from the Expo Center on Seventeenth Avenue to the stadium. This shuttle runs from three hours before the game to two hours afterward. Visit *www.cota.com* for schedules and information. The Greyhound station is located at 111 East Town Street.

TAXIS: Local taxi companies include Acme Taxi (614-299-9990), Yellow Cab (614-444-4444), and Bobcat Taxi (614-481-0388).

ACCOMMODATIONS

HOTELS: Many downtown hotels include a free shuttle service to OSU games. They include Hyatt (75 E. State St. / 614-228-1234 / $249), Hilton (3900 Chagin Dr. / 614-414-5000 / $249), Embassy Suites (2700 Corporate Exchange Dr. / 614-890-8600 / $239), and Sheraton (201 Hutchinson Ave.

/ 614-436-0004 / $109). Hotels close to campus include Red Roof Inn (441 Ackerman Rd. / 614-267-9941 / $74), Fairfield Inn (3031 Olentangy River Rd. / 614-267-1111 / $124), Holiday Inn Express (701 E. Hudson St. / 614-263-7725 / $117), and Hilton Garden Inn (3232 Olentangy River Rd. / 614-263-7200 / $199).

TICKETS

Good luck. Students can purchase ticket packages in April, while alumni tickets go on sale in May. Tickets for the general public go on sale in July. Visit the Ohio State University athletic website at *www.ohiostatebuckeyes.com* in early summer for the exact date. These tickets sell out faster than a Rolling Stones concert, so you'll probably have to purchase them through an online ticket broker or by visiting *www.stubhub.com*. Plan to spend at least $150 per ticket.

What to Pack
- Hand warmers
- Buckeye apparel
- Cornhole game equipment
- "Ann Arbor is a Whore" T-shirt

party tip

The Ohio State Marching Band is not your traditional conglomeration of band geeks. They call themselves "TBDBITL," or The Best Damn Band In The Land, they conduct rookie hazing, and they hold rock star status at OSU. One of the best things you can do is attend the famed Skull Session held across the street from Ohio Stadium two hours before kickoff in the St. John Arena. This final band rehearsal is an adrenaline-filled mega-sized pep rally for the 10,000 fans that show up.

Oklahoma

OKIE NOODLING TOURNAMENT

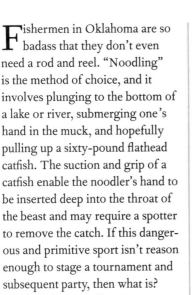

⭐ Pauls Valley, Oklahoma
Last weekend in June
www.paulsvalley.com/test/noodling.html

Fishermen in Oklahoma are so badass that they don't even need a rod and reel. "Noodling" is the method of choice, and it involves plunging to the bottom of a lake or river, submerging one's hand in the muck, and hopefully pulling up a sixty-pound flathead catfish. The suction and grip of a catfish enable the noodler's hand to be inserted deep into the throat of the beast and may require a spotter to remove the catch. If this dangerous and primitive sport isn't reason enough to stage a tournament and subsequent party, then what is?

The Okie Noodling Tournament is an annual hand-fishing challenge that draws thousands of revelers and grows exponentially every year. The tournament first took place in 1999, and it has quickly become a major cause for celebration in rural Oklahoma.

Pauls Valley plays host to the June event that celebrates the skilled ritual of hand fishing.

Participation is taken very seriously and should not be undertaken by those who've read a brief description of the sport and think that they can hang with the locals. In fact, noodling is often passed down through generations and can involve diving to depths of as much as twenty feet in murky water. Alligators, beavers, and snapping turtles often share this bottom-dweller space, and the experienced noodler is always on the lookout. Purists use no oxygen tanks or gloves, but the tournament permits the use of scuba gear with those competitors being placed in a separate category.

The nucleus of Okie noodling is Bob's Pig Shop, a glorified barbecue shack where the final fish weigh-in takes place. A grandstand of bleachers outside of Bob's overflows into the barricaded street as onlookers clamber for a spot to gaze into the huge metal tubs filled with live catches. The competition calls for twenty-four hours of hand fishing with all live catches required to be at Bob's by 7:30 P.M. on Saturday. Crowds gather and cheer as the catfish are tossed onto the scales. ESPN, documentary crews, the Food Network, and countless other press members snap pictures of the good ol' boys and the fruits of their noodling. The crowd eventually spills into Main Street, virtually taking over Pauls Valley with house party celebrations and good times in the multiple barbecue restaurants throughout town—Shot Gun Dave's, Punkin's, and Stevenson's to name a few.

TRANSPORTATION

AIR: Book flights into Will Rogers World Airport (OKC / *www.flyokc.com*), located one hour from Pauls Valley. Car-rental agencies are available.

BUS / TRAIN: Believe it or not, Pauls Valley has its own Amtrak (S. Santa Fe St. and E. Paul Ave.) and Greyhound (1002 N. Ash St.) stations.

ACCOMMODATIONS

HOTELS: Local hotels include Comfort Inn (103 S. Humphrey Blvd. / 405-207-9730 / $81), Days Inn (2606 W. Grant Ave. / 405-238-7548 / $76), Economy Inn Express (1409 S. Chickasaw / 405-238-3321 / $30), Garden Inn (700 Copperfield Dr. / 405-238-7313 / $169), Relax Inn (2506 W. Grant / 405-238-7545 / $30), and Sands Inn (2415 W. Grant Ave. / 405-238-6415 / $30).

TICKETS

Find an entry form on the event's website, *www .okienoodling.com*.

What to Pack
- Barbecue bib
- Sleeveless shirt
- Febreze—for your photo-op with the catch of the day

party tip

Noodlers are treated with a boatload of respect during the Okie tournament. Everywhere they go, the ladies follow. So guys, put some fake blood on your forearm, rough up your knuckles, and enjoy the "faux noodler arm" that just may pull in a catch for the weekend.

ROCKLAHOMA

⭐ Pryor, Oklahoma
Second weekend in July
www.rockfeverfest.com

Hair metal, circa the 1980s, makes a triumphant return to the stage in Pryor, Oklahoma, for an annual glam rock festival that has breathed new life into the hairspray industry. "Feel the Noize" for three days in mid-July, where band after forgotten band squeezes into leopard-print spandex, cranks their amplifiers to eleven, and reminds us that '80s metal ain't "Nothin' but a Good Time"!

Hair metal had a meteoric rise, led by bands like Warrant, Ratt, Twisted Sister, and Poison, with a simple formula—find a heartthrob lead singer, apply eye shadow, mix in the occasional love ballad, and sell out stadiums across the country. But it crashed and burned with the "alternative rock" movement of the mid-1990s. However, it has recently enjoyed a revival as a plethora of hero-to-zero bands have cleaned up their acts, teased their manes, and brought sleaze rock back to the mainstream. In 2007, the first annual Rocklahoma

sold over 100,000 tickets to skid row bums, cherry pie connoisseurs, and patients of *Dr. Feelgood*, for a three-day festival that's guaranteed to kickstart your heart.

About 30,000 fans per day fill a 400-acre farm from Friday to Sunday, for the largest 1980s metal event in the world. Sleeveless Def Leppard T-shirts, slashed jeans, large-hoop earrings, and sweatbands are the apparel of choice, and the rock is around the clock. Rocklahoma's inaugural lineup featured Slaughter, Quiet Riot, Ratt, and Poison on Friday, Warrant, Skid Row, Winger, and Vince Neil on Saturday, while L.A. Guns, Great White, and Twisted Sister rocked on Sunday. The first power chord is struck before lunch, and the final guitar is smashed just before midnight. Some groups are as fierce as they were twenty years ago, while others utilize pyrotechnics to disguise deteriorated instrument playing. Either way, the crowd loves it.

Single-day, three-day, and VIP passes are available. The three-day VIP ticket, although a couple of hundred dollars more than a general admission pass, is an excellent value. Up-front seating, free catered meals in the hospitality tent, and complimentary beer and mixed drinks will offset the savings from a general admission ticket. All fans have access to "Picture Alley," a stage-front area that allows up-close photography. The camping area is a party all day long, especially after the concerts. Spend some time decorating your site to give it that "Home Sweet Home" feel.

TRANSPORTATION

AIR: Book flights into Tulsa International Airport (TUL / *www.tulsaairports.com*), located approximately forty-five miles from Pryor. Car-rental agencies are available—call a couple of months in advance to book a car.

ACCOMMODATIONS

CAMPING: Passes can be purchased for $45 and must be accompanied by at least one three-day ticket. Campsites are dry; there are no electricity or water hookups. The sites measure 20' × 40', and they have access to hot showers, fresh water, trash service, RV dumping stations, and port-a-potties. There is a convenience store and twenty-four-hour security. Each campsite comes with one free vehicle pass.

HOTELS: Although in its infancy, this festival sold out every hotel room in Pryor during its first year. If you are not going to camp, then book a hotel room early. Options are limited, but they include Microtel Inn & Suites (315 Mid America Dr. / 918-476-4661 / $75), Comfort Inn (307 Mid America Dr. / 918-476-6660 / $100), Days Inn (6800 S. Mill St. / 918-825-7600 / $95), Best Western (106 Holiday Lane / 918-479-8082 / $180), and Monterey Motel (400 S. Chouteau Ave. / 918-476-5060 / $40). If you cannot find a room, try Claremore, located sixteen miles away.

TICKETS

Three-day general admission passes cost $110, single-days cost $50, and three-day VIP passes cost $325. Camping passes are $45 per vehicle. Purchase VIP passes early, as a limited number are available. Call 866-310-2288 or purchase online at *www.rockfeverfest.com*.

What to Pack
- Acid-washed jeans
- Jean jacket with "Faster Pussycat" iron-on patch
- Case of Aqua Net
- Mascara (men and women)
- Guns N' Roses' *Appetite for Destruction*

party tip

In the real world, it is often difficult to formulate an intelligent, interesting ice-breaker when approaching members of the opposite sex. This is not an issue at Rocklahoma. Common pickup lines include, but are not limited to, the following:

I like your big hair.
You're so much cuter than Dee Snider.
Where did you get that codpiece?

South Dakota

BLACK HILLS MOTORCYCLE RALLY AT STURGIS

★ Sturgis, South Dakota
First week in August
www.sturgis.com

Sturgis is the ultimate biker party in the United States. Each year a half million black-leather-clad motorcycle maniacs pour into this otherwise quiet town for a week of major league debauchery. Whether you own a Harley Davidson or are just interested in witnessing this revved-up counterculture gathering, Sturgis is one event for your to-do list.

Sturgis is located in the Black Hills of South Dakota, a region known for breathtaking scenery and wide-open roads. The town itself is quiet, with a population of about 6,600 people, but Sturgis balloons to seventy-five times this size during the rally. Bikers from all across the globe pour into South Dakota the first week in August for the opportunity to show off their

rides, compare tattoos, and celebrate life on the road.

The schedule is jam-packed each day with events such as motorcycle races, motorcycle shows, Ms. Sturgis contests, bull fights, and live rock 'n' roll acts, to name a few. The town of Sturgis, the campgrounds, and the neighboring towns are home to these organized events. Feel free to float back and forth, as there will be something happening everywhere at all hours! The streets and bars are constantly abuzz, and you will not have to look far to find entertainment. Check the website for a complete schedule.

The atmosphere at Sturgis is very positive, and a true feeling of community and comradery exists among partygoers. Nonbikers are accepted and welcomed, and you should not feel threatened showing up in a minivan. Despite an often rough exterior, most bikers are great people with warm hearts. You will never be stranded should you need a ride to a concert that is taking place a few miles outside of town.

TRANSPORTATION

Sturgis partygoers are encouraged to make this a road trip via motorcycle, car, or RV. If you do ride a motorcycle, then we suggest a day trip through the Devils Canyon and to the Crazy Horse Monument, a Mount Rushmore-like depiction of the Lakota leader, which is currently being carved into the side of a mountain. You can also take a ride to three neighboring towns that are host to some major partying themselves; Deadwood (twelve miles), Spearfish (seventeen miles), and Rapid City (thirty-four miles).

AIR: You can book a flight into Rapid City Regional Airport (RAP / *www.rcgov.com/Airport/ pages*) and rent a car from there, but if you are going to fly, you should make reservations twelve months in advance. Rapid City Regional Airport is located forty-five minutes southeast of Sturgis. Carriers are SkyWest, Northwest, United, and Allegiant Air.

ACCOMMODATIONS

HOTELS: Are you kidding? You will need to reserve a spot at one of the major campgrounds, as the waiting list for hotel rooms can be as long as *nine years.*

CAMPING: The campsites are about four miles from the town of Sturgis, and some of the wildest partying takes place on these grounds. Cost is approximately $15–$20 per night, and reservations should be made by February. Large breakfast tents are set up at the campgrounds for early morning beer and eggs.

For a list of campgrounds visit *www.sturgis .com* and click on the "Places to Stay" link.

Partygoers report enjoying the Glencoe Campground (*www.glencoecamp.com* or 800-272-4712). Glencoe provides clean shower and restroom facilities and excellent security. Reservations can be made online or by phone. Buffalochip Campground (*www.buffalochip.com*) is another site with a great reputation. Buffalochip campers will have access to flush toilets, nice shower facilities, and fast-food restaurants, which set up shop on the campground. This campground is home to the main concert events, and campers get free concert tickets on the nights they camp. Go online for reservations.

RV: RV parking is also available for the Glencoe and Buffalochip sites. Good reports come from the Katmandu Campground (*www.katmandu campground.com* or 866-776-0758), which runs a shuttle from its grounds into Sturgis. Reservations can be made online or by phone.

The importance of making your camping reservations as early as possible cannot be emphasized enough. This is a gigantic event in a small town and the space fills quickly. Many of the campgrounds will only allow entrance to those who have reservations and will not allow visitors. Get your group of friends organized way ahead of time!

TICKETS

Tickets are not necessary for the motorcycle races and rallies; however, you will need tickets for the concerts, which do sell out on a regular basis. Recent performers have included Lynyrd Skynyrd, Kid Rock, Tom Petty and the Heartbreakers, Alice N Chains, David Lee Roth, and the Steve Miller Band. Visit *www.ticketmaster.com* for tickets and concert information.

What to Pack

- Lots of black
- Harley Davidson raincoat
- Cut-off denim vest

party tip

Nonbikers should memorize the following motorcycle lingo in order to blend in:

- Back Door—The most experienced rider in a group rides "back door." His job is to watch over the entire group.
- Blue Hair—An elderly driver who may have trouble driving due to regressing eyesight and motor skills.
- Iron Butt Association—Someone who's ridden 1,000 miles within twenty-four hours.
- Iron Butt Gold Association—Someone who's ridden 1,000 miles a day for ten consecutive days.
- Pillion—To ride on the back of a bike. "My wife rode pillion for the past 500 miles."
- Yard Sharks—Annoying dogs that run after a biker. "We were riding in my neighborhood and a yard shark bit me in the leg."

Wisconsin

OPENING DAY AT MILLER PARK

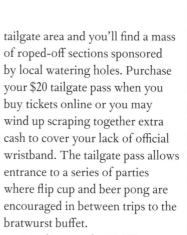

★ Milwaukee, Wisconsin
Early April
www.milwaukee.brewers.mlb.com

Beer, bratwurst, and baseball, what's not to like? Legions of die-hard fans, a new domed stadium, and a surplus of local brews are a recipe for a good time in Milwaukee, Wisconsin. Simply stated, the Brewers play host to the greatest opening day celebration in major league baseball. The city may be small, but the fandom is not. Granted, the Brewers have not exactly been the perennial champions of baseball, but they are top of the heap in the tailgating division. Pick up some hometown gear or you'll stick out like a sore thumb among the mass of fans littering Miller Park in early April.

While most modern-day ballparks are essentially a concrete field with a massive stadium on the horizon, Miller Park is located in a woodsy suburban landscape. Cross the bridge from the ballpark to the tailgate area and you'll find a mass of roped-off sections sponsored by local watering holes. Purchase your $20 tailgate pass when you buy tickets online or you may wind up scraping together extra cash to cover your lack of official wristband. The tailgate pass allows entrance to a series of parties where flip cup and beer pong are encouraged in between trips to the bratwurst buffet.

Fans buy out the 42,000 opening-day tickets, and unknown thousands of others show up just for the parking lot scene. In fact, Brewers management seems to think that they could sell out the Rose Bowl on opening day. Arrive as early as 9:00 A.M. with folding chairs and a miniature grill in tow, claim your parking space, and get ready for a citywide celebration. Oh yeah, there's a baseball game too.

TRANSPORTATION

AIR: Flights should be booked into General Mitchell International Airport (MKE / *www.mitchell airport.com*). The airport is located just three and a half miles from the stadium, which is three miles west of downtown Milwaukee. Multiple car-rental agencies are available at the airport.

Ⓑ BUS: The Greyhound station is located downtown at 606 North James Lovell Street (414-272-2156).

Ⓣ TAXIS: The overwhelming majority of fans drive to the game, as taxi and bus service is minimally provided. However, if your ride is unable to perform their specified duties due to overly reveling in a Brewer's victory, finding a taxi is not necessarily a lost cause. Walk past the Little League stadium toward the main highway and your odds of catching a ride are dramatically increased. A ride from Miller Park to downtown is no more than $20. Yes, taxi prices are significantly lower than comparable charges in other major cities. Public transportation is provided, but not especially well marked, if you're headed back downtown. Try Yellow Taxi (414-271-1800), Airport Cab Mobile Services (414-794-3188), Airport Car Service (262-377-9210), American Airport Car Service (414-421-3882), or American United Taxi (414-220-5000).

ACCOMMODATIONS

🛏 HOTELS: The following hotels are within walking distance or a short ride from Miller Park:

Ramada Inn Downtown (633 W. Michigan St. / 414-272-8410 / $89), Holiday Inn Milwaukee City Center (611 W. Wisconsin Ave. / 414-273-2950 / $98), Hyatt Regency (333 W. Kilbourn Ave. / 414-270-6000 / $139), and Courtyard Milwaukee Downtown (300 W. Michigan St. / 414-291-4122 / $109). For a complete list of nearby hotels and availability visit *hotel-guides.us/wisconsin/miller-park-wi-hotels.html*.

TICKETS

Visit *www.milwaukee.brewers.mlb.com* when February comes around for game ticket and tailgate ticket purchases.

What to Pack
- Warm clothes—too early for typical baseball weather
- Brewers gear is an absolute must
- An empty stomach to increase game-day sausage consumption

party tip

If and when you need a bathroom in Miller Park, avoid the long lines by walking down the corridor to the next series of restrooms. Some men's rooms have twenty-minute lines while their neighboring facility is virtually empty.

SUMMERFEST

⊛ Milwaukee, Wisconsin
End of June to beginning of July
www.summerfest.com

Only one annual celebration has earned the right to claim the prestigious title of "World's Largest Music Festival." This honor was bestowed upon Milwaukee's forty-year-old, massive Summerfest in 2001, when the *Guinness Book of World Records* reported over 1 million visitors! This mega-gathering of the Midwest's most dedicated music-loving, beer-drinking, good-timers is proof that some parties get better with age.

Summerfest is an eleven-day event that takes place in Henry Maier Festival Park, a gigantic property that sits on the shores of Lake Michigan, in close proximity to downtown Milwaukee. There are nine stages at the seventy-five-acre Festival Park, each hosting a separate genre of music, with food and entertainment tents set up in between. Each day, visitors from across the country pour through the gates to listen to the heaviest hitters in the music industry; from

the Doors in the 1960s to the Bangles in the 1980s to Destiny's Child in 2006. Headliners play the Marcus Amphitheater, a 23,000-seat venue known for its steep, grassy seating areas and superb views of the lake. The often televised "Big Bang" fireworks display kicks off the first night of the festival.

The gates open each day at noon, and tickets are priced very reasonably. Spend some time bopping around the park, poking your head into different onsite bars and sampling the wonderfully famous food of Summerfest. The wide variety of ethnic eateries includes German, Greek, Chinese, Italian, Thai, Mexican, and just about every other country you can name. Do not leave the park without having tried Milwaukee's famous fried eggplant from the Venice Club, the tastiest at the festival. Also worth mentioning are the scrumptious humongous turkey legs, which resemble Fred Flintstone's club.

For an excellent lake view during your meal, take the surprisingly uncrowded Lakeshore Path, to the picnic table section. Caribbean steel drum bands and South American pan-pipe musicians play outside of international bazaar tents, which offer merchandise from around the world.

TRANSPORTATION

AIR: Flights should be booked into General Mitchell International Airport (MKE / *www.mitchell airport.com*). The airport is located just eight miles from the festival grounds, which are a fifteen-minute walk from the city. Multiple car-rental agencies and taxis are available at the airport.

TAXIS: Take a taxi from the airport to your hotel in downtown Milwaukee and walk to the festival. Oftentimes it is difficult to hail a cab in the city, so phoning a cab may be a good idea should you need one. Yellow Taxi (414-271-1800), Airport Cab Mobile Services (414-794-3188), Airport Car Service (262-377-9210), American Airport Car Service (414-421-3882), and American United Taxi (414-220-5000).

BUS: The Greyhound station is located downtown at 606 North James Lovell Street (414-272-2156).

CAR: If you will be driving your car, please reference the "shuttle" section below.

SHUTTLE: There are many shuttles and buses that provide service to the festival grounds from park-and-rides and bus stops throughout the greater Milwaukee area. If you will be driving a car, you should utilize this service, as leaving the festival on weekend evenings can be a nightmare. No matter which direction you'll be coming from there will be a bus stop. Visit the "getting here" portion of the *www.summerfest.com* site for a listing of all the exact "Freeway Flyer" stops.

Shuttle times: Weekdays—11:30 A.M. to 5:00 P.M. every thirty minutes, 5:00 P.M. to 12:30 A.M., departing every fifteen minutes. Weekends—11:30 A.M. to 12:30 A.M., departing every fifteen minutes. Parking is free and round-trip fare is $6.

ACCOMMODATIONS

HOTELS: The following hotels are within walking distance or a short ride from Summerfest: Ramada Inn Downtown (633 W. Michigan St. / 414-272-8410 / $129), Holiday Inn Milwaukee City Center (611 W. Wisconsin Ave. / 414-273-2950 / $171), Hyatt Regency (333 W. Kilbourn Ave. / 414-270-6000 / $149), and Courtyard Milwaukee Downtown (300 W. Michigan St. / 414-291-4122 / $199). For a listing of hotels with special Summerfest rates visit *www.visitmilwaukee.org* or call 800-231-0903.

TICKETS

Buy tickets into Henry Maier Festival Park at the gate. During the week, from noon to 4:00 P.M., tickets are $8. After 4:00 P.M. and on weekends tickets cost $15. Two-day passes are available for minimal savings.

Tickets for many of the Marcus Amphitheater concerts must be purchased separately (always for the big-name headliners) in advance through *www.ticketmaster.com*. The larger shows sell out, so visit the event website early, find out who's playing, and purchase tickets before your trip. Ticketmaster tickets include your entrance into the Henry Maier Festival Park after noon on the day of the show.

party tip

While you're in town check out the Holler House (2042 W. Lincoln Ave. / 414-647-9284), home of the nation's oldest functioning bowling alley. Two lanes are located in the basement of this historic establishment, where beer is not available on tap, but Pabst Blue Ribbon cans are in no short supply. Call ahead so management can arrange for a pin setter. Don't expect electronic scorekeeping either.

FREAKFEST

★ Madison, Wisconsin
Saturday before Halloween

Those with even limited knowledge of infamous party towns know that Madison's reputation precedes itself. This eclectic city houses over 220,000 residents, serves as the cultural capital of Wisconsin, and is home of the University of Wisconsin Badgers. Madison inhabitants are quite aware that they reside in a special place, and they definitely celebrate life on a regular basis—just check out their Halloween celebration.

Since the 1970s, marauders have lined State Street for a Halloween that has left countless bits of costumes in its wake. The notorious reputation of the party swelled as time went on, as did the number of revelers. Estimates suggest that as many as 100,000 people gathered in the heart of the city in the early 2000s, on the Saturday before October 31. Arrests, property damage, swollen expenditures on policing costs, and riots forced city officials to change the party in 2006. Change is usually met with dismay, but Halloween in Madison, although a bit more structured, is still a wonderful assemblage of costumed party freaks.

Renamed locally as "Freakfest," Halloween officially takes

place on State Street from 7:30 P.M. to 1:30 A.M. Unofficially the party begins on Friday night. State Street connects the University of Wisconsin to the State Capitol and serves as the main artery into the center of the city. On Saturday night, State Street is fenced off, and only those revelers holding tickets are granted access. This may be the only official Halloween celebration in the country for which one can contact Ticketmaster for access. Those who arrive before 7:30 P.M. (wink, wink) will not be forced to leave State Street, although they cannot leave and return. Two stages are set up for a Battle of the Bands; one near Capitol Square and the other at Gorham and State Streets. The organization of Halloween in Madison has been met with some protest, and attendance has dropped off from those glory days of looting and pepper spray. Currently 35,000 freaks flood the downtown, which proves that the ghosts of a good costume party can't be bottled up.

TRANSPORTATION

AIR: You can fly directly into Madison's Dane County Regional Airport (MSN / *www.msnairport .com*) from most major U.S. cities. Fares can be more expensive than flights into General Mitchell Inter-national Airport (MKE / *www.mitchellairport.com*), located about seventy-five miles away in Milwaukee. Both airports have car rental available.

BUS FROM AIRPORT: Badger Coaches takes passengers from Mitchell airport to Madison with departures every two and one-half hours from 9:00 A.M. to 10:00 P.M. The bus can be picked up outside of the baggage claim. Round-trip tickets cost $34. Visit *www.badgerbus.com* or call 608-155-1511.

DRIVING/ TAXIS: Driving into the downtown area is not recommended. Many of State Street's surrounding blocks and adjacent streets are "No Parking Zones" during Freakfest. You're better off taking a taxi. If you need to drive, access downtown via the Beltline and use exit 263. Local cab companies include Union Cab (608-242-2000) and Madison Taxi (608-255-8294). After the party hail a taxi from any of three designated taxi stands. They are located on Langdon Street between North Park and North Lake Streets, on North Francis Street between West Johnston Street and University Avenue, and on East Johnson Street between North Carroll Street and Wisconsin Avenue.

BUS: Madison Metro Transit runs buses to all points in Madison. Bus 24 goes to and from Dane County Regional Airport. Visit *www.cityofmadison .com/metro* for information. The Greyhound station is located at 2 South Bedford Street.

ACCOMMODATIONS

HOTELS: The ones within walking distance to State Street include Best Western (22 S. Carroll St. / 608-257-8811 / $134), Doubletree Hotel (525 W. Johnson St. / 608-251-5511 / $159), Hilton (9 E. Wilson St. / 608-255-5100 / $360), and Quality Inn (2969 Cahill Main / 608-274-7200 / $130). Rooms should be booked one month in advance. For a further listing of Madison hotels, most of which are located within a few minutes drive from State Street, visit *www.hotwire.com*.

TICKETS

Tickets cost $5 in advance or $7 at the door. Tickets go on sale in early October at the Coliseum box office in Madison. Out-of-towners can purchase tickets by calling Ticketmaster at 608-255-4646 or by visiting *www.frankproductions.com*. On the day of the party you can purchase tickets at booths located at Library Mall (200 block of W. Gilman St.) and at Capitol Square, on North Carroll St.

What to Pack

- Two forms of ID for out-of-state residents
- Ron Dayne jersey
- "Ghost of Madison Past" costume
- Cheesehead

party tip

Are you a man with limited creativity in the Halloween costume department? Light a pair of pajamas and a bathrobe on fire for a few seconds and wear the burnt clothing. Mess up your hair, rub soot on your face, and be "the guy who didn't take the fire alarm seriously."

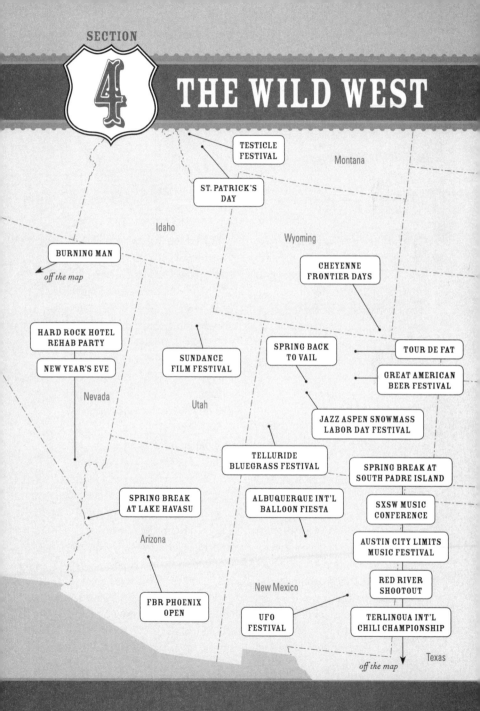

TESTICLE FESTIVAL

Montana

ST. PATRICK'S DAY

Idaho

Wyoming

BURNING MAN

off the map

CHEYENNE FRONTIER DAYS

HARD ROCK HOTEL REHAB PARTY

NEW YEAR'S EVE

SUNDANCE FILM FESTIVAL

SPRING BACK TO VAIL

TOUR DE FAT

GREAT AMERICAN BEER FESTIVAL

Nevada

Utah

JAZZ ASPEN SNOWMASS LABOR DAY FESTIVAL

TELLURIDE BLUEGRASS FESTIVAL

SPRING BREAK AT SOUTH PADRE ISLAND

SPRING BREAK AT LAKE HAVASU

ALBUQUERQUE INT'L BALLOON FIESTA

SXSW MUSIC CONFERENCE

AUSTIN CITY LIMITS MUSIC FESTIVAL

Arizona

RED RIVER SHOOTOUT

New Mexico

FBR PHOENIX OPEN

UFO FESTIVAL

TERLINGUA INT'L CHILI CHAMPIONSHIP

off the map

Texas

Arizona

FBR PHOENIX OPEN

★ Phoenix, Arizona
Super Bowl weekend, usually early February
www.phoenixopen.com

The Greatest Show on Grass is an elephant of a party, with a little bit of golf thrown in for good measure, and the highlight of Arizona's social calendar for the entire year. Nine irons, leader boards, and respect for the game take a backseat to the raucous social scene that goes on above the course.

Held at the Tournament Player's Championship Course in Scottsdale, the seven-day match reaches its party peak on the Friday and Saturday of Super Bowl weekend. The Phoenix Open is the most heavily attended stop on the PGA tour, as over 160,000 spectators make their way into this midday nightclub on a golf green. Whereas observation is limited at many professional tournaments, the hills above this course lend themselves perfectly to bird's-eye views of the action.

The dress code at this wild invitational is anything but what you'd expect at a golf course. Women walk the greens in high heels and miniskirts, while men slap on cologne and dress to the nines. Sixth-grader Alex Gross was one of the lone sober folks who attended the 2007 event. "It was totally crazy. Everyone was acting like they were at a rock concert," he testified.

The most famous hole in golf is the sixteenth hole in Phoenix. You'd swear you were at a football tailgate if there weren't little white balls rolling around on neatly trimmed Kentucky bluegrass. Enormous bleachers surround the cup, and spectators head over there, the epicenter of the tournament, between 12:00 P.M. and 2:00 P.M. This par-3 is a true testament to the mental focus of the golfers, as screaming and bantering from the crowd is expected, even encouraged. Some pros break down and flip off the crowd, while others refuse to show up altogether. Tiger Woods, for example, stopped playing in the tournament. The hometown favorite, ASU graduate Phil Mickelson, is perhaps the only golfer who doesn't receive constant hazing from the fans.

Head to the main food court behind the tenth hole after the sixteenth-hole party has ended at 3:00 P.M. This area is the place to be for those without VIP or hospitality tent privileges. Beers and mixed drinks are reasonably priced at around $7, and burgers, brats, and hot dogs are for sale. It's a time to relax and catch your second wind before the legendary Bird's Nest.

Between 5:00 P.M. and 10:00 P.M. every single person in the Phoenix area flocks to the Bird's Nest. Many will skip the match and just swoop into this gigantic outdoor party, which takes place in a fenced-in lot outside of the course. Famous musicians such as Sheryl Crow play underneath a huge tent. A $20 cover charge gets you into this most famous of post-golf parties.

TRANSPORTATION

AIR: Book flights into Sky Harbor International Airport (PHX / *www.skyharborairport.com*), located twenty-four miles from the TPC course. Taxis and car-rental agencies are available at the airport.

PARKING: From the west head toward Loop 101 and Hayden Road. Exit the 101 eastbound on Hayden Road and drive south into the parking lot. From the east take Frank Lloyd Wright Boulevard to Bell Road and head north. Turn east on Ninety-fourth Street and follow signs to the parking lot at WestWorld.

SHUTTLES: Free shuttle buses run spectators from the parking lots to the course. On the weekends they operate from 6:30 A.M. to 11:00 P.M. These buses stop running at 6:30 P.M. on Sunday.

TAXIS: Local cab companies include Scottsdale Cab (480-994-1616) and Scottsdale Taxi (480-994-4567).

BUS: The Greyhound station is located in Phoenix at 2115 East Buckeye Road.

ACCOMMODATIONS

HOTELS: The Arizona suburbs are much livelier than the city. You can stay in Phoenix, but Scottsdale and Tempe are logistically better choices, offering more in terms of restaurants, shopping, and nightlife. Scottsdale hotels include Holiday Inn (3131 N. Scottsdale Rd. / 480-675-7665 / $138), the beautiful Fairmont Scottsdale Princess (480-585-4848 / $699), Hyatt Regency (7500 E. Doubletree Ranch Rd. / 480-991-3388 / $379), and Chaparral Suites Resort (5001 N. Scottsdale Rd. / 480-949-1414 / $169). Visit *www.priceline .com* for further options.

TICKETS

General admission tickets cost $25 and can be purchased on the event website, by visiting *www*

.ticketmaster.com, or by calling 480-784-4444. They are sold in advance until late January, or you can purchase tickets on the day of the event.

The Champion's Pavilion package is a great option. It includes pavilion badges for four people for each of the seven days of the tournament. These badges give you access to large tents on the second and ninth greens that are similar to sports lounges, with large plasma televisions, comfortable seating, and a special parking pass. Food and drinks are not free. The $750 package is for sale on the event website.

The Members Club package also includes four badges for each of the seven days, and a special parking pass. Ticket holders have access to four Members Club tents, located on holes nine, twelve, seventeen, and eighteen, where they will enjoy free food and drinks with excellent views. The $1,800 package is for sale on the event website.

Bird's Nest tickets can be purchased at the gate; however, lines tend to be lengthy. You can save time by purchasing tickets as soon as you enter the Phoenix Open early in the day. Look for the ticket booth when you cross over the bridge. VIP Bird's Nest tickets are available for $150, which includes dinner and drinks, and a private VIP area.

> **What to Pack**
> - Sunglasses
> - Cash—ATMs have $4 surcharges
> - Binoculars to watch the players cringe as they approach the sixteenth hole
> - A 1970s vintage tuxedo—it'll make quite the impression

party tip

Tiger Woods gets a bad rap for skipping the Phoenix Open; however, you can hardly blame the guy. He used to tee up at the Greatest Show on Grass, but 1999 probably put a bad taste in his mouth. A heckler who followed Tiger around the course became so abusive that he was restrained by security guards. On the same day, Tiger was settling in for a putt when someone hurled an orange at his head.

SPRING BREAK AT LAKE HAVASU

✪ Lake Havasu City, Arizona
First two weeks in March
www.golakehavasu.com

Located on the California and Arizona border, Lake Havasu is the most revered spring-break destination in the western United States. College-aged and postgraduate party people from Arizona, California, Colorado, and Nevada pour into Lake Havasu for an overwhelming combination of sun, sports, and crazy times on land as well as in the water. Although any summertime weekend on the lake is a lesson in gluttony, early March beckons the area's true desert wildlife to the water in search of fun.

The first stop is Lake Havasu City, otherwise dubbed "the personal watercraft capital of the world." This fifty-horsepower hub is a five-hour drive from L.A. or a 150-mile jaunt from Las Vegas. Once in town you can rent any and all types of water-based recreational vehicles to make your spring break as accident-prone as you'd like. The most interesting aspect of the city is that the actual London Bridge was moved here in the 1960s due to the structure's inability to handle the increasing traffic over the Thames. "The Channel" is the boat-launching area and social hot spot in the morning. The morning is also the best time of day for water skiing on the pristine lake glass. Five miles south of Lake Havasu City is Copper Canyon, home of the infamous floating boat parties. Most party barges make a beeline to this cove, which is surrounded by looming red canyon walls from which cliff diving is the major spectator sport. Fill your boat with enough supplies to last the day and tie it to a group of boats in Copper Canyon.

Another popular party area is the sandbar, located fifteen miles north of the London Bridge. The water level is low, which allows people to get out of their boats and wander about, as though they're at a nightclub with a soggy floor. At the end of the day a large contingent of castaways gathers beneath the London Bridge to recount tales of their day on the water and make plans for the evening. Nighttime hot spots include Kokomo (1477 Queens Bay), a behemoth 10,000-square-foot club/bar with four stories, a swimming pool, dance music, and twenty-one places from which to grab a drink. Red Room (1519 Queens Bay) is another common dance club with DJs and pool tables, the Naked Turtle (on the water, across from London Bridge) is a beach bar within a floating water park, and Mad Dog's Bar & Grill (2048 McCulloch Blvd.) is a spring breaker's heaven with the occasional live band.

TRANSPORTATION

AIR: The closest airport is Las Vegas McCarran International Airport (LAS / *www.mccarran .com*), located 150 miles away. There is a shuttle company, Havasu Vegas Express Company, which runs a door-to-door charter bus service from the airport to Lake Havasu City. Rates vary depending on group size. Call 800-459-4884 or visit *www .havasuvegasexpress.com* for information. Car-rental agencies are also available.

® RECREATIONAL VEHICLE RENTALS: If you don't have a trailer with your own boat, WaveRunner, or Jet Ski, don't fret. There are a ton of watercraft rental shops in Lake Havasu City that rent everything from houseboats to water skis. Do not come into town without having first made a reservation! Book early for spring break—six months is usually safe. Some of the more reputable companies include Arizona Watersports (928-453-5558), Paradise Boat Rentals and Sales (928-854-4214), and Champion Rentals (928-855-8088). Club Nautical Houseboats (928-885-7000) specializes in houseboats that will negate the need for a hotel room. The prices are steep, but you'll be sharing the costs with your entire group.

ACCOMMODATIONS

When it comes to accommodations, you have a few options. Many people take their houseboats to a secluded cove, drop an anchor, and sleep onboard. Others stay at hotels, some of which are lakefront party spots, or less expensive chain hotels without the waterfront views. Another popular option is to camp at a number of private campgrounds located on the lake.

🏠 HOTELS: The Nautical Inn Resort (1000 McCulloch Blvd. / 928-855-2141 / $139) is on the water with a private dock for guests. This luxury resort has a heated pool, a golf course, a store for stocking up on beer, and some excellent bars. The London Bridge Resort (1477 Queens Bay / 928-855-0888 / $197), located beside the London Bridge (surprise, surprise), has a full spa and boat access, and it is in close proximity to the nightclub Kokomo. The Sandman Inn (1700

McCulloch Blvd. / 928-855-7841 / $40) is basic but is in the middle of the nighttime action. Other hotels that are less expensive and a little bit farther off the lake are Hampton Inn (245 London Bridge Rd. / 928-855-4071 / $113), Quality Inn (271 S. Lake Havasu Ave. / 928-855-1111 / $80), and Super 8 (305 London Bridge Rd. / 928-855-8844 / $125). For a further listing of hotels visit *www .lakehavasuhotels.reservetravel.com.*

🔥 CAMPING: Lake Havasu is a state park and therefore camp sites are in abundance. The sites cost between $15 and $25 per night and should be reserved in advance; permits are required. Visit the Arizona State Parks website at *www .azparks.gov* or call 928-855-2784. Once in Lake Havasu City you can visit the office at 699 London Bridge Road to pick up your permit. There are also many private camp sites that do not require permits. Visit *www.golakehavasu.com* for listings of private campgrounds.

What to Pack
- Nose plugs
- Waterproof camera
- Cooler
- Water balloon launcher

---

party tip

When cliff diving, it is not recommended that you enter the belly flop competition. Be safe and stick with cannonballs and can openers. Furthermore, your bathing suit may be ejected once you hit the water. Although this can be embarrassing, it usually evokes cheers and applause from the onlookers.

Colorado

SPRING BACK TO VAIL

⊛ Vail, Colorado
Usually mid-April
www.springbacktovail.com

Sun-soaked spring skiing conditions, killer "corn" snow, and the inevitable April dump in Colorado beckon to Vail anybody with an urge to earn more turns. And if the lure of the sport isn't motivation enough, the greatest end-of-the-ski-season party in the country offers plenty of excuses.

Spring Back to Vail, voted the number one ski party in North America by *Skiing* magazine, is a two-week bash that's adored by rope-ducking locals and weekend gapers alike. The party usually kicks off early in the month and concludes two weeks later at the base of Vail Resort after its run of live music, slope-side antics, adrenalized competitions, and après-ski indulgences. The final week of Spring Back to Vail is forecast to provide the perfect wintry mix of swooshing down the mountain during the day and celebrating at night, among thousands of fleece-wrapped revelers.

Vail Resort has arguably the sickest (bro-local lingo) combination of ski terrain and nightlife in the United States. The mountain's expansive acreage, which includes world-famous "back bowls," thirty-three chairlifts plus a gondola, 121 runs, and recent addition "Blue Sky Basin," provides heaps of options for skiers of all levels. Vail Village, the resort's base area, is modeled after a Bavarian town—evident in its cobblestone streets, A-framed shops, and picture-perfect rustic mountain backdrop. Advanced, intermediate, and beginner partiers should head directly into the heart of Vail Village for a slew of free evening street concerts that take place throughout the week.

Recent performers have included Maceo Parker, Toots and the Maytals, and Mix Master Mike of the Beastie Boys. Other notable events include the screening of a Warren Miller movie, the NCAA Final B-Ball and Beers party at the Tap Room (333 Bridge St.), and Malay Day competitions at the Terrain Park. You can also head over to the Streetwater Brush Battle and Body Art Competition at Samana Lounge (228 Bridge St.), featuring artists who take their time while painting the Bacardi girls' bodies. The winner is determined by crowd applause.

The final day and evening are definitely the highlights of Spring Back to Vail. The World Pond Skimming Championships take place at the base of Golden Peak, attracting a huge crowd of onlookers. Racers come flying down the mountain and must cross a frigid pond on skis without sinking into the icy water. The winner is celebrated like a downhill gold medalist while the losers go home frostbitten. Later that evening is the major outdoor concert held at Ford Park. Well-known acts like Snoop Dogg, Kid Rock, Blues Traveler, and G Love & Special

Sauce have played in the past. Visit the event website for a complete two-week schedule. Samana and 8150 are the best dance clubs in the Vail Village—perfect places for late-night frolics.

TRANSPORTATION

AIR: You can fly into Denver International Airport (DEN / www.flydenver.com), which is an hour and a half away. Those who don't mind spending the extra cash can connect through Denver and fly into Eagle County Regional Airport (EGE), located just outside of Vail. Car-rental agencies are available at both airports.

SHUTTLE: Colorado Mountain Express offers rides in large ten-person vans from D.I.A. to Vail for $78 per way. This is an excellent idea if you don't want to rent a car. They will also pick you up at Eagle County Airport for $47 per way. Call 970-296-9800 or visit www.ridecme.com for reservations.

TAXIS: Local cab companies include High Mountain Taxi (970-524-5555) and Summit County Taxi (970-453-8294).

BUS: Vail has an excellent bus system that runs throughout the valley and into the ski area, providing easy access for those staying in houses and condos outside of Vail Village. Buses service each stop every twenty minutes and run almost twenty-four hours a day.

ACCOMMODATIONS

HOTELS: Staying at a hotel inside Vail Village is an excellent experience, though you'll pay for it. There are hotels outside of town, although you may have to drive or take a taxi back and forth. Hotels in Vail Village include Evergreen Lodge

(250 S. Frontage Rd. / 970-476-7810 / $187), Vail Mountain Lodge & Spa (352 E. Meadow Dr. / 970-476-0700 / $225), the Lodge at Vail (174 E. Gore Creek Dr. / 970-476-5011 / $349), the Tivoli Lodge (386 Hanson Ranch Rd. / 970-476-5615 / $259), Vail Plaza Hotel (100 E. Meadow Dr. / 970-476-5622 / $299), Manor Vail Lodge (595 E. Vail Valley Dr. / 970-476-5651), and Marriott (715 W. Lionshead Circle / 970-476-4444 / $329).

⌂ RENTAL HOMES: Renting a condo or house in Vail Valley is a good idea because you'll be able to take the public buses around town. Condos typically start at $180 per night and houses go for $250. Visit *www.skivailcolorado.net*, a great website with lots of options.

TICKETS

The street concerts are free and tickets to the large headlining show cost $30 if purchased early, or $40 at the gate. Tickets go on sale in late March through *www.springbacktovail.com*. A single-day lift ticket at Vail costs a whopping $85. Prices go down slightly if multiple days are purchased at once. The day after the headlining

concert usually signals the beginning of Spring Skiing Specials—lift tickets fall to $33 a day during the final week of the season.

What to Pack
- Skis and poles (but leave good skis at home—lots of rocks poking up this time of year)
- Spring skiing attire
- Camera to take "action shots" during your China Bowl descent

party tip

Do not board a chairlift with a skier wearing blue jeans, an NFL jacket, and aviator sunglasses rather than goggles. This getup marks the wearer as someone who could pose major hazard concerns. Your safety will be at risk when you both disembark the chair, and he barrels into you, rented ski poles flailing and snow flying. Just to be on the safe side, wave this guy ahead and jump on the next lift.

TELLURIDE BLUEGRASS FESTIVAL

⊛ Telluride, Colorado
Third weekend in June
www.bluegrass.com

If Norman Rockwell had been a westerner, Telluride would have been a likely subject.

Imagine winding your way through the Colorado Rockies and the San Juan Mountains, then emerging into a colorful town ensconced among majestic peaks and sprawling green prairies. Add 10,000 attendees, a stage that protrudes from the base of a mountain, four days of world-class bluegrass music, and a delectable beer selection from local micro-breweries and you have the Telluride Bluegrass Festival. Since its inception in 1973, the Telluride Bluegrass Festival has grown into arguably the best bluegrass gathering in the United States—with unarguably the most breathtaking scenery. In 2004 B. B. King remarked from the stage, "Out of the ninety different countries I've been to, I've never seen anything more beautiful than what you have here."

The festival begins on Thursday and goes through Sunday evening underneath the full moon of the summer solstice. The music kicks off each day at around 10:00 A.M., and the day's final headliner plays until midnight. Be sure to get to the perimeter of the festival by 10:00 A.M. with your tarp and blankets in hand. It's a mad dash to claim a section of grass once the gates open. Recent performers have included Alison Krauss, Sam Bush Band, Bela Fleck, Yonder Mountain String Band, Ani DiFranco, Bonnie Raitt, Bruce Hornsby, Jerry Douglas, Tim

O'Brien, the Decemberists, and Barenaked Ladies (see the website for upcoming schedules and performers). Spend the daytime taking in the music and the scenery, playing Frisbee on a luscious green lawn, and absorbing the positive spirit that's entirely unique to Telluride.

NightGrass is a series of late-night shows held in specific Telluride watering holes. The historic Sheridan Opera House, Fly Me to the Moon Saloon, and Las Montanas, all on Colorado Avenue, house the nightly after-hours performances. Tickets to the late-night shows must be purchased separately from festival tickets.

The main drag of Telluride is home to a wide array of restaurants, shops, and bars. The Fred Shellman Memorial Stage is a quick ten-minute walk to the town. Don't leave town without taking the ski gondola to Mountain Village for more breathtaking views. The Telluride Conference Center in Mountain Village hosts special high-altitude shows throughout the weekend.

With world-class music on stage, interesting workshops and educational booths, unbelievable surroundings, late-night Night-Grass bar shows, and campground jam sessions, this festival beckons attendees to the Telluride Bluegrass Festival year after year.

TRANSPORTATION

AIR: Getting to this festival can be somewhat of a challenge, as it lies in the middle of the mountains. The closest major airport is Albuquerque International Sunport (ABQ / *www.cabq.com*), located five hours away. Denver International Airport (DEN / *www.flydenver.com*) is over six hours away. A number of small regional airports are closer. The closest is Telluride Regional Airport (TEX / *www.tellurideairport.com*). Others include Montrose (one hour / *www.airport.co.montrose.co.us*), Cortez (one and a half hours / *www.cityofcortez.com/airport.shtml*), and Durango (two hours / *www.durangogov.org/services/airport.html*)

All airports have car-rental agencies, and Telluride Central Reservations can provide detailed travel information depending on your route. Visit *www.telluride.com* or call 888-605-2578 for driving directions from the airport of your choice.

RV/VAN: This destination makes for an ideal road trip. The scenery is such that boredom will not set in and an RV or large van will only add to the memory. This will also make a more enjoyable trip for those who prefer camping over hotels.

PARKING: You will not be able to drive into town or park on the streets beginning on the Tuesday before the festival. If you're staying at a hotel, it will provide a special "town access" sticker for your vehicle. If you're camping, follow signs to the festival parking lot, which is located just outside of town. A free shuttle will take you from the parking lot to your campground and the festival.

ACCOMMODATIONS

CAMPING: Camping is a very popular option at the Telluride Bluegrass Festival. Camping tickets are sold per vehicle and per person, not per site. If you want to camp next to your car, then be prepared to purchase a camping pass plus a vehicle pass (see "tickets"). Expect to camp fairly close to your neighbor, and sites are on a first-come-first-serve basis. Showers are available from 8:00 A.M. to 1:00 P.M. at the Telluride High School for $3.50. Visit the main website for camping and parking passes.

HOTELS: Hotel Telluride (199 N. Cornet St. / 970-369-1188 / $479, three-night min.), Peaks Resort and Golden Door Spa (136 N. Country Club Dr. / 970-728-6800 / $212), and San Sophia (330 W. Pacific Ave. / 970-728-3001 / $170) are first-class hotels. The Mountainside Inn (333 S. Davis St. / 888-728-1950 / $239) is an affordable hotel. Visit *www.telluride.com* for a complete array of lodging options. Hotels in town fill very quickly, so book months in advance if possible.

RENTAL HOMES: The *www.vrbo.com* site has a list of available condos and houses for rent during the festival. One-bedroom condos typically start in the mid-$200s per night.

TICKETS

Tickets go on sale in early December and always sell out. Tickets are sold as a four-day pass or single-day tickets—two- and three-day passes do not exist. A four-day festival pass costs $145. Town Park is the camping area adjacent to the festival grounds, where campers can sleep next to their vehicle. Four-day Town Park camping passes with festival pass and Town Park vehicle pass included are sold via online lottery due to high demand. Lottery entries are accepted via the event website from late October to early November. The Warner Field tent camping area is also located adjacent to the concert grounds. Four-day Warner Field camping plus a four-day pass costs $245 (bring your own tent). Other campsites, located farther away, cost $50 for the weekend—a festival ticket must be purchased separately. RV parking costs $150, and a separate four-day pass must also be purchased. All tickets are available through *www .bluegrass.com*.

NightGrass tickets go on sale in the spring through their Web site at *www.bluegrass.com*. They can often be purchased during the festival; however, it's recommended to get them early as they sell quickly.

What to Pack
- Typical summer clothing for the daytime
- Warm fall clothing for the evening
- Extra warm clothing—the mountain weather can be unpredictable

party tip

Partying in Telluride is not to be taken lightly. The altitude can intensify the effects of those Colorado microbrews, so out-of-towners should go slow.

JAZZ ASPEN SNOWMASS LABOR DAY FESTIVAL

⊛ **Snowmass, Colorado**
Labor Day weekend
www.jazzaspen.com

An internationally renowned festival takes place in one of the more pristine and magnificent spots in the United States. September in Aspen calls for a soul-cleansing mix of sunny warm days, cool fall evenings, and colorful mountain foliage—the scenery is simply phenomenal. Add an always-impressive lineup of musicians playing on an outdoor stage at the base of a ski resort and the result is a reason to join 10,000 others for a Labor Day trip to the Rocky Mountains.

Taking place in Snowmass Village, about fifteen miles northwest of Aspen, the festival begins late in the day on Friday and goes through Monday evening. Friday's music typically starts at 6:00 P.M., while acts start earlier on Saturday, Sunday, and Monday, at 1:00 P.M. The final act takes the stage at 7:00 P.M., giving festivalgoers the opportunity to enjoy the area's wonderful array of restaurants and shops. The Jazz Festival always attracts an eclectic mix of top-notch musicians. Recent performers have included Ben Harper and the Innocent Criminals, Michael Franti and Spearhead, Kanye West, Jack Johnson, LeAnn Rimes, and Los Lonely Boys. Headliners play on one main stage, with two side stages featuring local musicians.

The festival grounds are located at the base of the road that winds up into Snowmass Village. Local restaurants set up shop on the grass, as do vendors that sell a variety of Colorado trinkets. Relax on the lawn or throw the Frisbee around, while gazing up at Capitol Peak, which sits directly above the stage. Capitol Peak is one of Colorado's famed "14ers," indicating its 14,000-foot altitude.

The crystal-clear mountain night, aided by the elevation and unpolluted air, makes for excellent stargazing. The Aspen / Snowmass villages also make for some human stargazing during the Jazz After Dark shows. Many of the local bars feature postshow performances in an extremely intimate setting. Kelly Shanahan of Aspen recalls, "There was a rumor that Jack Johnson was going to play the After Dark show in a small bar in Snowmass. I went, and he was there, playing to a tiny crowd. It was amazing." These shows are typically announced right before or during Labor Day weekend. Venues in Snowmass include the Cirque (105 Snowmass Village Mall), Mountain Dragon (67 Elbert Ln.), and the Artisan (300 Carriage Way). Belly Up (450 S. Galena St.) is the best venue for live music in Aspen; it typically houses some big-name postshow performances.

Aspen is teeming with shops, bars, and restaurants—be sure to spend some time walking the streets of this high-altitude Hollywood.

TRANSPORTATION

You can fly directly into Aspen, or into Denver and drive three and a half hours. Flights into Aspen will cost an extra couple hundred dollars; however, the lack of rental car or shuttle ride may be worth the more expensive plane ticket. You will not need a car in Aspen, as the public bus system is excellent; it runs to the Jazz Festival in Snowmass Village. Highway 82 connects the two towns, which are separated by fifteen miles.

✈ **AIR:** Book flights into Aspen/Pitkin County Airport (ASE / *www.aspenairport.com*), which has taxi service and car-rental agencies. You'll most likely connect on United from Denver or Delta from Salt Lake City. Denver International Airport (DEN / www.flydenver.com) is 185 miles away.

SHUTTLE: Colorado Mountain Express runs a shuttle from Denver's airport to Aspen for $112 each way, or $180 round-trip. Discounts may be given for groups. Call 800-525-6363 or visit www.cmex.com/aac.htm for information.

BUS: All points in Aspen and Snowmass Village can be reached by the RFTA bus system, which services myriad bus stops in both towns. Call 970-925-8484 for schedules and information. You can get around easily and without having to drive a car by using this bus. If staying in Snowmass, take the bus to the festival.

PARKING: The one advantage to driving is a nice parking lot tailgate scene. Parking costs approximately $20.

ACCOMMODATIONS

HOTELS/LODGES: It's easiest to stay in Snowmass Village, although staying in Aspen has its perks as well. The after-concert scene is strong in both places, but Aspen is larger and has a wider variety of things to do. Affordable options in Snowmass include Pokolodi Lodge (25 Daly Ln. / 970-923-4202 / $119), Silvertree Hotel (100 Elbert Ln. / 970-923-3520 / $119), Snowmass Inn (67 Daly Lane / 970-923-2819 / $99), or Wildwood Lodge (40 Elbert Ln. / 970-923-3550 / $189). Visit www.stayaspensnowmass.com for a variety of hotels in Snowmass and Aspen. For lodging / ticket packages visit www.snowmassvillage.com.

TICKETS

Your best bet is to purchase the four-day ticket for $150. Single-day passes can be purchased for approximately $50, and they cost an additional $5 if purchased at the gate. Tickets go on sale in early April. Many people purchase the "blind faith pass" in December, before the headliners are announced. This is a four-day pass that sells for $100. The headliners are always great, so this pass is not much of a gamble. VIP passes are available beginning at $1,250. They include reserved seating, nightly open bars, and catered meals each day. Visit the event website or call 855-527-8499 for ticket purchases.

What to Pack
- Blanket and low-back chair
- Water—stay hydrated at this altitude
- Backpack with change of clothing for the evening
- Glitzy Aspen nightlife-scene attire

party tip

An excellent ending to this trip is a stop in Glenwood Springs, where Interstate 70 meets Colorado 82, forty miles outside of Aspen. The natural hot springs have been channeled into the largest and most soothing pool in the United States. Another idea is to hit Woody Creek Tavern (2858 Woody Creek Rd.), Aspen's greatest dive bar, which was frequented by Dr. Gonzo himself, Hunter S. Thompson. Three-quarters of a mile west of Snowmass Village on Colorado 82 is Smith Road. Turn right, and then make a left at the fork.

TOUR DE FAT

⭐ Fort Collins, Colorado
Usually the third Saturday in September
www.newbelgium.com

The world's largest bicycle parade is a rolling carnival on wheels that's sponsored by a brewery with a conscience—and riders' outfits make Halloween seem like a yawn. The Tour de Fat is part costume party, part pedaling pandemonium, and 100 percent chaotic originality in Fort Collins, Colorado.

The Tour de Fat has been taking place since 2001, steadily picking up major steam each year since, evident by the increasing number of jet-set participants. Ingenuity, imagination, and positive vibes rule this Colorado fiesta, which encourages the use of bicycles for local transportation beyond the one-day party.

In 2007, the spectacle smashed the *Guinness Book of World Records* statistic for the largest bike parade. Over 4,800 participants arrived at New Belgium Brewery on September 22, dressed in purple wigs, pink boas, top hats, beekeeper outfits (flanked by friends dressed

as bees), bridal veils, gorilla costumes, and glam rock attire. Some rode plain old mountain bikes, while others pedaled the most outrageous homemade contraptions imaginable. In 2008, over 7,000 people attended, growing the party by over 40 percent in one year!

New Belgium Brewery, a privately held beer company, is responsible for the tour. Located in Fort Collins, they brew a host of the tastiest beers distributed throughout the West—Fat Tire being the flagship product. New Belgium's concern for the environment is as great as their concern for brewing delectable suds. Their green brewing plant is the first U.S. brewery to operate on wind power. A fully functioning sustainable operating program keeps their eco-footprint minimal, but the beer's flavor leaves quite a mark.

Stay in "Old Town" Fort Collins on Friday night, and awaken on Saturday to the sight of costumed participants biking toward the brewery for an 11:00 A.M. start time. The parade is slow moving, as it winds its way through the streets, past throngs of cheering onlookers, and on to the Colorado State University campus. Once at CSU, a morning dance party erupts for a half hour before the 12:00 P.M. return to "The Mothership." From noon to 6:00 P.M., the brewery is hopping with parade participants, plus those who couldn't handle the four-mile jaunt. Bands play all day long, unicycle jousters punish each other, and dancers on stilts wander above the crowd. The atmosphere is that of a hip carnival or a rock 'n' roll circus, where people of all ages revel in the opportunity to party in a costume all day long. Fort Collins resident Jennifer Edwards commented, "Walking into the after-party feels like walking into a Dr. Suess book."

TRANSPORTATION

AIR: Book flights into Denver International Airport (DEN / *www.flydenver.com*), located one hour from Fort Collins. Car-rental agencies are available, but a taxi ride is expensive. Airlines typically charge $80 per bike.

SHUTTLE: The Shamrock Shuttle runs a cheap, convenient shuttle from the Denver airport to Fort Collins and back. Make a reservation in advance and pick it up outside of door 504 on the west side of the airport. Shamrock will take you to a number of hotels for $28 per way, or to a specific address for an additional $5. Bikes must be packed in boxes. Call 970-482-0505 for information and reservations, or visit *www .rideshamrock.com.*

BIKE PURCHASE/RENTAL: You can purchase an official New Belgium Fat Tire road cruiser at Lee's Cyclery (202 W. Laurel / 970-482-6006), voted Best Bike Shop in Fort Collins. Recycled Cycles (527 Mathews St. / 970-491-9555) will rent bikes for the day.

ACCOMMODATIONS

HOTELS: Try to stay in or close to Old Town. The Hilton (425 W. Prospect Rd. / 970-482-2626 / $139) is a short ride from the brewery, as is Best Western (914 S. College Ave. / 970-484-1984 / $85).

B&BS: Other easy access accommodations include bed-and-breakfasts. Try Edwards Historic House (402 W. Mountain Ave. / 970-493-9191 / $99) or Inn at City Park (1734 W. Mountain Ave. / 970-672-4725 / $125).

What to Pack

- Cash to purchase wooden coins
- A combination of your last five Halloween costumes
- A bottle of Coyote Gold Margaritas—locally produced and all the rage in Ft. Collins

---

party tip

Steer clear of roaming bands of sword-wielding gladiators. They ride the length of the parade swinging wooden sticks and various clubs of destruction at one another, taking out countless innocent bikers in their path.

GREAT AMERICAN BEER FESTIVAL

⊛ Denver, Colorado

First or second weekend in October

www.beertown.org

In an extraordinary effort to conserve water, thousands of environmentalists head to the mile-high city for the largest beer festival on planet Earth. *The Guinness Book of World Records* has officially declared the Great American Beer Festival as the largest selection of suds in the world—whether you prefer dark, amber, or think that blondes have more fun, the GABF will undoubtedly provide something to cure what "ales" you.

Over 1,800 different brews from more than 400 breweries are sampled by 41,000 connoisseurs who roam the 188,000-square-foot floor of the Denver Convention Center. Think these numbers are staggering? Then just wait until you have to select your favorite of the lot. Your inner Homer Simpson will be hard at work as you sample wheats, stouts, ales, ambers, lagers, pilsners, pumpkin and chili beers, beers infused with watermelon and cherry, vanilla-flavored beers, and just about every other concoction under the sun. Breweries compete for gold, silver, and bronze medals in over seventy-five categories, which include Aged, American Cream Ale, Scottish Ale, Classic Irish, Coffee Beer, Experimental, German Pilsner, Oatmeal Stout, and Herb and Spice, to name a few. Test-drive them all as you roam through the never-ending hallways of suds. Some attendees complain that their one-ounce plastic cup is too small; however, others realize that this is the only way to increase the number of samples.

This three-day extravaganza begins on Thursday and runs until Saturday. The doors open at 5:30 P.M. and close at 10:00 P.M. Wine festivals are known for serving up cheese and crackers while Mozart plays in the background, but nothing could be further from the scenario in Denver. Attendees in flip-flops and T-shirts will have their choice of barbecued ribs or burgers, while classic rock fills the convention center. Expect to fill your pockets with freebies like coasters, key chains, and bottle openers. The floor is arranged geographically so that you can sample specific styles of beer from different parts of the country. However, the West's reign as the microbrew master is obvious, as most booths showcase beers from Colorado, California, Oregon, and Washington.

Don't drop your glass. The roar of 41,000 voices fills the air whenever someone lets a plastic tumbler slide through their fingers. Cheers are also raised throughout the convention center as a troupe of Scottish bagpipers parade the floor every hour.

TRANSPORTATION

AIR: Book flights into Denver International Airport (DEN / *www.flydenver.com*). The airport is about twenty-five minutes from downtown. Taxis and rental cars are available.

SUPERSHUTTLE: This service charges $19 for one-way and $28 for round-trip rides from the airport to Denver hotels. Grab the shuttle on the baggage-claim level.

TAXIS: Local cab companies include Metro Taxi (303-333-3333), Freedom Cab (303-292-8900), and Yellow Cab (303-777-7777). Cabs arrive quickly in Denver.

PARKING: If driving, you can park at the Convention Center parking garage for $7 for the day. The garage is located on the west side of the building; enter from northbound Speer Boulevard.

BUS / TRAIN: A Greyhound station is located at 1055 Nineteenth Street. The Amtrak station is located at 1701 Wynkoop Street.

ACCOMMODATIONS

HOTELS: Staying in the city and walking or taking a taxi to the Convention Center is the best idea. Nearby hotels include Plaza Denver City Hotel (1450 Glenarm Pl. / 303-573-1450 / $187), Comfort Inn (401 Seventeenth St. / 303-296-0400 / $219), Hyatt Hotel (650 Fifteenth St. / 303-436-1234 / $145), and Adam's Mark (1550 Court Pl. / 303-893-3333 / $159). Visit the event website for a list of hotels that offer special rates for Great American Beer Festival attendees.

TICKETS

Tickets must be purchased separately for each session, Thursday through Saturday from 5:30 P.M. to 10:00 P.M. Tickets can be purchased on the event website at *www.beartown.org*, by calling 303-477-0816, or by visiting *www.ticketmaster.com*. Prices per day are $45 in advance, or $50 at the door. The Great American Beer Festival does sell out, so purchase tickets in advance if possible.

What to Pack

- Comfortable clothing
- Steady hands (don't drop your glass)
- Pants with large pockets for giveaway items (backpacks are not allowed at the event)
- A pen and paper to write down your favorite beers

party tip

The morning after the festival you'll probably wake with a hankering for a great breakfast. Nothing's better than some eggs, bacon, and hash browns after a night of beer drinking. Head to the Bump & Grind (439 E. Seventeenth Ave.), where transvestite servers, a flashy décor, and male cooks in high heels serve up one of the best breakfasts in town. A line is inevitable, but it's worth the wait!

Montana

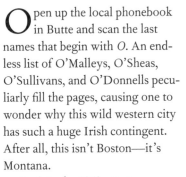

ST. PATRICK'S DAY

★ Butte, Montana
March 17

Open up the local phonebook in Butte and scan the last names that begin with *O*. An endless list of O'Malleys, O'Sheas, O'Sullivans, and O'Donnells peculiarly fill the pages, causing one to wonder why this wild western city has such a huge Irish contingent. After all, this isn't Boston—it's Montana.

Back in the 1860s, Butte was a virtually nonexistent mound of dirt. Then, the discovery of gold and silver in the area led to an influx of immigrants with fantasies of striking it rich. Although wealth was attained by some, many miners' frustrations grew as they repeatedly stumbled upon Butte's abundant, yet worthless supply of copper. However, the advent of the telephone in the 1870s changed the value of this commodity, as the enormous demand for copper

phone lines turned Butte into an overnight boomtown. It became one of the most prosperous cities in the country, with a notorious red light district where any man's vice could be instantly satiated. Bordellos, booze, gambling, and carousing were the copper miners' hobbies of choice. The descendants of those Irish excavators still reside in Butte, and that wild blood still courses through their veins.

Butte's version of St. Patrick's Day lasts about a month, although March 17 is when Irish eyes are really smilin'. Thirty thousand "Butteants" begin to assemble in the historic Uptown streets to get their Shamrock on. The party is so monumental that buses shuttle Celtic kin into Butte from myriad Montana cities to enjoy the parade, the music, the dancing, the food, and the merriment.

The Irish Parade serves as a starting gun for a truly bacchanalian day in Uptown. Amid a rowdy emerald crowd, the procession gets underway at the intersection of Mercury and Colorado streets, near Uptown Pork Chop John's, at 11:00 A.M. Leprechauns, potato pickers, bagpipers, and frolicking fiddlers wind their way around town, ending at Mercury and Dakota Streets. At the parade's conclusion, local bartenders crack their knuckles, grease up the Guinness tap, and await the imminent Paddy onslaught.

Bars like Maloney's (112 N. Main St.), Irish Times Pub (2 E. Galena St.), and the ever-popular Silver Dollar Saloon (133 S. Main St.) get so packed that you can only do the jig with your lower body. Live music explodes out of watering holes, as does the crowd, which fills the streets with a copper-miner ferocity. Partial or full nudity is to be expected, so don't be surprised if a Butteant shows you where the real pot of gold is.

TRANSPORTATION

This party makes for a great excuse to visit one of the more pristine and beautiful states in the country. If you live in the west, consider making a road trip.

AIR: The closest major airport is Missoula International Airport (MSO / www.flymissoula.com), located 125 miles away. The drive takes just under two hours. Butte has a regional airport named Bert Mooney Airport (BTM / www.butteairport.com). Two Delta flights per day arrive from and depart to Salt Lake City. Often the flights into Butte will be cheaper. Both airports have car-rental agencies, but make reservations because selections are limited.

ACCOMMODATIONS

HOTELS: The party takes place in historic Uptown, but most hotels are a couple of miles away. Things are less expensive in Butte than in other parts of the country, so staying in the grandest hotel in town may be within your budget. The Finlen Hotel (100 E. Broadway / 406-723-5461 / $58) is a towering building with a history dating back to 1889, and rooms around $50. It's in the middle of Uptown, and famous guests have included John F. Kennedy and Theodore Roosevelt. Other hotels on the outskirts of Uptown include Comfort Inn (2777 Harrison Ave. / 406-494-8850 / $94), Days Inn (2700 Harrison Ave. / 406-494-7000 / $119), Hampton Inn (3499 Harrison Ave. / 406-494-2250 / $109), Holiday Inn Express (1 Holiday Park Dr. / 406-494-6999 / $134), and Best Western (2900 Harrison Ave. / 406-494-3500 / $150).

What to Pack
- Green Stetson
- Green spurs
- Green Evel Knievel stunt helmet (he was from Butte)

party tip

Butte's incredibly rich history is evident in its abundance of historic landmark buildings and a slew of eerie ghost tales. The spirits of cowboys, robbers, outlaws, easy women, and thousands of miners who died for copper, are said to haunt every corner of the Uptown district. Take some time to visit Venus Alley, a brick-lined passage that served as the rear entrance to the Dumas Brothel, one of the oldest prostitution houses in the United States. The alley was once lined with overhanging "cribs," each entrance lit by a single light bulb. The alley still remains, and is now a tourist attraction.

TESTICLE FESTIVAL

⊛ Clinton, Montana
First weekend in August
www.testyfesty.com

Each year, a rowdy congregation of bikers, mountaineers, and curious everyday folks head to the place where the birds fly and the bulls cry. If ever there was a reason to road-trip to Big Sky Country, this is it. For over twenty-five years, the "Testy Festy" has enjoyed its position as one of Montana's top parties, in spirit and name alike.

The Rock Creek Lodge, located about twenty-two miles east of Missoula, is the birthplace and home of this five-day celebration, which draws around 5,000 people. The festival gets its name from Rocky Mountain Oysters, a local delicacy, consisting of battered and fried bull testicles. Word to the wise—don't expect an inhibited crowd or an uptight atmosphere. Nudity and bestial behavior are as much a part of this celebration as the two tons of bull testicles that will be consumed. If you are a bit shy, maybe you'll loosen up after witnessing the hairy chest competition, the wet T-shirt contest, oil wrestling, "bull shit bingo," or the body painting and tattoo events. The Testicle Festival typically begins on a Wednesday and runs through Sunday.

Many of the events and much of the carrying on takes place in the fields surrounding the lodge. Live blues and rock 'n' roll acts play outdoors, while the party picks up steam as the evening approaches. Friday and Saturday nights are the most rowdy of the festival, so be sure not to burn yourself out over the first couple of days. Don't forget to pack extra pairs of underwear, as ladies can trade panties for free drinks on Wednesday or Thursday. The safest and most clever event is the motorcycle competition, during which contestants must bite Rocky Mountain Oysters off of a fishing pole as they drive by on their Harleys.

It's best to camp at or drive an RV to the Rock Creek Lodge, and park for the duration of the festival. Campsites are available on a first-come-first-serve basis—no reservations. A breakfast of eggs, bacon, and hash browns is available each morning, as is food from a number of outside vendors who set up shop around the lodge. Be sure to sample the infamous "nut kabobs," a stick of oysters marinated in Jack Daniels. A truck is raffled off on Saturday at midnight, but you must be present and coherent to win. Plan a trip to the Rock Creek Lodge in early August, and you're guaranteed to have a ball.

TRANSPORTATION

✈ AIR: Flights can be booked into Missoula International Airport (MSO / *www.flymissoula.com*). There are only a few car-rental agencies at the airport, and reservations should be made ahead of time: National (406-543-3131), Alamo (406-543-3131), Avis (406-549-4711).

ⓣ TAXI / ⓑ BUS: You can take a taxi or a bus from the airport to the business district, and take a shuttle to the festival from here. Taxis include Yellow Cab (406-543-6644) and All Valley Cab (406-388-9999). Buses include Mountain Line (406-721-3333) and Beach Transportation (406-549-6121)—call for schedules and pickup times.

🚐 SHUTTLE: The festival organizers run an around-the-clock shuttle from Missoula to the Rock Creek Lodge and back. The shuttle is free and runs every hour on the hour, from 8:00 A.M. to 2:00 A.M.

ACCOMMODATIONS

🔥 CAMPING: Cars and vans can be parked outside of the lodge for the entire five days for $20 per person. Campsites cannot be reserved, as they are available on a first-come-first-serve basis. Bring your own tent. Recently the festival has brought in trailers with showers; however, they have not worked too well. You can head a half mile south on Rock Creek Rd. to a campsite with shower facilities. This site charges approximately $5 for shower usage.

🚐 RV: RV parking is also available on a first-come-first-serve basis for $40 per person. You can park for the entire five-day festival. There are no hookups. See the "camping" section for shower information.

🏨 HOTELS: You can stay in Missoula and take the free shuttle bus back and forth. Hotels in town include the Mountain Valley Inn (420 W. Broadway / 800-249-9174 / $89), Red Lion Inn (700 W. Broadway / 406-728-3300 / $119), Days Inn (201 E. Main St. / 406-543-7221 / $79), and Best Western Grant Creek Inn (5280 Grant Creek Rd. / 406-543-0700 / $150). Visit *www.hotel-rates.com/us/montana/missoula* for further hotel listings.

TICKETS

Your five-day camping pass includes entrance into the festival each day. The same holds true with the RV pass—do not throw away your wristband or you will have to pay again! A five-day entrance pass costs $15 for those who are not staying on the lodge grounds.

What to Pack
- Sleeveless Harley Davidson shirt
- Sleeveless flannel shirt
- Dental floss

party tip

Many people tend to cringe when they imagine biting into a chewy Rocky Mountain Oyster, but they actually taste like hush puppies or chicken nuggets. The origin of eating animal genitalia can be traced back to ancient Rome, when it was done for medicinal purposes. The theory was that a man who ingested the meat could correct a "dysfunctional" situation that he may be experiencing. Why spend all that money on Viagra when you can just head to the Testicle Festival?

Nevada

HARD ROCK HOTEL REHAB PARTY

⊛ **Las Vegas, Nevada**
Memorial Day weekend, on Sunday
www.hardrockhotel.com

The Hard Rock Hotel is home to the wildest, craziest, most hedonistic pool party in the country, end of story. Officially dubbed "Rehab," the Hard Rock pool party is the perfect way to kick off the summer.

Hard bodies featuring the best tans that money can buy, iron-pumped pecs accentuated with tribal tattoos, and breasts that look conspicuously too large for the bodies they inhabit, fill the 4.7-acre pool area, which the hotel plans to expand over the next few years. DJs spin the day away, while partygoers spend $35,000 an hour on beer, bubbly, and cocktails. From noon to 7:00 P.M. the Rehab party is an untamed midday celebration that lets over 3,000 oil-covered bodies slide through its gates for shenanigans rivaled only by scenes in *Animal House*. The pool

is enormous, and "Rehabbers" have their choice of floating in the lazy river, hitting the hot tubs, getting a soothing massage, or playing swim-up blackjack. This party has become such a force that many people retire early for a good night's sleep on Saturday—imagine that!

Getting into Rehab presents an interesting set of options, especially over Memorial Day weekend. Hotel guests, up to four per room, are allowed into the pool area at 9:00 A.M. for free. If the Rehab party is tops on your list for the weekend, then do yourself a major favor and stay at the hotel. Nonguests begin to line up at 8:30 A.M., and may be waiting a while before entrance is granted. The girl-to-guy ratio is kept in check, with groups of women always taking priority over the men. So guys, don't travel in packs of twelve, and girls, help your guy friends get in.

The absolute best way to be assured a spot at Rehab, other than staying at the Hard Rock Hotel, is to reserve a cabana. These little private huts are a poolside status symbol and a surefire way to get quick service. The cabanas start at approximately $1,000 for the day and go up to $5,000, depending on size and deck space. Under normal circumstances you must call at least one week in advance to book (702-693-5555), but it's best to give three or four weeks notice before Memorial Day weekend. When reserving a cabana there are a couple of important points to keep in mind. First, do not call ahead with a large group of men, as you will be laughed at and then denied. Make sure there are some women in your group, even if it means putting your smallest male friend in a string bikini. Secondly, there are minimum drink orders for these high-roller huts. More information is available at www.hardrockhotel .com by clicking the word "Rehab."

TRANSPORTATION

✈ **AIR:** Book flights into Las Vegas McCarran International Airport (LAS / www.mccarran.com). Many airlines are constantly running special fares to Vegas so shop hard. The airport is located just five miles south of the strip, so take a taxi to your hotel.

ACCOMMODATIONS

🛏 **HOTELS:** If you can, try to stay at the Hard Rock Hotel (4455 Paradise Rd. / 702-693-5000 / $429), which is just a few blocks off of Las Vegas Boulevard, or the Strip. Prices are steep over Memorial Day weekend, although multiple people can make it easier to swallow. Less pricey hotels within a stone's throw include Super 8 Koval (4250 Koval Lane / 702-794-0888 / $115), Alexis Park Hotel (375 E. Harmon / 800-582-2228 / $209), and AmeriSuites (4250 Paradise Rd. / 866-870-3246 / $209). Hotel and general Las Vegas information is available at www.vegas.com.

TICKETS

If you are not staying at the Hard Rock Hotel, then be in line early. The crowd starts forming at 8:30 A.M., sometimes earlier. The general cover charge is $20 for women and $30–$40 for men.

> **What to Pack**
> - Hair get
> - Tanning oil
> - Sunglasses—for inconspicuous people watching

party tip

If your skin hasn't seen the light of day in months or you haven't felt the burn of the gym in twice that time, maybe Rehab isn't your best bet. There are plenty of places in Vegas that won't exploit your lack of musculature. So saddle up at a nickel slot and watch the pool party from the comfort of the casino floor.

BURNING MAN

⭐ **Black Rock City, Nevada**
Monday before Labor Day through Labor Day weekend
www.burningman.com

Attending Burning Man is like boarding a spaceship, abandoning all preconceived notions of life and societal norms, and exiting into a world that is nothing like the one left behind. This eight-day festival in the Nevada desert encourages communal participation in a spontaneously created liberal society. Since it's inception in the mid-1980s, Burning Man has become the ultimate road trip for hipsters of all ages who wish to escape the confines of "normal" America, if for just a week.

Burning Man is held in Black Rock City, located in the Black Rock desert, ninety miles north of Reno. This area is the largest expanse of flat land in North America. Over 47,000 people, including belly dancers, tribal drummers, fire-eaters, sculptors, painters, outcasts, businesspeople, accountants, and housewives load their cars with supplies to weather the desert for a week and hit the sand-blown road. The city is burned to the ground following the conclusion of the festival, in accordance with the "leave no trace" principle. The highlight is the ritualistic burning of a gigantic wooden statue on the Saturday night before Labor Day, from which the gathering takes its name.

Visionary art that knows no boundaries is one of the main attractions. Festival volunteers assist in setting up these imaginative pieces, which add to the surreal landscape on the playa. Examples include gigantic human heads jutting from the desert floor, monstrous multicolored animal sculptures, televisions surrounded by sofas in the sand, and countless works of modern art. Tie-dyed vehicles, coffins on wheels, and golf carts dressed as lobsters serve as motorized transportation along the city grounds. Participants who wish to bring a "Mutant Vehicle" must submit their plans to the festival DMV, or "Department of Mutant Vehicles," for approval before the Burning Man.

Theme camps and villages make up the playa's massive sea of shelters. You can either register your theme camp officially on the event website or build it without registration. If you plan on meeting friends, then go ahead and register so they can find you. Be creative on this front, and pick a theme that will add something to the community.

Center City serves as the location of the Burning Man statue, a wooden temple, and the midpoint of Black Rock City. This is the only place where you can purchase goods with cash—however you're limited to ice and coffee.

It is extremely important that you visit *www.burningman.com* before attending. A very informative website, it gives specifics about safety and vehicle maintenance, a survival guide, and rules. This is not a stroll in the park—you're literally in the middle of a harsh desert. Civilization, as you know it, is far away, and awareness of surroundings is important.

TRANSPORTATION

AIR: The closest airport is Reno / Tahoe International Airport (RNO / *www.renoairport.com*) located 127 miles from the gathering.

RV: Bringing an RV is a good idea. You'll have a bed, a shower, protection from the infamous wind storms, and a lack of dust in your food. It's recommended that you decorate your RV (nothing that will make you forgo your rental deposit) in a colorful manner. Park on the outskirts of your theme camp to help protect the tents from windstorms.

RV servicing is available for $50 to $60, depending on the size of your camper, payable only with cash.

BIKE: Bring a bike! This is absolutely mandatory, no exceptions. If you're taking a small car, then buy a bike rack. Don't bring a $1,200 cycle—a prehistoric hunk of metal with a basket will do. Attach a flashlight, or better yet, bring a headlamp.

SHUTTLE: You can purchase a $5 shuttle ticket to Gerlach. The ticket office is in Center City, and buses run from mid morning to late afternoon.

ACCOMMODATIONS

CAMPING: Campsites are available on a first-come-first-serve basis. Do not get back in your car and drive around after you've arrived. There are no showers on site.

Most people bring wood to construct a solid structure or they camp in tents. Remember that gusts up to forty miles per hour are common. The event organizers recommend Rebar stakes be used to secure tents to the desert floor. You can purchase Rebar at a hardware store, but tape the top or cap it off to prevent injuries.

Experienced Burning Man attendees tend to construct geodesic domes for their theme tents. Visit *www.burningman.com* to learn how. Wood is another popular choice—bring a hammer and some nails. Afterward you can donate the wood or burn it in massive cleanup fires.

VILLAGES: Groups of 150 to 300 campers will become a village. Villages should be planned out carefully and should adopt some sort of common theme. Make your village stand out by allowing it to contribute to the greater community. Construct entrances and exits, build a main stage for music, befriend fellow villagers, and allow the artists to convert it into a visual experience. It's just as important to work on your village as it is your theme camp.

TICKETS

There is one type of ticket to Burning Man but the tickets are sold at different levels, from $200 to $280, depending on your economic situation. There is no differentiation in the status these price levels afford—it's an honor system. Buy tickets in advance through the event website at *www.burningman.com.* You can purchase tickets at the gate before 11:00 P.M. on Thursday, when the gates close; however, the prices are much higher. Gates open at 12:01 A.M. on Monday—no early entrance.

What to Pack

- Camping gear
- Trash bags
- One gallon of water per day
- Water basin
- Goods to trade

party tip

Various road hazards can put a damper on your week before it even starts. If you need to pull over then do not do so in the soft sand because you will get stuck. Don't speed on your way into the festival—no matter how excited you may be. When pulled over for exceeding the speed limit in Indian Territory, pay the fine right away with cash. Burning Man may not encourage the use of dollars, but area police certainly do. Furthermore, don't drive a thirteen-year-old car with a transmission that's been replaced three times—the only thing that will be burning will be your temper and your wallet as you wait to have it serviced in a town with one gas station.

NEW YEAR'S EVE

★ Las Vegas, Nevada
Dec. 31
www.vegas.com

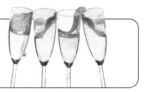

There's only one city that rings in the New Year as if the world was going to end on January 1. Sin City pulls out all the stops for the country's largest New Year's Eve celebration, and invites hundreds of thousands of its closest friends to join in. Imagine the brightest town on planet Earth overflowing with humanity, while fireworks illuminate the sky and the masses dance in the streets.

The casinos are elbow to elbow, the streets shut down to host the largest block party you've ever seen, the nightclub MCs include Kid Rock and Pamela Anderson, and the showrooms are full of A-list entertainers. This surreal, adrenaline-pumping experience is something that everyone should take part in at least once. In fact, it makes that silly ball drop in New York seem like a small gathering of friends sitting around a piano while singing "Auld Lang Syne."

Priority number one is getting to the Strip as early as possible.

This four-mile-long boulevard of bodies shuts down automobile passage, allowing pedestrians only, thus transforming itself into mayhem central on New Year's Eve. Party hungry revelers begin to infiltrate the Strip as early as 6:00 P.M., just as vacationing grandmothers play their final penny slot before indulging in a late dinner buffet. The center Strip area, by Harrah's and Mirage, is where you'll find the most concentrated crowds. Move in either direction and things tend to spread out. A must-see bombastic fireworks display blows up the air above the Strip while rock bands play on the ground.

If you're the type of person who needs to go clubbing, then listen up. Three words describe Vegas's infamous nightclub scene on December 31—crowded, baby, crowded. Most casinos on the Strip close their doors around 9:00 P.M. to anyone who isn't staying at the hotel, due to capacity issues. This means that you must get yourself inside a casino and stay there before this happens. The lines are long, and cover charges can be as high as $250. Large groups can opt to spend half their night in line or purchase a VIP table before they board the airplane. These tables demand a high price on New Year's Eve; many require a six-bottle minimum, which can total $2,000. Popular clubs include Rain at The Palms, Tangerine at Treasure Island, Tao inside the Venetian, and Jet at the Mirage.

TRANSPORTATION

It's Vegas taboo to go to sleep before the sun rises on New Year's Day. Combine this late night with the fact that January 1 is the zenith of outbound traffic, and the result is painful. It's recommended that you relax by the pool and enjoy the first day of the year while everyone else scrambles to make their flight home. Book your travel plans on January 2.

✈ **AIR:** Make plane reservations as soon as possible. Book flights into Las Vegas McCarran International Airport (LAS / *www.mccarran.com*). Many airlines are constantly running special fares to Vegas so shop hard. The airport is located just five miles south of the Strip, so take a taxi to your hotel.

ACCOMMODATIONS

🏨 **HOTELS:** Book your hotel right now, especially if you want to stay on the Strip. Not only do hotels sell out fast, but rates are increased as the holiday approaches. Booking online through *www.i4vegas.com* or *www.vegas.com* usually gets the best rates. Hotels in the center of the action, on the Strip, include Treasure Island (3300 S. Las Vegas Blvd. / 800-288-7206 / $449), Mirage (3400 S. Las Vegas Blvd. / 800-374-9000 / $250), Caesar's Palace (3570 Las Vegas Blvd. / 866-227-5938 / $700), Bellagio (3600 Las Vegas Blvd. / 888-987-6667 / $699), New York New York (3790 Las Vegas Blvd. / 866-815-4365 / $350), MGM Grand (3799 Las Vegas Blvd. / 877-880-0880 / $200), Bally's (3645 Las Vegas Blvd. / 877-603-4390 / rate unavailable), Harrah's (3475 Las Vegas Blvd. / 800-214-9110 / $400), Venetian (3355 Las Vegas Blvd. / 877-883-6423 / $399), and Planet Hollywood Resort (3667 Las Vegas Blvd. / 702-785-5555 / $250).

TICKETS

Visit *www.vegas.com* or *www.nightclubs.com* to purchase VIP nightclub tables as well as line-cutting passes, which are highly recommended. They go on sale about one month in advance. A $50 tip for the bouncers can also help your cause.

What to Pack
- Line-cutting passes
- Cigars
- Cash (you've gotta bet big to win big)

party tip

Wait until you get home to make your New Year's resolution. Las Vegas is the last place on Earth that you want to make a personal pledge or commitment to better yourself in any way. A piece of yard art stands a better chance of weathering a hurricane than your New Year's resolution stands lasting a weekend in Sin City.

New Mexico

UFO FESTIVAL

⭐ Roswell, New Mexico
First weekend in July
www.roswellufofestival.com

Thousands of UFO enthu-siasts and alien conspiracy theorists put their Xbox on pause and inform their boss that they'll be back to the video store in a few days. They come from all across the world to explore the darkest secrets of the universe with like-minded Fox Mulder fanatics, in a place where little green men hold a godlike status.

The Roswell Incident took place in July of 1947, when an unidentified flying object crashed in the desert outside of this New Mexico town. Ever since the army's supposed cover-up of the crash site, Roswell has become a hotbed of extraterrestrial research, flying saucer investigation, and gift shops that sell alien key chains.

If you believe in UFOs, you're not alone. In fact, 35,000 to 50,000 truth seekers make the annual pil-grimage to Roswell, doubling the city's population for the weekend. This festival has been taking place since 1992, drawing over a million earthlings since that time, while abducting every single hotel room in town during the first weekend in July. The four days of explora-tion include lectures from highly respected UFO experts, glow-in-the-dark disc golf tournaments, music concerts, crash-site tours, costume contests, parades, museum exhibits, and outdoor evening film showings—the most popular film is *Close Encounters of the Third Kind*. Many events take place on the grounds of the UFO Museum and Research Center. Visit the event website to download a print-able schedule of events.

This conglomeration of beings makes for the best people-watching you could ever hope for.

The atmosphere resembles that of a carnival, as the entire town gets into the spirit. Shops display huge flying saucers that appear to be crashing into the roof, restaurants have signs that say "aliens welcome," and street lights are replaced by little green spaceman heads. Don't leave without having attended one or two lectures! They are interesting and typically end in a heated debate between the extraterrestrial equal rights activists and those from a more conservative school of thought. You couldn't dream up a better excuse to take a road trip.

TRANSPORTATION

✈ **AIR:** Book flights into El Paso International Airport (ELP / *www.elpasointernationalairport.com*) or Albuquerque International Airport (ABQ / *www.cabq.gov*). Both airports are approximately 200 miles from Roswell, so base your decision on airline ticket price. Rental-car agencies are available at both airports.

🚌 **BUS:** There is a Greyhound Bus station located at 1100 North Virginia Avenue in Roswell.

ACCOMMODATIONS

🏨 **HOTELS:** They fill up extremely fast. Book a hotel by February at the latest. Hotel options include Days Inn (1310 N. Main St. / 505-623-4021 / $85), Best Western (2000 N. Main St. / 505-622-6430 / $80), Fairfield Inn (1201 N. Main St. / 505-624-1300 / $149), Comfort Inn (3595 N. Main St. / 505-623-4567 / $130), Ramada (2803 W. Second St. / 505-623-9440 / $79), and Holiday Inn (2300 N. Main St. / 505-627-9900 / $110).

Visit *www.hotels-rates.com/Roswell/NM/usa* for a complete listing of hotels.

🚐 **RV:** RV parking is available at three main campgrounds: Spring River Estates and RV Park (1000 E. College Blvd. / 505-623-8034), Trailer Village Campgrounds (1706 E. Second St. / 505-623-6040), and Red Barn RV Park (2806 E. Second St. / 505-623-4897). Space should be reserved at least three months in advance.

TICKETS

Most events are free, although some charge a small admission fee at the gate. The concerts, which have included recent headliners like War and the Alan Parsons Project, are ticketed events. Tickets can be purchased on the event website for $20 or at the gate for $25.

> **What to Pack**
> * Camera
> * Tin foil
> * Green body paint
> * Ray gun
> * "I break for Martians" bumper sticker

party tip

Most extraterrestrials are honest, law-abiding folk who go out of their way to make you feel comfortable. However, you may cross paths with one who's looking for trouble. Fortunately, there is a reliable solution that always stops an overly aggressive alien in his tracks. The Vulcan Nerve Pinch, when applied to most life forms, is an effective way to gain submission while preventing permanent damage to your enemy. Apply pressure near the base of neck, above the shoulder blade, to instantly render your opponent unconscious. It's effectiveness against reptilian-human hybrids has not yet been established.

ALBUQUERQUE INTERNATIONAL BALLOON FIESTA

⭐ **Albuquerque, New Mexico**
First weekend through the second weekend in October
www.balloonfiesta.com

Some of the phrases used to describe the Albuquerque International Balloon Fiesta include, "Mardi Gras in the air," "the most colorful celebration in the world," and "the country's highest party." One simply needs to look upward to see why this extraordinarily awe-inspiring festival is the most photographed event in the world.

The festival began thirty years ago when thirteen balloons were launched from a shopping mall parking lot. Since that time its popularity has risen quicker than hot air. It now takes up a seventy-eight-acre lot, or fifty-four consecutive football fields; attracts a half million visitors; and showcases over 700 balloons. The A.I.B.F. is the single largest international event in the United States.

Albuquerque is the perfect location for this prismatic party. The city's serene southwestern charm,

warm adobe buildings, and rich American Indian and Mexican heritage make for an already brilliant, multicolored landscape. Add nine consecutive days of kaleidoscope-like effects looming from the heavens above and the result is simply magical. The crisp fall weather and deep blue New Mexican skies make October the prime month to witness this floating parade.

It's recommended that you arrive for the first weekend of the fiesta, before the initial launch on Saturday morning. This weekend is the most celebratory time throughout the city, as a wide variety of events kick off the balloon festival. The opening ceremonies take place at Balloon Fiesta Park at 6:45 A.M., before the incredible 7:00 A.M. Mass Ascension. The park is located seven miles north of downtown Albuquerque.

Your neck will undoubtedly stiffen up after a few hours of

watching the vivid air show. Gobbling a couple of Tylenols is an option, but an even better move is to head to the Fiesta Del Vino, the annual New Mexican Wine festival, which takes place during the first weekend of the Balloon Fiesta. New Mexico is home to some of the most underrated vineyards in the country, which produce award-winning reds, whites, and sparkling wines. The wine exposition begins at noon, ends at 8:00 P.M., and is held on the Balloon Fiesta Park grounds.

Balloon glow is a term that was coined in Albuquerque in 1979, when local pilots fired their burners on Christmas Eve as they floated above the city. The result appears to be gigantic Christmas tree ornaments lighting up the sky. This effect is the most astonishing scene in the entire Balloon Fiesta. The balloon glow begins at 5:45 P.M., ends at 7:30 P.M., and is followed by a fireworks display that's rivaled only by the hovering balloons themselves.

TRANSPORTATION

AIR: Book flights into Albuquerque International Sunport (ABQ / *www.cabq.gov/airport*). This four-runway airport is serviced by seven major carriers (American, Continental, Delta, Frontier, Northwest, Southwest, US Airways), and flights can be booked directly from thirty-nine major cites. All major car-rental agencies as well as taxis are available. The airport is located four miles from downtown Albuquerque.

SUNPORT SHUTTLE: Provides twenty-four-hour service to any address in the Albuquerque area from the airport, and back (505-833-4966).

BUS / TRAIN: The Greyhound station is located at 320 First Street SW. The Amtrak station is located at 214 First Street SW.

PARK-AND-RIDE: You can either drive seven miles north of downtown to the festival grounds or you can take a shuttle from an Albuquerque park-and-ride. Call 888-422-7277 for locations and departure times.

BALLOON RIDES: Rainbow Ryders is the only company that offers balloon rides for the general public during the festival. This unique opportunity to soar beside the professionals should be booked well in advance by visiting *www.rainbowryders.com* or by calling 800-725-1111.

ACCOMMODATIONS

HOTELS: Downtown Albuquerque hotels include Doubletree (201 Marquette Ave. / 505-247-3344 / $109), Hotel Blue (717 Central Ave. NW / 505-924-2400 / $77), Embassy Suites (1000 Woodward Pl. NE / 505-245-7100 / $219), Hilton (1901 University Blvd. NE / 505-884-2500 / $159), Quality Inn (411 McKnight Ave. NW 505-242-5228 / $119), and Hyatt Regency (330 Tijeras Ave. NW / 505-842-1234 / $160). Visit *www.nmtravel.com* for further hotel listings and travel information. Book a hotel by July.

RV: RV facilities are available within walking distance of the launch field. The four levels of camping include standard (dry camping), premium (low water pressure and 20 amps of electricity), VIP (dry camping adjacent to launch field with entry passes included), and President's Compound (on a bluff overlooking the launch field with water and 30 amps of electricity). Rates vary depending on level and number of nights. Call 888-422-4277 for reservations and pricing.

TICKETS

Tickets can be purchased at the gate for $6 per day or in packs of five for $25 by calling 888-422-7277 ext. 303. Gates open at 4:30 A.M. for morning events and 3:00 P.M. for evening festivities. Parking passes cost $10.

The VIP ticket is called "Gondola Club." This ticket grants a special parking pass, VIP seating, and either breakfast or dinner buffet in a hospitality tent. Gondola Club costs $100 per session (either morning or evening) for the first person and $40 for each additional person. Visit the event website to purchase Gondola Club tickets.

What to Pack
- Folding chair
- Warm clothing and raincoat
- Binoculars
- 800- or 1,000-speed film
- Digital camera with a high-powered zoom or telephoto lens

party tip

Your festival photos stand a great chance of winding up on your wall with some helpful hints: You'll capture the best color when the sun shines from behind you as you're photographing the balloons. Use 1,000-speed film during the twilight hours during the balloon glow—you'll need high-speed film in this low-light situation. Many people feel they need to squeeze ten different balloons in each frame; however, one single balloon in front of a simple blue sky is enough for the perfect photo.

Texas

SPRING BREAK AT SOUTH PADRE ISLAND

⭐ **South Padre Island, Texas**
Mid-February to mid-March
www.springbreak.sopadre.com

South Padre is the ultimate getaway for guys who wear their baseball hats backward and for the women who adore them. The twenty-five-mile stretch of beach at the southern end of Padre Island brings over 250,000 amped-up college students to Texas each February and March. Located about two miles from the southernmost coast of Texas and twenty-six miles from Mexico, South Padre is the premier spring break destination in the United States. Beautiful beaches, an abundance of daytime activities and nightlife options, and camera crews from MTV and *Girls Gone Wild* have solidified South Padre's reputation among the college crowd. They have also caused instant panic in countless parents when the phrase, "Mom, can I go to South Padre Island for spring break?" is uttered over the phone.

An immensely popular beach party takes place at the Radisson Hotel (500 Padre Blvd.). Otherwise known as Coca-Cola Beach, this copious celebration bills itself as the largest beach party in Texas. All-day dancing, bikini contests, and concerts keep the coeds coming back for more. Drinking is legal on the beach, and barrels of beer beneath the sand are an inviting target for those who believe that keg stands should be an Olympic event.

Also available are a host of beach activities including diving, parasailing, Jet-Skiing, volleyball, golf, dolphin spotting, or just hanging out. Uncle Buggie's Beach Buggy Rentals (1612 Padre

Blvd. / 956-751-6162) rents dune buggies to cruise the Padre strip, or to off-road on the dunes. A number of local companies offer two- or three-hour booze cruises to Mexico, complete with an onboard DJ and unlimited drinks. Ben's Liquor Store (1004 Padre Blvd.) has the best deal on kegs.

Louie's Backyard and Grill (2305 Laguna Blvd.) is the epicenter of South Padre's nightlife scene. The huge must-go-to bar is constantly packed and hosts many big-name musical acts throughout spring break. Louie's taunts students with nonstop giveaways, bungee jumping, nightly Hawaiian Tropic Bikini Contests, and all-you-can-eat prime rib and seafood buffets. Tequila Frogs (205 W. Palm St.) is an indoor-outdoor club and another island hot spot. It has been voted "best beach party" by *Playboy*. Club Chaos is a wild ride that lives up to its name. It combines seven separate clubs underneath one roof, each bursting at the seams.

TRANSPORTATION

Most people fly into South Padre Island, but those who go to school in Texas can drive—San Antonio is 285 miles away. Many spring break travel companies offer free airfare for those who can convince a group of friends to make the trip. Check online for spring break travel packages. Flights into South Padre are reasonably priced, but flights into Miller International Airport may be considerably less expensive. You do not need a car.

AIR: There are three airports on the island. Brownsville-South Padre International Airport (BRO / *www.flybrownsville.com*) is a half hour away, Valley International Airport (HRL / *www.flythevalley.com*) is fifty minutes away, and McAllen International Airport (MFE / *www.mcallenairport.com*) is an hour and a half from South Padre. Taxi and shuttle services are available at all airports.

TAXIS: South Padre cab companies include J.J. Taxi (956-761-9292) and Brownsville Taxicab (956-761-1040).

ACCOMMODATIONS

HOTELS: Directly on the beach are Holiday Inn (100 Padre Blvd. / 888-897-0088 / $77), Sheraton (310 Padre Blvd. / 956-761-6551 / $229), Padre South Hotel (1500 Gulf Blvd. / 956-761-4951 / $199), and La Copa Inn (350 Padre Blvd. / 956-761-6000 / $69). If you want to be near major beach-party action, get a room at the Radisson (500 Padre Blvd. / 888-201-1718 / $129). Within walking distance of the beach are Howard Johnson Inn (1709 Padre Blvd. / 956-761-5658 / $199), America's Best Value Inn (3813 Padre Blvd. / 956-689-5900 / $69), Comfort Suites (912 Padre Blvd. / 956-772-9020 / $140), and Holiday Inn Express (6502 Padre Blvd. / 888-772-3222 / $79).

RENTAL HOMES: You can also rent a house or condo. Two bedroom / two bathroom condos that sleep eight people usually range from $1,200 to $1,800 per week. Condos on the beach are naturally more expensive. You'll have to fork over a damage deposit, so don't do any damage. Visit *www.pirentals.com* or *www.vrbo.com* for a wide range of available properties.

party tip

Many college women go to a tanning salon before a trip to the beach with their friends. This is understandable because society places an extraordinary amount of aesthetic pressure on young women, and they naturally want to fit in. Be suspicious, however, of a man who has hit the tanning beds. These confidence-lacking fellows are easily distinguished if they reside in a landlocked state and have an orangey bronze hue.

SOUTH BY SOUTHWEST MUSIC CONFERENCE

⊛ Austin, Texas

Usually the second week in March
www.sxsw.com

The live music capital of the world erupts with volcanic force every spring as 1,400 bands rock and roll into town for this one-of-a-kind four-day festival. South by Southwest is one of the largest musical events in the country, the largest industry gathering of its kind, and one heck of a great excuse to visit Austin.

South by Southwest is Austin's largest revenue-producing event, overshadowing Austin City Limits and Texas Longhorn football games. Over a half million people converge on the city for this landmark party. It's all things to all people—an industry showcase for up-and-coming bands, a huge marketing opportunity for well-established stars, and spring break for air guitarists everywhere. The acts top the bill at forty-plus venues over the course of four days. Do the math. There's something happening 24/7. This is your chance to catch tomorrow's superstars today, a welcome reason to visit this culturally rich college town, and definitive proof that your town may need more burrito stands per capita.

Daytime events are centered around the Austin Convention Center, where industry players hold trade shows, conventions, interviews, and introductions to the latest in music technology. The networking opportunities are abundant for unknown musicians seeking producers, label connections, and the ever-elusive chance to get discovered. However, for most "SXSW" attendees, Sixth Street is where you'll be partaking in the rock star lifestyle, minus the challenge of songwriting or performing.

Over recent years, South by Southwest has evolved into a progressive yet high-voltage street party in downtown Austin. Sixth Street has always been a musical focal point, but it reaches the zenith in March, as every single bar features a nonstop rotation of undiscovered or very much discovered bands. The SXSW website posts specific venue and band schedules in February. Outside the bars, the streets are chock-full of fans who rave about the group they just heard, and industry insiders who pass on information about the location of sought-after late-night parties. Celebrity sightings are frequent, and the energy level is enough to power a freight train.

Industry outsiders, and even many insiders, can have a particularly difficult time getting into the venues, especially for well-known acts like Iggy Pop, Arctic Monkeys, and Wolfmother. South by Southwest operates on a strict badge system, with the platinum and music badges providing all-access admittance into any show. The problem is that these badges start at around $425 (when purchased months in advance), and sell for $900 during the festival. Noncredentialed attendees are forced to wait in long lines and pay $100 for a wristband. If there is an act you're dying to see, get in line two hours early!

TRANSPORTATION

✈ **AIR:** Book flights into Austin-Bergstrom International Airport (AUS / *www.ci.austin.tx.us*) located nine miles from downtown Austin. Car-rental agencies are available, but totally unnecessary. Take a taxi.

🚕 **TAXIS:** Austin cab companies include Yellow Cab (512-452-9999), American Yellow Checker (512-434-7700), Austin Cab Co. (512-478-2222), and Lone Star Cab (512-836-4900).

🚐 **SHUTTLE:** SuperShuttle will take passengers from the airport to downtown Austin for $13 for the first person and $10 for each additional passenger. Call 512-258-3826.

🚂 **TRAIN:** The Amtrak station is located at 250 North Lamar Boulevard.

ACCOMMODATIONS

🏨 **HOTELS:** Make a reservation no later than December, but preferably much earlier. Hotels near the Sixth Street action include Courtyard by Marriott (300 E. Fourth St. / 512-236-8008 / $259), Hilton Garden Inn (500 N. I-35 / 512-480-8181 / $289), Hilton (500 E. Fourth St. / 512-482-8000 / $389), Hampton Inn (200 San Jacinto Blvd. / 512-472-1500 / $199), Sheraton (701 E. Eleventh St. / 512-478-1111 / $189), Super 8 (1201 N. I-35 / 512-472-8331 / $150), Doubletree (303 W. Fifteenth St. / 512-478-7000 / $329), and Radisson (111 E. Caesar Chavez St. / 512-478-9611 / $269). Hotel San Jose (1316 S. Congress / 512-444-7322 / $105) is the funkiest place in town and a guaranteed destination for many SXSW musicians. Call on November 1 at 1:00 P.M. to get on their waiting list.

TICKETS

The platinum badge gets you into the interactive sessions at the Austin Convention Center during the day, and it makes for a speedy entry into all evening shows. It goes on sale in September, starting at $650. On Sept. 29 the cost is raised $50, and increased at $70–100 increments from there, until it reaches a $950 walk-up rate. The music badge allows for line-cutting into the evening shows. It begins at $425 and is raised at similar increments until a $600 walk-up rate. Wristbands into individual shows can cost $100, but prices vary depending on the act. Visit *www.sxsw.com* to purchase.

What to Pack
- Funky clothing
- Printout of the show schedule
- Camera for rock star sightings
- MP3 recording device
- Demo tape

party tip

One SXSW secret is to find a venue that is part restaurant and go there for dinner. You'll gain free admittance if you hang around after your meal. Once you get in, stay in! Keep your ear to the ground for the late-night party locations—this incredible event is all about meeting people, getting in the know, and allowing the night to take you where it pleases.

AUSTIN CITY LIMITS MUSIC FESTIVAL

⭐ **Austin, Texas**
Second weekend in September
www.aclfestival.com

A longside Bonnaroo and Coachella, the Austin City Limits Music Festival has blossomed into one of the top rock festivals in the country. This three-day show should be a priority for lovers of rock, reggae, blues, folk, indie, soul, funk, and just about every other genre imaginable.

Austin is the Texas version of Berkeley, California, or Boulder, Colorado. It's a lush green bohemian city, with an eclectic population and a healthy dose of culture. It comes as no surprise that the self-described "live music capital of the world" should host a festival of this magnitude. The ACL origins date back to 1976, when PBS began airing the show as part of its live concert TV series. Back then, the focus was on Texas-born country and folk musicians. As the festival has evolved, so has the PBS special, which is now the country's longest-running concert TV program.

Over 130 bands play on eight stages in Zilker Park during the second weekend in September, bringing in 65,000 attendees each day. The stages are set a healthy distance apart from one another, so be prepared to do some walking. A good idea is to print up a schedule from the event website so that you can plan your day in advance. Zilker Park is an enjoyable grassy field that sits in the middle of Austin, convenient in location and pleasant in ambiance. Bringing a lawn chair is a must. Some fans tend to relax on the lawn sipping wine, playing chess, or reading, while the music fills the air. Others get as close to the stage as possible and dance the day away.

Headliners over the past five years have secured ACL's top-notch, grade-A festival status. They have included Ben Harper, the Shins, Ween, Willie Nelson, the Allman Brother's Band, Arcade Fire, Ryan Adams, Bob Dylan, My Morning Jacket, Queens of the Stone Age, Bjork, the Killers, G Love & Special Sauce, Raconteurs,

Tom Petty, Decemberists, Kings of Leon, Clap Your Hands Say Yeah, and Trey Anastasio. Visit *www.aclfestival.com* for upcoming schedules.

Unlike other major music festivals, there is no camping at ACL due to its urban location. Shuttle buses will take concertgoers the short distance between downtown Austin and Zilker Park. The sheer volume of people waiting for buses in the evening can turn this small jaunt into a lengthy ordeal. For this reason it is highly recommended that you bring or rent a bike, and take the well-lit Town Lake Hike and Bike Trail from Zilker Park to downtown—it's easy, fun, and adventuresome. Head to Austin's Sixth Street after the concert, where many of the ACL bands play more intimate shows.

TRANSPORTATION

AIR: Book flights into Austin-Bergstrom International Airport (AUS / *www.ci.austin.tx.us*) located nine miles from downtown Austin. Car-rental agencies and taxis are available.

TAXIS: Austin cab companies include Yellow Cab (512-452-9999), American Yellow Checker (512-434-7700), and Austin Cab Co. (512-478-2222).

SHUTTLE/PARKING/PASSENGER DROP-OFF: There is no parking at the festival. There is a passenger drop-off area at the north end of the Mopac Pedestrian Bridge on Stephen F. Austin Drive. The free shuttle picks passengers up at Republic Square, at the corner of Fourth and Guadalupe streets. Shuttles begin to run at 10:00 A.M. and stop at 11:00 P.M.

BIKE: Bike racks are located near the festival gates but you must bring your own lock. The Bicycle Sport Shop (517 S. Lamar / 512-477-3472) and Hampton Inn (200 San Jacinto / 512-472-1500) rent bikes from their downtown locations.

BUS / TRAIN: The Greyhound station is located at 916 East Koenig Lane. The Amtrak station is located at 250 North Lamar Boulevard.

ACCOMMODATIONS

HOTELS: You should stay in downtown Austin at any number of hotels. Located close to the Town Lake bike path, which leads to Zilker Park, are Radisson Hotel (111 E. Cesar Chavez St. / 512-478-9611 / $215), Embassy Suites (300 S. Congress Ave. / 512-469-9000 / $169), Hyatt Regency (208 Barton Springs / 512-477-1234 / $309), and Four Seasons (98 San Jacinto Blvd. / 512-478-4500 / $410). A little bit farther, but still very convenient are the Hampton Inn (200 San Jacinto Blvd. / 512-472-1500 / $209), Hilton (500 E. Fourth St. / 512-482-8000 / $249), and Courtyard Marriott (300 E. Fourth St. / 512-236-8008 / $199). The two swankiest, hippest, and most unique hotels in town are the Hotel San Jose (1316 S. Congress Ave. / 512-444-7322 / $95) and the Austin Motel (1220 S. Congress Ave. / 512-441-1157 / $70). Both sell out during the ACL, so book months in advance.

TICKETS

The ACL limits entrance to 65,000 to 75,000 per day, although the demand is higher. Three-day passes cost $145 and should be purchased as soon as they go on sale through *www.aclfestival.com*.

Ticket brokers tend to gobble up passes and raise the rates very quickly. Single-day passes sell for approximately $50 and should also be purchased in advance. A VIP pass provides access to food servings, beer and wine, minispa and misting lounge, VIP seating, air-conditioned restrooms, and VIP parking pass. They cost about $850 per ticket.

What to Pack

- Sunglasses and sunscreen
- Two sealed bottles of water
- Toilet paper
- Bottle opener to sample the local brew, Shiner Bock
- Stevie Ray Vaughn mix

party tip

If you have a free night in Austin, head to the Congress Avenue Bridge at dusk to watch the "bat show." This must-see spot attracts a crowd of visitors every night from March until November to watch a real-life "Animal Planet" show. The 1.5 million bats that live underneath the bridge fly out each evening in a huge, black cloud. The Congress Avenue Bridge is supposedly the world's largest urban bat colony.

RED RIVER SHOOTOUT

★ **Dallas, Texas**
Saturday, in late September to early October
www.attcottonbowl.com

The early season contest between the Texas Longhorns and the Oklahoma Sooners presents a rivalry so fierce that the Hatfields and McCoys pale in comparison. It's the sports world's Godzilla vs. King Kong, and it dwarfs that petty tiff between the Boston Red Sox and the New York Yankees. This game is more than a typically heated college football border war; it's a religion, and the ritual is held once a year in Dallas.

For over 100 years these two college pigskin powerhouses have been duking it out on the gridiron in what has been dubbed the "Red River Shootout." The Red River separates Texas and Oklahoma, two states that consider football to be as vital to life as air or water. The most interesting aspect of the rivalry is the fact that it takes place on neutral ground, with fandom being equally represented by both schools. Over the past sixty-five years, either one or both teams have been ranked in the top twenty-five nationally, lending added significance.

The Cotton Bowl plays host to the shootout. This ancient and somewhat dilapidated stadium has been in existence almost as long as the Alamo, and its worn-down exterior seems a perfect fit for the gritty battle that takes place inside. Its cramped, narrow seats hold over 79,000 blood-thirsty fans. Historically, Oklahomans filled the south side of the stadium and Texans the north side, with the fifty yard line acting as the boundary. This division has recently been changed to an alternating system, so check the website for specifics, depending on who you want to root for.

The game is played in the middle of the Texas State Fair, which surrounds the Cotton Bowl. Your game ticket also serves as a ticket into the fair, adding a new dimension to the tailgate experience. Arrive very early to enjoy the parking lot as well as the fair-grounds. The parking lot scene is a massive party, complete with scores of tailgates and alumni festivities. Bring a grill, some comfortable chairs, and enjoy the lightning before the storm. Afterward head into the fair for games, rides, and fried everything. Kickoff is usually around 6:30 P.M.

Don't leave town without having eaten at Texas De Brazil (2727 Cedar Springs Rd.), an all-you-can-eat meat-lover's paradise. The waiters, or gauchos, bring skewers full of mouth-watering beef, pork, alligator, and shrimp wrapped in bacon, until you say stop.

TRANSPORTATION

AIR: Book flights into Dallas Fort Worth International Airport (DFW / www.dfwairport.com) located eighteen miles from downtown Dallas. Taxis and car-rental agencies are available at the airport.

COMMUTER RAIL: The TRE train runs between the airport and the downtown Dallas Union Station for a low fare. Visit www.trinityrailwayexpress.org for schedules.

TAXIS: Local cab companies include Cowboy Cab (214-428-0202), Yellow Cab (214-426-4000), Dallas Yellow Cab (214-350-4445), and Freedom Cab (214-956-0800).

BUS / TRAIN: The Greyhound station is located at 205 South Lamar Street. An Amtrak station is located at 401 North Houston Street.

ACCOMMODATIONS

🏨 **HOTELS:** All downtown hotels are located a short distance from the Cotton Bowl. They include Hotel Indigo Dallas Aristocrat (1933 Main St. / 214-741-7700 / $120), Spring Hill Suites (1907 N. Lamar St. / 214-999-0500 / $279), Hotel Lawrence (302 S. Houston St. / 214-761-9090 / $249), and Sheraton Suites (2101 Stemmons Freeway / 214-747-3000 / $179). For competitive rates visit *www.dallas.hotelscheap.org.*

TICKETS

The game is a sure sellout. Face-value seats usually go to students and season ticket holders. Although remaining tickets typically sell on the OU and Texas websites, they are nearly impossible to obtain. You will probably be forced to purchase through a ticket vendor or on eBay for $250 to $800 per seat. Parking is $10 at the lot entrances.

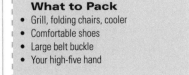

What to Pack
- Grill, folding chairs, cooler
- Comfortable shoes
- Large belt buckle
- Your high-five hand

party tip

This game is a blast, even if you have no allegiance to either team. It's advisable to root for Texas because the nightlife scene in Dallas is definitely more supportive of Longhorn fans. If you choose to become a Texan for the weekend, there is a hand signal you need to learn. Close your hand in a fist while keeping the pointer and pinkie fingers extended. This may be the international symbol for "heavy metal," but in Texas it signifies Longhorn pride. Besides, the Red River Shootout makes an Ozzy Osbourne concert seem like child's play.

TERLINGUA INTERNATIONAL CHILI CHAMPIONSHIP

⭐ Terlingua, Texas
First Saturday in November
www.krazyflats.com

The self-proclaimed grand-daddy of all chili cookoffs is a hot 'n' spicy, fire breathin', bullwhip-crackin' hootenanny that takes place, as it should, in West Texas. Anyone in the chili cookin' business will admit that an award-winnin' bowl of chili ain't worth its weight in red beans until it makes an appearance in Terlingua.

This four-day fragrant festival takes place in the middle of nowhere, thus the perfect road trip for free souls with time on their hands and gas in their tank. Terlingua was an abandoned ghost town until the late 1960s, when the first cookoff took place. Legend has it that a Midwesterner named H. Allen Smith wrote an article for *Holiday* magazine in 1967 titled "Nobody Knows More about Chili Than I Do," which sent huge sparks flying in Texas. Wick Fowler, the Texan who created Three-Alarm Chili, called Mr. Smith's bluff, and the two met in Terlingua to settle the score. "The Great Chili Confrontation" was a heated duel that ended in a draw, but more importantly it started the ball a rollin'. This World Series of chili has been feeding the masses and keeping the local antacid market in business for over forty years.

These days Terlingua is a 360-person boomtown with a jail, a general store, and more dust than the Sahara Desert. Not to mention the fact that there's a Wal-Mart—150 miles away. But things change in November, as 10,000 longhorns head to town for four days of stomach-rumblin', five-alarm madness. The annual party begins on the Wednesday before the first Saturday in November and ends with the final grand competition

on Saturday. Maybe it's the location, maybe it's the beer, or maybe the "natural fumes" have gone to everyone's head, but the scene is crazier than a sack of weasels.

Two mouth-watering, tear-jerking battles take place in Terlingua, with the larger of the two occupying a 320-acre sprawl four miles west of the Terlingua ghost town in Rancho CASI (Chili Appreciation Society International) de los Chisos. El Rancho (the ranch) is divided into the Cooks Area, the Old 320 Area, and the spectator's area—otherwise known as Krazy Flats. Convoys of trailers, RVs, trucks, and campers invadee Krazy Flats on Wednesday, turning the land into redneck paradise. Concession stands are available. Ice is also for sale to cool your carried beverage supply. If you need groceries, you'll have to go eleven miles east to Study Butte. You can pick up an Internet signal at Krazy Flats Saloon, but good luck getting cell phone service.

TRANSPORTATION

You will definitely need to drive. The festival is located in West Texas, near the Mexican border, in the Big Bend area of the state—just above Big Bend National Park. Rancho CASI de los Chisos is nine miles west of the FM-170 and Texas 118 intersection in Study Butte, or four miles west of Terlingua ghost town. Make sure you have a spare tire and that someone in your group knows how to change one.

✈ **AIR:** The closest airport is Midland International Airport (MAF / *www.flymaf.com*), located 246 miles from Terlingua. Rent a car at the airport.

ACCOMMODATIONS

🔥 **CAMPING:** In order to truly experience this thing you should stay in Krazy Flats, where dry camping is available on a first-come-first-serve basis. No reservations. Port-a-potties are available, and the local sanitation company can pump out campers or RVs. Bag your trash each evening and it'll get picked up in the morning.

🚐 **RV:** There are RV parks in Study Butte and Terlingua with hookups, although you'll have to travel ten to fifteen miles away from the cookoff. The closest is Terlingua Oasis RV Park (432-371-2218) at Texas 118 and FM-170 with full hookups. Terlingua Ranch Lodge RV Park and Campground (423-371-2416) has full hookups, located twelve miles north of 118 and 170. Located five miles east of the intersection of 118 and 170 with full hookups is BJ's RV Park (423-371-2259). Study Butte RV Park (432-371-2259) has electricity and plumbing along 118, south of the 118 and 170 intersection. Make your reservation as early as possible.

🏠 **MOTELS:** There are motels in Terlingua and Study Butte; however, rooms are tough to come by. Many attendees, concessionaires, and chili fanatics make their reservations for next year's event as this one is ending. Motels are scattered around the Terlingua area, and you will have to drive on the cookoff each day. Don't count on the Ritz Carlton. Try Big Bend Motor Inn (Texas 118 / 432-371-2218 / $76, three-night min.), Badlands Motel (Hc 70 Box 400, Terlingua / 432-424-3451 / $76 / has RV spots as well as a motel), and the nicer Ten Bits Ranch (6000 N. Country Club Rd., Terlingua / 432-371-3110 / $159). You can send an e-mail to *mayor@krazyflats.com* for further motel recommendations if these are full.

TICKETS

Tickets are purchased at the entrance. Wednesday through Saturday costs $25, and Saturday only is $10. This fee includes Krazy Flats camping.

What to Pack
- Alka-Seltzer
- Tent
- Imodium
- Cowboy hat
- Milk of Magnesia
- Lawn games
- Kaopectate
- Pico de gallo
- Rolaids

party tip

Although it may not be Wick Fowler's Three-Alarm special, this recipe is sure to dazzle the taste buds of chili lovers everywhere:

4 lbs. chopped sirloin
2 cans finely chopped fresh tomatoes
7 cloves garlic
1 chopped green bell pepper
3 chopped onions
1 tablespoon ground cumin
1 teaspoon fresh basil
1 tablespoon oregano
3 tablespoons chili powder
2 chili pods
Sea salt and black pepper to taste

Brown meat in butter in a 3- or 4-quart pot, throw everything else in, let simmer for 2.5 hours, and serve.

Utah

SUNDANCE FILM FESTIVAL

⭐ Park City, Utah
Mid- to late January
www.festival.sundance.org

Park City, Utah, is known to the ski world as home of arguably the best powder and expert terrain in the United States. Like all ski towns, it attracts those with an affinity for arctic outdoor recreation, and the motto is simply "go big or go home." However, for ten days in mid- to late January, Park City sheds its ski-bum image and rolls out the red carpet, Hollywood style.

Over the course of twenty years, the Sundance Film Festival has evolved into the most important and well-respected display of independent films in the country. For ten days viewers have a chance to preview films that fly underneath Hollywood's big-budget movie radar alongside some of the biggest stars in the industry. You get all of this entertainment, and it takes place nowhere near Los Angeles.

Naturally the film festival draws an eclectic crowd. The streets and bars are hopping all week long, and this could be the perfect time for you to take a rustic ski vacation. A week in this winter wonderland is guaranteed invigoration for the body along with a healthy dose of relaxation for the mind. There's excellent opportunity for a healthy combination of hitting the slopes, watching some films, and enjoying the nightlife. The Canyons, Park City Resort, and Deer Valley Resort are the three places to ski.

If you feel like doing some celebrity watching, find "Moto on Main." This Motorola-sponsored lounge is temporarily created on Main St. each year, and each year it earns the reputation as the best celebrity hangout. The corporate-sponsored events, which attract the A-list crowds, are by invitation only, but anything is worth a try, right? Acts such as the Beastie Boys and Metallica have been known to play these private parties. Outdoor live music from up-and-coming acts is becoming more and more popular on Main Street. "Commoners" can attend these street parties, which take place once the chairlifts have finished their day's work.

TRANSPORTATION

AIR: Independent film critics and ski bunnies alike should book flights into Salt Lake City International airport (*www.slcairport.com*).

SHUTTLE: From the airport you can take a shuttle into Park City. The shuttle bus costs $30–$50 each way, and arrangements should be made via the airport website before you arrive.

TAXIS: If you need a taxi try calling City Cab (801-363-5550), Ute Cab (801-359-7788), or Yellow Cab (801-521-2100). Renting a car is not advisable, as parking is tough during the film festival. You do not need a car to go skiing or to get around town.

BUS: The city transit buses stop frequently around town. Buses begin running at 7:30 A.M. and stop at 10:30 P.M. Routes and stops are clearly marked, and the system is set up to provide access to all areas.

ACCOMMODATIONS:

HOTELS: It's recommended to find lodging located as close to Main Street as possible. This is the center of the nightlife scene, and since a car can be a burden, Main Street offers the luxury of easy transit to town, to the film showings, and to skiing. There is an excellent website, *www.skiparkcityutah.net*, that allows you to plug in your lodging preference and price range. During the festival, rooms start at approximately $180 and go into the $400s per night at a wide variety of hotels.

RENTAL HOMES: Condos, another great option, start in the mid-$200s for two bedroom lofts. See the hotels website above for condo rentals as well. Although it gets crowded, the sheer number of hotels makes it possible to book last-minute lodging.

TICKETS

Tickets to the multitude of films, which show at different sites around town, can be purchased in advance through the Sundance website (*www.festival.sundance.org*) and can range anywhere from $15 to $50 per ticket. They tend to sell out fast, so try eBay or a ticket broker's website if you have your heart set on a particular sold-out film screening. If you prefer to wait until you've arrived in town, stop by the Main Information Board off Main Street for a list of all movies, their screening times, and places. You also have the option of simply showing up to a screening site for a film that is already sold out, and taking a number. These numbers are given out based upon no-shows. Arrive a couple of hours early so you can get a low number. Numbers will be called about a half hour before showtime. Ticket prices to sold-out shows can go through the roof if you purchase through a scalper.

party tip

Celebrity spotting isn't limited to the downtown swag booths, where the rich and famous pocket freebies before partying the night away. Many celebrities take time to get out on the slopes, so be sure to look for them there as well. While they may look stunning at the Oscar awards, most Hollywood types have horrible fashion taste on the mountain. If you see a skier in a shiny neon-green one-piece (commonly referred to as a "onesie") and sporting earmuffs, then it may be your favorite actor. If the outfit isn't a dead giveaway, look for individuals snow-plowing down a black diamond with a few beefy bodyguards in tow.

Wyoming

CHEYENNE FRONTIER DAYS

⭐ Cheyenne, Wyoming
Last ten days in July
www.cfdrodeo.com

Nicknamed "the daddy of 'em all," this festival is a massive week-and-a-half-long tribute to all things Western. If you have an itch to see a massive bucking bull throw a fearless cowboy through the air like a rag doll and then charge him like a runaway freight train, there is only one place to go. If you want to hear the biggest stars in country music play an adrenaline-filled arena alongside thousands of cowpokes, there is but one choice. Cheyenne Frontier Days is the undisputed largest outdoor rodeo and western festival in the world, so saddle up, partner, and head to Wyoming for ten days of bronco busting and buckshot.

Over 550,000 attendees saunter in from all across the West, while many come from around the world to watch elite cowboys wrangle, wrestle, and rope their way into Cheyenne's Cowboy Hall of Fame. Frontier Days is known as the most fast-paced, most dangerous rodeo anywhere—rodeo great Lane Frost lost his life at Frontier Days in 1989. An enormous number of contestants alongside forty raging bulls and seventy buckin' broncos make their way into the arena each afternoon starting at 1:00 P.M., although you can take your seat at noon. Some of the wildest events include Saddle Bronc, Bareback Bronc, Steer Wrestling, the Wild Horse Race, Bull Riding, and Chuckwagon Races. Another noteworthy aspect is the Indian Villages that are assembled in Frontier Park. Native Americans from New Mexico and South Dakota demonstrate dancing, crafts, and teepee assembly.

At nighttime, after the rodeo events have wound down, the

musical portion of Frontier Days commences. Taking place in the outdoor rodeo pavilion, the 2007 lineup included Bon Jovi, Reba McEntire, LeAnn Rimes, Los Lonely Boys, Big & Rich, and Def Leppard. General admission tickets start at around $25, and choice seating goes up to $75.

Downtown Cheyenne is located 2.28 miles away. Keep in mind that this city is fairly quiet most of the year, but it's bursting at the seams during Frontier Days. Check out the Snake River Pub and Grill (115 W. Fifteenth St.) for the city's largest selection of ales, stouts, and porters; the Crown Bar (222 W. Sixteenth), with two levels, the top being an R&B and rock 'n' roll, the lower being hip-hop music; or Cowboy South (312 S. Greeley Hwy.), a true Wyoming bar experience.

TRANSPORTATION

✈ **AIR:** Book flights into Denver International Airport (DEN / *www.fly.denver.com*), located an hour and forty-five minutes away. All major car-rental agencies are available.

ACCOMMODATIONS

🛏 **HOTELS:** Hotels fill up extremely early; book a room by February to be safe. Hotels in downtown Cheyenne include the Days Inn (2360 W. Lincoln Way / 307-778-8877 / $200), Holiday Inn (204

W. Fox Farm Rd. / 307-638-4466 / $210), and Roadway Inn (5401 Walker Rd. / 307-632-8901 / $170). The Historic Plains Hotel (1600 Central Ave. / 307-638-3311 / $129) is the picture of western elegance with very affordable rooms during Frontier Days. For a complete listing of hotels visit *www .priceline.com*. If you are too late to reserve a room in Cheyenne, try Fort Collins, Colorado, a forty-five minute drive south. The Comfort Inn (601 SW Frontage Rd. / 970-407-0110 / $89) and Ramada (3836 E. Mulberry St. / 970-484-4660 / $99) are the two closest options.

TICKETS

Rodeo tickets cost $15 for bleacher seats at the end of the arena, $20 for seats closer to the roping gates, and $25 for center stage. Concert tickets start at around $25 and go to $70 for premium seats for the big-name acts. All tickets should be purchased online at *www.cfdrodeo .com* by early May.

What to Pack
- Denim
- Stetson
- Raincoat
- Willie Nelson CD
- More denim

party tip

There is an interesting motor vehicle exterior decorating fad currently taking place in Cheyenne. Be on the lookout for pickup trucks sporting a pair of chrome testicles dangling below the license plate. Young male angst rears its macho head in many different ways, and this is Wyoming's equivalent of tattoos or Mohawk hairdos. While it may be better than a Mohawk, keep in mind that dozens of chrome bulls are now roaming the open range without their manhood.

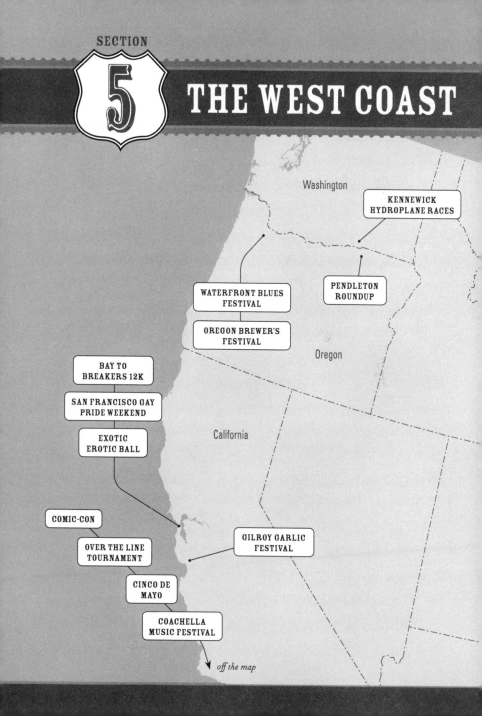

Washington

KENNEWICK
HYDROPLANE RACES

WATERFRONT BLUES
FESTIVAL

PENDLETON
ROUNDUP

OREGON BREWER'S
FESTIVAL

Oregon

BAY TO
BREAKERS 12K

SAN FRANCISCO GAY
PRIDE WEEKEND

EXOTIC
EROTIC BALL

California

COMIC-CON

GILROY GARLIC
FESTIVAL

OVER THE LINE
TOURNAMENT

CINCO DE
MAYO

COACHELLA
MUSIC FESTIVAL

off the map

California

COACHELLA MUSIC FESTIVAL

⊛ Indio, California
Last weekend in April
www.coachella.com

The inaugural Coachella festival took place just months after the overly muddy (and overtly commercialized) Woodstock 1999. However, where cloudy skies and testosterone-driven rock rained supreme in upstate New York, Coachella fosters an atmosphere of sun and inspiration in the California desert. The three-day festival has played host to some of the largest and most energetic live acts in music today. Beck, Rage Against the Machine, the Pixies, and Tool have all graced the Coachella stage under the crisp Indio, California, sky. Art installations and electronic-driven acts are also present at what many consider the premier live music festival in North America.

Coachella has developed a reputation as the rock reunion venue du jour. Look for big acts from the past headlining alongside today's rising stars. Taking place annually in late April, Coachella has only grown since its inception, an impressive feat considering the struggles of alternative music festivals such as Lollapalooza and Woodstock.

The festival begins mid morning on Friday and ends on Sunday evening. Two main stages and three enormous stage-containing tents are scattered throughout the Polo Grounds, giving fans easy access to the multitude of bands which play throughout the course of the weekend. Typically the headliners take the stage later in the night, while newer buzz bands provide the day's music. Beyond the open-air stages are DJ and house music gardens, which seldom slow their rhythmic pulse. Beer gardens are plentiful, although you should not attempt to listen to your favorite band from these areas.

Coachella nights are a wonderful display of laser lights and installation art. The grounds are enough to make one feel as though they've entered Alice's Wonderland. Expect to see your fair share of tattooed bodies with dreadlocks juggling fire and dancing as though they are in a world all their own.

TRANSPORTATION

Located approximately 150 miles east of Los Angeles and 25 miles east of Palm Springs, Indio offers partygoers a variety of travel choices. The most important fact to keep in mind is that Interstate 10 is the only vein into the festival. Therefore traffic becomes an issue regardless of your mode of transportation. Many a horror story is reported from people who flew into Palm Springs International Airport and then sat for three hours in traffic during the final leg of the trip. The absolute best way to avoid this situation is to arrive on Thursday night, before the first band hits the stage on Friday.

AIR: Book flights into Palm Springs International Airport (PSP / www.palmspringsairport.com).

BUS / TRAIN: There is a Greyhound Bus station in Indio located at 45-524 Oasis Street (760-347-5888). From here you can take a cab, ask for a ride, or walk approximately three miles to the festival.

The Amtrak Indio station is located on the corner of Highway 111 and Monroe Street. The station is approximately 3.5 miles from the main festival area.

TAXIS: American Cab (760-416-7447), California Cab (760-776-9878), City Cab (760-416-2594), Country Club Taxi (760-779-5937), Indio Yellow Cab (760-347-7777), and Suntaxi (760-340-3071).

ACCOMMODATIONS

CAMPING: The Coachella Festival offers partygoers a very nice, lush, green campground, which is directly adjacent to the main concert entrance. The cost for four nights is $45 per person and tickets must be purchased on www .ticketmaster.com, separately from concert tickets. Camping is the most popular choice of accommodation, and it is recommended that *each* person make their camping reservation as far in advance as possible.

The grounds are equipped with male and female restroom trailers as well as free showers.

Tents are not provided, so bring your own. Each person will have approximately fifty square feet of personal space for a tent. A general store that carries the essentials is onsite, and all entrants to the campgrounds must have a wristband. If you've chosen "will-call" then pick up your camping tickets and wristband before your concert tickets.

HOTELS / MOTELS / RENTAL HOMES: Partygoers who prefer a hotel and do not mind traveling back and forth to the concert grounds have a large selection. The closest hotels in Indio are approximately four miles from the concert gates. Indian Wells (seven miles), Palm Desert (twelve miles), and Thousand Palms (thirteen miles) have a wide range of hotels, motels, and condos as well. Visit the Coachella website for a long list of local hotels and condos or call the hotel hotline at 800-537-6986. Many area residents flee Indio for the weekend, renting out their houses for the festival. For approx. $1000 per night you can rent an incredible four-bedroom home with a saltwater swimming pool and hot tub. An optimal rental is located within two miles of the Polo Grounds, and a bicycle serves as ideal transportation back and forth. Check *www.vrbo .com* for listings.

🚐 **RV:** A multitude of RV parks make this option quite feasible. The Outdoor Resorts Motorcoach Resort and Spa (760-357-0073) is the closest, at three miles from the concert gate. The Indian Wells RV Park (760-347-0895) is just beyond that, and the Lake Cahuilla Recreation Area (760-564-4712) is five miles away. Reservations must be made in advance, and space tends to fill up quickly. Visit the Coachella website for further RV parking information.

TICKETS

Three-day passes run about $250 while single-day tickets are available on a limited basis for $85. Despite its impressive size, the festival *does* sell out. Posted set times and a highly informative FAQ section make *www.coachella.com* an impressive resource. Generally it is wise to purchase tickets at least three months in advance, and three-day passes are not available during the festival. Visit *www.ticketmaster.com* to purchase tickets.

What to Pack
- Cash—credit cards aren't accepted and ATM lines are longer than just a song or two
- Plenty of sunscreen, soap, and shampoo
- A pillow, a headlamp, a money belt, and tent
- An extra pair of flip-flops in case one flop disappears

---

party tip

The people who camp out for four days to see the hottest new acts in music tend to be huge fans who know a lot about the bands and would do anything to meet them. With a little creativity and the right approach one could certainly have some fun in this arena. Some band T-shirts with the words *security* or *entourage* on the back coupled with a fake backstage pass could help you make friends for all the wrong reasons.

How to make a fake backstage pass: Order some name badges from a corporate meeting vendor. You are interested in the badges that come inside a plastic sleeve with a string that loops around the neck. Next, print up a band logo that you've found online. Go to your local copy shop and have that logo transferred onto cardboard. Include the words *All Access Backstage* in large lettering, and put this into your name tag sleeve.

CINCO DE MAYO

★ Old Town San Diego, California
May 5
www.fiestacincodemayo.com

Delectable margaritas mixed with top-shelf tequila and homemade lime juice, mariachi music carrying through the air, and carne asado tacos grilled fresh before your eyes. Welcome to the ideal execution of Cinco de Mayo, a San Diego fiesta that is often imitated but never replicated.

The first lesson you must learn before a trek to the biggest celebration of Mexican heritage in the United States is that Cinco de Mayo is not the Mexican Independence Day, as it is often believed to be. Rather it is a commemoration of the Mexican victory over a larger and more intimidating French occupational force on May 5, 1862, at the Battle of Puebla. History lesson concluded.

It makes perfect sense that San Diego is home to this awesome celebration, which draws an estimated 250,000 attendees. It's a city that sits on the border and has the necessary capacity to play the role of obliging host. The fiesta typi-

cally kicks off around May 2, with a multitude of music-, food-, and art-based events that take place in San Diego's Old Town district. The Old Town Fiesta is ground zero up until the evening of the fifth, although dates tend to change each year, depending when the actual holiday falls. The Old Town Fiesta is a free, multi-day festival that assaults the senses with over 200 colorful performers at eight different venues, 100 handcraft and specialty booths, and a glut of establishments that serve authentic Mexican cuisine to mobs of happy patrons. Try Café Coyote (2461 San Diego Ave.) for the largest selection of margaritas. The more casual local favorite, Fred's Mexican Café (527 Fifth Ave.), has won "Best of San Diego" awards for its food and drink. Make your way to Old Town San Diego State Historic Park and San Diego Avenue and visit *www.fiestacincodemayo.com* for exact dates and start times. For information call 619-296-3236.

Head to the Gaslamp Quarter at 5:00 P.M. on May 5 for the zenith of the Cinco de Mayo festivities. The Five-on-Five Block Party takes place on Fifth Avenue, between Island Avenue and J Street, and on J Street between Fifth and Sixth avenues. Here you'll witness go-go dancers, pro skateboarders executing top-notch tricks on the skate ramp in the X-Games lounge, and a variety of DJs and live bands. Tickets are necessary for this twenty-one-and-over affair—they can be purchased early for $15 or at the gate for $20. This Latino-grooves booty-shaking block party lasts until midnight. Bring your sombreros and hold on tight!

TRANSPORTATION

✈ AIR: Flights should be booked into San Diego International Airport (SAN / *www.san.org*). All major car-rental agencies are available at the airport.

🚕 TAXIS: Local companies include Yellow Cab (619-234-6161), American Cab (619-234-1111), Orange Cab (619-291-3333), and San Diego Cab (619-226-8294).

🚈 TROLLEY: San Diego has a convenient trolley system that runs from most downtown San Diego areas to the major attractions, and into Old Town. Trolleys run until 2:00 A.M. and fares are approximately $1 each way. They do not go to the airport.

Ⓑ BUS / 🚆 TRAIN: The Greyhound Bus station is located at 120 West Broadway in downtown San Diego. You can take a trolley into Old Town from there. The Amtrak station is located at 1050 Kettner Boulevard.

ACCOMMODATIONS

🏨 HOTELS: You should book in the Old Town district for easy access. The Western Inn Old Town (3889 Arista St. / 619-298-6888 / $99), Holiday Inn Express (3900 Old Town Ave. / 619-299-7400 / $139), La Quinta Inn (2380 Moore St. / 619-291-0265 / $109), Courtyard Marriott (2435 Jefferson St. / 619-260-8500 / $199), and Best Western Hacienda Hotel (4041 Harney St. / 619-298-4707 / $149) are all located nearby with swimming pools and rates under $150. Visit *www.sandiego.org/event/ Visitors/270* for a complete listing of hotels.

TICKETS

The Old Town Fiesta is free; however tickets must be purchased for the Five-on-Five Block Party. At the gate ticket prices are $20. You can purchase in advance for $15 by visiting *www.myspace .com/gaslamp5on5, www.mcfarlaneproductions. com,* or by calling 619-233-5008.

What to Pack
- Summer clothing
- Sunscreen
- Piñata
- Cuervo Gold

party tip

Cinco de Mayo partygoers in San Diego seem to have a genetic predisposition for salsa dancing. If you don't, then prepare yourself to be out-danced by about 90 percent of this party. If and when this happens, do not retreat into the corner and sulk. As with anything in life, approach with confidence and poise, and remember to move your hips.

BAY TO BREAKERS 12K

⊛ San Francisco, California
Third Sunday in May
www.ingbaytobreakers.com

A roaming party: The country's most infamous 10K running race is moving mayhem, or a 7.5-mile-long block party. Welcome, ladies and gentlemen, to the Bay to Breakers.

This 75,000-person gathering is centered around a race in San Francisco that has been taking place since 1912. The B to B starts at 8:00 A.M., and every year approximately 50,000 people sign up for the race; they are joined by 25,000 others who show up and complete as much of the course as they can. The goal of this race is to finish *as slowly as possible* because the fun is actually to be had along the way. As you wind your way through the streets of San Francisco you can expect invitations into the multitude of house parties taking place along the course. And the infamous rolling tiki bar is equipped with enough bartenders to keep all of the "racers" happy.

Many partygoers run and walk in all sorts of costumes—or even naked without a care in the world. This party is a great opportunity for creative self-expression, as you can get away with any sort of outfit or costume that you can dream up. In fact, the B to B has been dubbed "an early morning Mardi Gras." Groups of friends will dress as superheroes, the seven dwarves, or simply construct a float upon which they ride the length of the course.

The course starts at sea level and quickly rises to about 215 feet between Fillmore and Steiner streets. Halfway up Hayes Hill be sure to stop and look down over all of the costumes and floats below you. This is an awesome spot to take a photo, and enjoy the lunacy of this event. The final five miles is a gradual downhill through Golden Gate Park.

After the race everyone will wind up at the "Footstock" party in Golden Gate Park. This is a time for some to fall asleep on the lawn while others visit beer gardens, listen to live music, and watch the costume contest. Footstock lasts until about 3:00 P.M. and buses will bring you from Golden Gate Park back to downtown San Francisco.

TRANSPORTATION

AIR: Fly into San Francisco International Airport (SFO / *www.flysfo.com*) or Oakland International Airport (OAK / *www.flyoakland.com*).

TAXIS: S.F. cab companies include Bayshore Cab (415-648-4444), DeSoto Cab (415-970-1300), Metro Cab (415-920-0715), Yellow Cab (415-626-2345), American Taxi Co (415-775-3315), and Veterans Cab (415-552-1300).

Driving to this race is not recommended because it is very difficult to find a space on the streets or in a lot. You can jump in a cab and ask to be dropped off near the starting line at Embarcadero and Howard Street.

BUS: The Greyhound station is located at 425 Mission Street.

ACCOMMODATIONS

HOTELS: You can stay anywhere in San Francisco and easily get to the starting point by cab. The closest hotel to the starting point is the Hyatt Regency SF (5 Embarcadero / 415-788-1234 / $339) located two blocks away.

TICKETS

Anyone can run the race without registering; however, only registrants are permitted on the start and finish lines. You must register online by May 14 in order to receive a race packet via mail.

What to Pack
- Water bottles
- Comfortable shoes
- The craziest combination of clothes that you own

party tip

Keep in mind that this is a fairly athletic party. Even if you walk the entire time you will get tired after seven miles. Make sure to stay hydrated and get some sleep the night before. Depending on your cardiovascular condition it may be a good idea to train a bit.

SAN FRANCISCO GAY PRIDE WEEKEND

★ San Francisco, California
Last weekend in June
www.sfgaypride.org

San Fran's annual Gay Pride Parade is the country's greatest celebration of all things rainbow. It easily ranks as one of the heaviest-attended events in the United States, bringing in over 750,000 members of humankind each year. Although the parade is held on the last Sunday in June, the weekend leading up to the flamboyant march is a spirited gathering, full of unrestrained merriment, unequalled wackiness, and good, old-fashioned, out-of-the-closet fun.

The weekend's heartbeat is San Francisco's famed gay neighborhood and business district, the Castro. An unfathomable number of colorful events take place from Friday to Sunday, and the rainbow flag is proudly flown above them all. Bar and club parties, political booths, art displays, warehouse raves, and everything in between fills the Castro at all hours. The vibes are powerfully positive, due to the massive crowd's effervescent unification. Crazy costumes are commonplace—200-pound men in high heels and g-strings, overweight topless lesbians with hairy legs. You may not want to see it, but you're going to anyway. Open-minded straight people are welcomed without question, as this party's individuality does not discriminate. San Franciscan Mark Christy explained, "It's a great party for anyone to come to. Straight people love it because it's all-inclusive and so festive. You'll see things you've never seen before and you'll be shocked, but that's part of the fun."

The Civic Center (355 McAllister Ave.) exemplifies the saying "gay people have more fun." From noon until early evening, the building is rocking with constant entertainment, including music, dance, and comedy acts. Performers like En Vogue, Third Eye Blind, Chaka

Khan, the Pointer Sisters, and Margaret Cho hit the main stage on Saturday and Sunday afternoons.

The Gay, Lesbian, Bisexual, and Transgender Parade on Sunday is the reigning "queen" event of the weekend. This spectacle rivals New York's Macy's Thanksgiving Day Parade—just substitute studs and leather for Snoopy floats and clowns. The procession begins at 10:30 A.M. on Market and Beale streets, and follows Market down to Eighth.

Plan to arrive an hour and a half early to get a decent viewing spot. "Dikes on Bikes," featuring loud Harleys and lesbians, is a highly anticipated motorcade that signals the start of the four-hour moving exhibition.

The atmosphere is jovial and high-energy, with undeniable displays of landmark achievements in the gay movement. These include blown-up marriage certificates mounted on posters, and the presence of many couples' children. Marching is more fun than watching—do some research on groups with connections to the event and contact them a couple of months prior.

TRANSPORTATION

✈ **AIR:** It's preferable to fly into San Francisco International Airport (SFO / www.flysfo.com); however, Oakland International Airport (OAK / www.flyoakland.com) is just a half hour away.

🚕 **TAXIS:** S.F. cab companies include Bayshore Cab (415-648-4444), DeSoto Cab (415-970-1300), Metro Cab (415-920-0715), Yellow Cab (415-626-2345), American Taxi Co (415-775-3315), and Checker Cabs (415-468-9090).

PUBLIC TRANSPORTATION: It is not wise to drive in the city during the parade. Streets are closed down, and the traffic is a nightmare. Take the BART (Bay Area Rapid Transit) trains around town—schedules are available on www.bart.gov. Another option is the MUNI train, which is known for short wait times, twenty-four-hour a day service, and $1.50 fares. Visit www.sfmuni.com.

🚌 **BUS:** The Greyhound station is located at 425 Mission Street.

ACCOMMODATIONS

🏨 **HOTELS:** You will have to plan to book ten months in advance to get a room at Renoir Hotel (45 McAllister St. / 415-626-5200 / $179), a gay-managed establishment located two miles from the Castro. Another popular hotel that markets to the gay population is Beck Motor Lodge (2222 Market St. / 415-621-8212 / $93), located in the Castro. Two other Castro options are Castro Hotel (705 Vallejo St. / 415-788-9709 / $165, shared bathrooms) and Inn on Castro (321 Castro St. / 415-861-0321 / $95). Hotels near the Civic Center, which offer proximity to the party yet some peace at nighttime, include Civic Center Inn (790 Ellis St. / 415-775-7612), Holiday Inn (50 Eighth St. / 415-864-4040 / $243), and Days Inn (465 Grove St. / 877-485-2038 / $130).

party tip

There's no better way to take in San Fran than a quick cruise around the harbor, and there's no better harbor cruise than Adventure Cat Sailing (*www.adventurecat.com*). A quirky German import named Hans will lead you on a smooth-sailing Catamaran tour around Alcatraz, toward Sausalito, under the Golden Gate Bridge, and back along the San Francisco waterfront with plenty of disco time left in your day. Bay cruises leave from pier 39, directly next to the sea lions.

OVER THE LINE TOURNAMENT

⊛ San Diego, CA
Middle two weekends in July
www.ombac.org/over_the_line/index.html

Jimmy Buffet's vision of paradise is tossed into a blender and mixed with a little bit of sport and a lot of skin. Welcome to OTL, the annual hormone-driven tournament during which teams play a uniquely San Diego-style ballgame while consuming adult beverages.

The tournament is played on the beach on Fiesta Island in gorgeous Mission Bay, and it has a history dating back over fifty years. The Old Mission Beach Athletic Club's main fundraising event entry is limited to 1,200 teams of three, who duke it out on fifty courts, resulting in over 55,000 players and sun-baked spectators. It's typically held over the middle two weekends in July, with the championship match taking place on the final Sunday.

The sport is similar to baseball, except players are forced to hit the foamy orange ball in a very small area of fair territory. There's no running, and every third hit counts as a run. The pitcher is on the batter's team, with the defenders playing for the opposing team. The batter must try to hit the ball "over the line," fifty-five feet into the sand before the other team catches it in the air. Hit it over the fielder's heads and it's a homerun. Bats must be "official" wooden softball or Little League bats, and gloves are only allowed in the women's brackets. Visit the event website for further explanation of the rules. Play begins at 7:30 A.M. and ends at dusk.

This event is more like a massive maniacal beach party than it is a competitive sport. The heat and the far-from-modest crowd are ingredients for a fair amount of nudity and over-the-line behavior, although organizers have recently attempted to curb this aspect. It's technically a BYOB bash, so load up a cooler but be sure not to bring any glass bottles. Burritos, margaritas, Jell-O shots, and sexual innuendo are in no short supply. OTL players historically utilize X-rated team names, and the tournament announcers do an exceptional job of enunciating them for the crowd to hear. Many people were surprised last year when the "Neverland Ranch Day Care" team didn't make it to the finals.

TRANSPORTATION

AIR: Flights should be booked into San Diego International Airport (SAN / *www.san.org*) located near the downtown area. All major car-rental agencies are available at the airport.

PARKING: There is only one road that runs onto and around the island, so plan to park and take a shuttle bus. Traffic is heavy, and the main parking lot off Route 5 fills early in the day. If you're lucky enough to find a spot at the Pacific Highway Lot at the island entrance, you can either take the island shuttle or walk approximately one mile to the beach. Otherwise shuttles run from lots at Sea World Drive and Mission Boulevard or at Pacific Highway and Sea World Drive. The Linda Vista Trolley Station at Friar's Road and Napa Street is the final pickup point; however, cars may not be parked at the trolley station. Shuttles begin running early in the morning and quit after the final person has left the beach.

TAXIS: Local companies include Yellow Cab (619-234-6161), American Cab (619-234-1111), Orange Cab (619-291-3333), and San Diego Cab (619-226-8294). Taking a taxi to the shuttle pickup points may be a wise idea.

BUS: The Greyhound station is located at 120 West Broadway in downtown San Diego. Visit *www .greyhound.com* for arrival and departure times.

RV: RV parking is available on a limited basis on Fiesta Island from Friday to Sunday. Cost is $100, and reservations are accepted after March 1. E-mail *rvparking@ombac.org* to find out availability and arrange payment.

ACCOMMODATIONS

HOTELS: Old Town is the hot spot in San Diego, and it's located in close proximity to shuttle pickup points as well as Fiesta Island. The Western Inn Old Town (3889 Arista St. / 619-298-6888 /

$129), Holiday Inn Express (3900 Old Town Ave. / 619-299-7400 / $157), La Quinta Inn (2380 Moore St. / 619-291-0265 / $149), Courtyard Marriott (2435 Jefferson St. / 619-260-8500 / $209), and Best Western Hacienda Hotel (4041 Harney St. / 619-298-4707 / $199) are all located nearby with swimming pools and reasonable rates. Visit *www.sandiego.org/event/Visitors/270* for a complete listing of hotels.

TICKETS

Entrance to the party is free; however team entrance fees are $75. Registration for out-of-state teams begins on December 1 and runs through May 1. Send a written request for an application to OTL Committee, 3990 Old Town Ave., Suite 205A, San Diego, CA 92110. Include a business-sized, self-addressed, stamped envelope. Sign ups begin in the San Diego area on May 3 at the Beachcomber and Pennant bars on Mission Boulevard in South Mission Beach. In Los Angeles sign up at Blackies by the Sea in Newport Beach at the beach pier on May 3.

> **What to Pack**
> - Cooler
> - Hilarious team uniform
> - Coordination

party tip

This sport is more about grace and bat control than it is about speed and power. We realize that you hit lots of home runs in your softball league, but swinging for the fences gets you nowhere in Over the Line. Avoid drafting players who tend to think that they're a weekend warrior version of Hank Aaron.

COMIC-CON

⊛ San Diego, California
Thursday to Sunday, usually late July
www.comic-con.org

Throngs of proudly self-proclaimed nerds ascend the steps of their parents' basements and make the annual trek to San Diego for what is now the premier comic convention in the entire world. However, to label Comic-Con as simply a pocket-protector party minimizes the cultural impact and lavish decadence of the event. Now in its twentieth year, the pop culture celebration has morphed into the premier venue for Hollywood to generate buzz over its forthcoming offerings. Stars mingle side by side with the costumed masses, hoping to court an audience for their latest comic-inspired film or television show.

Beyond the elaborate booths and X-Men costumes lies a massive celebration filled with 125,000 fanatics who pray to a god named Spock. Friendly rivalries perpetuate outstanding showmanship, and partygoers come from distant corners of the galaxy to prove that they are indeed the hottest Princess Leia. Hordes of alien life-forms, Power Rangers, Jedi knights, and flabby superheroes patrol 525,701 square feet of continuous exhibit space from Thursday to Sunday, in a collective effort to banish reality and the threat of a normal sex life. The Comic-Con will whet your appetite for all upcoming movie and TV offerings way before the general public knows just how cool they are. You're simply out of the loop if you're a comic fan who misses this elaborate and unrivaled event.

The massive floor space in the San Diego Convention Center houses a never-ending array of exhibitors and dealers who peddle every single comic book and related piece of memorabilia

known. Workshops, seminars, and artist autograph sessions promote a range of genres, which include horror, animation, science fiction, fantasy, collectible card games, and video games. The Comic-Con International Film Festival provides nerds with the opportunity to view blockbusters like *Shaun of the Dead* and *Ghost Rider*—a welcome change from normal weekends spent watching *Shaun of the Dead* and *Ghost Rider* at home. Lovers of Japanese anime are faced with the daunting task of deciding which of the new sword-wielding virtual temptresses would be the best kisser.

Two gaming outposts, one on the mezzanine of the Convention Center and the other at the Marriott Hotel, have become popular destinations. Gamers should spend at least six months training in a dark basement among half-empty cans of Mountain Dew prior to gaming in San Diego. Arrive early at Ballroom 20 for the Masquerade costume contest on Saturday night—the ballroom only holds 4,000 and is guaranteed to fill up. Elaborate hand-made costumes make the judging process quite difficult—those who dare show up in store-bought costumes are considered lesser life-forms. Download a signup form from the event website if you wish to participate in the contest.

TRANSPORTATION

AIR: Flights should be booked into San Diego International Airport (SAN / www.san.org). All major car-rental agencies are available at the airport. The San Diego Convention Center is located four miles away.

PARKING: Parking at the Convention Center is a nightmare and should be avoided like the plague. You can park at Qualcomm Stadium (9449 Friars Rd.), home of the San Diego Chargers, and take the trolley from there. You should also avoid parking a car in downtown San Diego. It's best to use public transportation.

TROLLEY / COMIC-CON SHUTTLE: San Diego's Metro Transit Shuttle runs trolleys every twenty minutes during Comic-Con. The trolleys stop at Qualcomm Stadium, Fashion Valley / Mission Valley, Old Town, the Convention Center, and the Gaslamp Quarter. It's a wise idea to purchase a one- to four-day trolley pass ahead of time at www.sdcommute.com. The Comic-Con free shuttle services a number of large San Diego hotels, running directly to the Convention Center. You can try to park at a nearby hotel and utilize this shuttle—they run throughout the downtown area all day long.

TAXIS: Local companies include Yellow Cab (619-234-6161), American Cab (619-234-1111), Orange Cab (619-291-3333), and San Diego Cab (619-226-8294).

B BUS / TRAIN: The Greyhound station is located at 120 West Broadway in downtown San Diego. The Amtrak station is located nearby at 1050 Kettner Boulevard.

ACCOMMODATIONS

HOTELS: Comic-Con negotiates rates for attendees with a number of nearby hotels. These special rates are posted on www.comic-con.org ahead of time, and the hotels sell out instantly following the post. In fact, most San Diego hotels are almost full within six months of Comic-Con. The Marriott (333 W. Harbor Dr. / 619-234-1500 / $435) is located next door to the Convention Center and fills up fast. Book at least ten months in advance. Within a mile are the Holiday Inn Harbor Bay (1355 N. Harbor Dr. / 619-232-3861, rate unavailable) and Holiday Inn Downtown (1617 First Ave. / 619-239-9600, rate unavailable). You can stay in nearby downtown San Diego at the Western Inn Old Town (3889 Arista St. / 619-298-6888 / $184), Holiday Inn Express (3900 Old Town Ave. / 619-299-7400 / $171), La Quinta Inn (2380 Moore St. / 619-291-0265 / $169), Courtyard Marriott (2435 Jefferson St. / 619-260-8500 / $249), and Best Western Hacienda Hotel (4041 Harney St. / 619-298-4707 / $199). Booking a hotel in Mission Valley will also put you close to the Convention Center.

TICKETS

Comic-Con's popularity has risen so quickly over the past few years that tickets are beginning to sell out. Purchase tickets on www.comic-con.org ahead of time, especially for Saturday's convention. A four-day adult ticket costs $65, which includes entry into Wednesday's preview night. A three-day ticket does not include admittance to Saturday's convention, and costs $55. Single-day admission is approximately $30 for Thursday and Friday, $35 for Saturday, and $20 for Sunday. The gates open at 9:45 each morning; although the entry line can get enormous—arrive by 8:30 A.M. to save yourself some major time in line.

party tip

Those who live in reality should memorize the following acronyms to better prepare themselves for conversation inside the Convention Center:

- LOL—laugh out loud
- BRB—be right back
- SUP—what's up?
- l8ter—later
- GTG—got to go
- ROTFL—rolling on the floor laughing
- SYS—see you soon

GILROY GARLIC FESTIVAL

⊛ Gilroy, California
Last weekend in July
www.gilroygarlicfestival.com

Mark Twain once said that "you can marinate a steak by hanging it on a clothesline anywhere near downtown Gilroy," and that concept is celebrated every summer in this quiet Northern California town. Garlic, the city's main cash crop, is Gilroy's lifeblood, equivalent to Nebraska's corn or Florida's oranges. Knowing that fact, Gilroy is officially the last place you'd expect to see Dracula hang his hat or many women kiss on the first date. Yes folks, this is the biggest garlic festival in the world (Europe has some big ones too) and one of the top food festivals in the country. Putting a "check" next to the Gilroy Garlic Festival on your life's list of things-to-do is priceless, as this event is as memorable as it is pungent. The townspeople and their cooking pots bring in 125,000 visitors from around the world each year for a party that is unmatched in both spirit and taste.

This three-day garlic gala begins at 10:00 A.M. in Christmas Hill Park and goes until 7:00 P.M.,

Friday through Sunday. Arrive early on Friday or on Thursday to beat the crowds, which jam the roads for miles. Over fifty booths are set up, selling souvenirs, crafts, and gourmet food seasoned with over two tons of garlic. Topping the "must-try" list is garlic ice cream, garlic French fries, garlic sausage, and fresh garlic prawns. Wash it all down with some garlic beer or garlic wine; just be careful not to inhale before your first sip. Pick up some garlic honey or garlic soap to send home for a Christmas gift, and wear a garlic braid around your neck to earn full-fledged participant status. Eclipse Gum, the festival's official breath saver, is available at each stop. This party is casual, so don't dress for success. You will not be permitted to bring food or beverages into the festival. Live music including rock, country, and blues is plentiful all weekend long.

TRANSPORTATION

✈ **AIR:** Book flights into San Jose Airport (SJC / www.sjc.org). Car-rental agencies are available.

Ⓑ **BUS / 🚆 TRAIN:** A Greyhound station is located at 7250 Monterey Street in downtown Gilroy. Amtrak is an excellent way to avoid the heavy traffic following the festival. An Amtrak station is also located at 7250 Monterey Street.

Ⓟ **PARKING:** You will be directed to one of a few large parking lots. Free shuttles bring patrons from the lots to the festival.

ACCOMMODATIONS

🏨 **HOTELS:** Book a room at least two months before the festival. Local hotels include the Hilton Garden Inn (6070 Monterey St. / 408-840-7000 / $239), Super 8 (8435 San Ysidro Ave. / 408-848-4108 / $170), and Comfort Inn (8292 Murray Ave. / 408-848-3500 / $140). For a complete listing of hotels visit *www.gilroy-california.com/hotels.*

🛏 **B&BS:** Bed-and-breakfasts are a nice option for Gilroy Garlic. Good reports come from Gilroy Fitzgerald House (7446 Rosanna St. / 408-847-6421 / $165). Space is very limited.

TICKETS

Tickets must be purchased at the gate for $12. Parking is free. Items sold at the festival tend to be pricey, so bring extra cash.

What to Pack
- Hat
- Sunscreen and sunglasses
- Extra cash
- Listerine

party tip

Do everyone around you a favor and try this home remedy for that garlic smell: Wash your entire body with salt and baking soda. Rinse and repeat. Next, wash your body with a coat of toothpaste. Rinse and repeat. After this, take a fork and rub it all over your body while underneath hot water—the metal actually helps to remove the smell! Finally, and this shouldn't have to be said, throw the fork away.

EXOTIC EROTIC BALL

⭐ **San Francisco, California**
Usually the weekend before Halloween
www.exoticeroticball.com

The kinkiest party around is held in the most sexually liberated city in the country over a holiday weekend where anything goes. The Exotic Erotic Ball is proof that sexy prevails over scary when late October rolls around in the City by the Bay. Whips, chains, lingerie, high-heeled boots, leather, and skin are the costumes of choice at this stimulating party, which E! Entertainment TV has dubbed "the world's number one wildest and sexiest party."

This skintight, leather-clad celebration of the flesh is not for the meek, the shy, or those who like clothing. Rather, it's a tribute to the most erotic depths of the human mind, where attendees are encouraged to don costumes that express their wild side. Due to increasing crowds, the venue was relocated in 2008 to Treasure Island, an enormous waterside property which served as a location for the 1939 World's Fair. With its

new setting in the middle of the San Francisco Bay, the E.E.B. estimates a weekend crowd of 30,000 masqueraders of all ages. Over a million people have attended since its inception in the 1970s.

The weekend kicks off on Friday at the Exotic Erotic Expo, which is the warmup to the huge party on Saturday. The expo features over 100 booths of erotic art and fashion, lingerie and costumes, adult products, adult film stars, and yes, a human petting zoo. It's important to note that this is not a porn convention but an event attended equally by men and women who enjoy the opportunity to escape the mainstream for a weekend. The expo is divided into two sessions, from noon to 6:00 P.M., and from 7:00 P.M. to 11:00 P.M. Many partygoers head to the Friday sessions to find an outfit for the masquerade ball on Saturday.

Victoria holds no secrets at the Exotic Erotic Ball that takes place on Saturday from 8:00 P.M. to 2:00 A.M. Creativity, lack of inhibition, and the desire to be outrageous make for an absolute one-of-a-kind experience. Multiple stages host big-name musicians, DJs, exotic dancers, and burlesque acts. Onstage games include Masochism Tango and Lesbian First Kiss, as well as the infamous costume contest, which awards $15,000 to the winners. Body painting, bondage, and other novelty acts perform in between the headlining bands that have recently included George Clinton, Snoop Dogg, Tommy Lee, and Flavor Flav. Loosen up your choker collar and wander around to a huge scope of performers and side shows.

TRANSPORTATION

AIR: Book flights into San Francisco International Airport (SFO / *www.flysfo.com*). Car-rental agencies and taxis are available.

TAXIS: It's highly recommended that you take a taxi from the airport to your hotel, and also use a taxi service to Treasure Island and back. San Francisco cab companies include City Wide (415-920-0700), Bayshore Cab (415-648-4444), Metro Cab (415-920-0715), Black and White Checker (415-468-9090), and Yellow Cab (415-626-2345).

PARKING: Due to limited space on Treasure Island, motorists must park at nearby Pac Bell park. From Pac Bell, patrons will be shuttled to the event in the lap of luxury by a fleet of 120 biodiesel limo-style buses.

BUS / TRAIN: Two Greyhound stations are located at 425 Mission Street and 155 Freemont Street. The Amtrak station is located at 425 Mission Street.

ACCOMMODATIONS

HOTELS: You can stay anywhere in San Francisco, or you can stay at one of two nearby fetish-friendly hotels which offer special deals to Exotic Erotic Ball attendees.

Downtown hotels include Holiday Inn Gateway (1500 N. Van Ness Ave. / 888-465-4329 / $135), Hyatt (345 Stockton St. / 415-398-1234 / $299), Fairmont (950 Mason St. / 415-772-5000 / $399), and Marriott (500 Post St. / 415-771-8600 / $269). Visit *www.priceline.com* for competitive San Francisco hotel rates.

For a true Exotic Erotic Ball experience check into Renoir Hotel (45 Mcallister St. / 415-626-5200 / $169, two-night minimum) or Hotel Whitcomb (1231 Market St. / 415-626-8000 / $175). Both are located just a few miles from Treasure Island and will provide lower rates if you mention the event.

TICKETS

Saturday general admission is $69 if you purchase tickets early on the event website. VIP tickets include red-carpet entry, backstage access to mingle with celebrities and adult film stars, access to the VIP lounge with finger foods and a private cash bar, and one free drink. These tickets cost $150 if you purchase early online. All tickets are also available through *www.ticketmaster.com*.

Tickets to the early Friday Exotic Erotic Expo session, from noon to 6:00 P.M. are $20. Entrance to the later session, from 7:00 P.M. to 11:00 P.M. is $35. Purchase tickets on the event website.

party tip

The Exotic Erotic Ball is just the tip of the iceberg in San Francisco over Halloween weekend. The city bursts at the seams with decadent costumed extravaganzas, and your ball outfit will work just fine wherever you go. The streets are full of hedonistic Halloweenists, as many nightclubs throw S&M-flavored celebrations.

WATERFRONT BLUES FESTIVAL

⊛ Portland, Oregon
Week of July 4
www.waterfrontbluesfest.com

The largest blues festival west of the Mississippi combines unparalleled music with a good cause, while preserving the environment. The positive atmosphere and gorgeous downtown Portland backdrop are enhanced by the festival's stellar location on the banks of the Willamette River. This multi-award-winning gathering is a music fan's opportunity to listen to the purest of blues at a top-notch festival.

Portland beckons fans from across the globe, who make the long pilgrimage to attend this highly recognized music industry event. As the recent recipient of the "Northwest Blues Event of the Year" award, this 120,000-person concert has established itself as a true heavyweight act. It started as a one-day gig in 1987, but has blossomed into five days, four stages,

and 150 musicians. The Waterfront Blues Festival separates itself from the pack not only by atmosphere and attendance, but in terms of the musical acts. Many "blues" festivals incorporate multiple genres of music, hoping to appeal to a wide array of people, and thus losing validity with true blues fans in the process. The Waterfront Blues Festival maintains the integrity of its name, while reigning as the second-largest blues festival in the country.

It typically beings on July 2 or 3, and runs for five consecutive days. Performances begin at noon and end at 10:00 P.M. Headliners of past festivals have included John Mayall, Buddy Guy, Etta James, Dirty Dozen Brass Band, Greyboy Allstars, Double Trouble, Ike Turner and the Kings of Rhythm, and Johnny Lang. The evenings are reserved for rhythm and blues dance parties or film tributes to artists such as Jimi Hendrix, which go until 1:00 A.M. On the evening of July 4 a massive fireworks display ignites the city skyline.

An absolute must is a trip on the "blues cruise." The *Portland Spirit*, a three-deck party ship, sets sail twice a day, at 2:30 P.M. and 10:15 P.M. The boat makes a trip down the Willamette River for two hours in the afternoon and about three hours in the evening. Headlining acts play aboard the ship while partygoers boogie, chasing the blues with brews. Tickets cost approximately $30 and should be purchased in advance, as this popular trip sells out fast. Cruise at least once, if not more.

All proceeds from the concert go toward the Oregon Food Bank. The week's net proceeds come in at approximately $500,000 plus close to 100,000 pounds of canned goods. In 2007 the Waterfront Blues Festival went green. Land Rover, one of the major sponsors, offsets the 124 pounds of carbon dioxide used by musicians to travel to the event through a carbon neutral program. This program restores native forests to replenish

what has been taken from the environment through travel. An Eco Shuttle transports artists using 100 percent biodiesel, carbon-friendly fuel. Furthermore, the festival is powered with renewable energy, which saves 11,000 pounds of CO_2.

TRANSPORTATION

AIR: Book flights into Portland International Airport (PDX / *www.flypdx.com*) located thirteen miles from downtown Portland.

TAXIS: It is easiest to take a taxi to your hotel, or to drive to your hotel and either walk or take a taxi to the festival. Local cab companies include Radio Taxi (503-227-1212) and Broadway Cab (503-227-1234).

PARKING: There are three parking lots that easily service the festival grounds. Motorists can park at the east bank of the river and walk across the Hawthorne Bridge or East Bank Esplanade. Lots are located at SW Fourth and Yamhill, SW Third and Alder, or SW First and Jefferson.

LIGHT-RAIL / STREETCAR: Portland's MAX Light Rail (*www.trimet.org*) and Portland Street Car (*www.portlandstreetcar.org*) are excellent ways to get to the festival and to tour the city. The MAX stops at SW First and Oak Street, just one block from the festival.

BUS / TRAIN: The Greyhound station is located at 550 NW Sixth Avenue, and the Amtrak station is located at 800 NW Sixth Avenue.

ACCOMMODATIONS

HOTELS: Many multiday festivals allow camping or RV parking; however, the urban location of the Waterfront Blues Festival restricts festivalgoers to hotels. The Marriott (1401 SW Naito Parkway / 503-226-7600 / $179) is located across the street, while the RiverPlace Hotel (1510 SW Harbor Way / 503-228-3233 / $311) is directly adjacent to the park. Visit *www.travelportland.com* for a further selection of hotels.

TICKETS

Tickets can be purchased on a day-by-day basis for $8 plus two cans of food at the gate. A five-day pass can be purchased for $25 by visiting *www.ticketswest.com* or by calling 800-992-8499.

The Blues Cruise tickets should be purchased a month in advance by visiting *www.ticketswest.com* or calling 800-992-8499. They cost approximately $30 per cruise.

party tip

While in Portland, take a ride on the sleek Euro-designed streetcar, which makes a 4.8-mile loop around some beautiful sections of the city. The RiverPlace neighborhood is the perfect stop for restaurants, shops, and galleries.

OREGON BREWER'S FESTIVAL

⊛ **Portland, Oregon**
Last full weekend in July
www.oregonbrewfest.com

The brewing industry has labeled Oregon "the beer capital of America," making it a destination location for barley and hops fanatics everywhere. It makes perfect sense that beer lovers from across the globe pour into Portland in the summertime for a brewer's festival with the most consistently high-caliber beer selection in the country.

The event begins on Thursday before the last weekend in July with Portland's mayor leading a brewer's parade down the city sidewalks. The procession of bagpipers, drummers, and beer guzzlers ends at Tom McCall Waterfront Park, where the mayor ceremoniously taps the first keg with the mighty swing of a wooden mallet. With the four-day beer free-for-all officially underway, Waterfront Park prepares for an invasion of 60,000 visitors and the $1.5 million they bring into Portland over the weekend. The gates open at noon and close at 9:00 P.M.—arrive early to avoid lines.

There are four entrances, the main entrance being at the corner of SW Oak Street and Bill Naito Parkway. Avoid the long lines here by entering under the Morrison Street Bridge, Bill Naito Parkway and Pine Street, and near the river walkway at Pine Street.

Head for the mug and token tents upon entering the park. You'll need to purchase a $4 mug in order to partake in the festival goodies—no need to bring your favorite goblet. Cash does not work, so trade dollars for wooden tokens. Four tokens, or four dollars, buys you a glass of beer, while one token buys a few ounces. A smart idea is to purchase one token worth of suds from an array of breweries, decide on your favorites, and revisit them for a full mug. Some keen observation has shown that three of the one-token pours usually are equal to a

four-token mug's worth of beer. You can save money by purchasing tastes over full mugs. Smart, efficient beer drinking is necessary at a brew-ha-hoedown like this.

Over seventy different breweries from fourteen states are represented at the festival. Unlike many beer festivals, each brewery is only allowed to submit one tasty beverage. The result is an incredibly high-quality showcase of talent, as only the cream of the crop is represented. The festival draws craft beer manufacturers rather than traditional brew houses. Craft brewing relies on malt and aging to enhance, rather than lighten, the flavor of beer. The results are aromas of citrus, flowers, and herbs. Crowd favorites from years past have included Hop Rod Rye Ale from Bear Republic Brewing Company, Zon from Boulevard Brewing Company, White Lightning Whiskey Stout from McMenamins, and Farmhouse Summer Ale from Jack Russell Brewing Company.

Good vibes, live music, a great crowd, and incredible brews have helped the festival to earn its well-deserved reputation as one of the top beer parties in the country. The crowd takes the short walk to Portland's bars immediately following the day's tasting. Hot spots include East Bank Saloon (727 SE Grand Ave.), the Bridgeport Brewing Company (1313 NW Marshall St.), Kells Pub (112 SW Second Ave.), and Dublin Pub (6821 SW Beaverton Hillsdale).

TRANSPORTATION

✈ **AIR:** Book flights into Portland International Airport (PDX / *www.flypdx.com*) located thirteen miles from downtown Portland.

🚕 **TAXIS:** It is easiest to take a taxi to your hotel, or to drive to your hotel and either walk or take a taxi to the festival. Local cab companies include Radio Taxi (503-227-1212) and Broadway Cab (503-227-1234).

🚲 **BIKING:** Finding a parking spot can be rough due to the sheer size of the event, and driving to a beer festival is never a good idea. There's a bike parking area on the northeast side of the park, along the seawall. Biking is a very common means of transportation in Portland. Waterfront Bicycle Rentals (315 SW Montgomery St. / 503-227-1719) rents cruisers from its downtown location.

🚋 **STREETCAR/LIGHT-RAIL:** Portland's MAX Light Rail (*www.trimet.org*) and Portland Street Car (*www.portlandstreetcar.org*) are excellent ways to get to the festival and to tour the city. The MAX stops at SW First and Oak Street, just one block from the festival.

ACCOMMODATIONS

🏨 **HOTELS:** Stay downtown to keep logistical planning to a minimum. You'll be spending most of your time hopping from hotel to festival to downtown bars and restaurants. The Marriott (1401 SW Naito Parkway / 503-226-7600 / $199) is located across the street, while the RiverPlace Hotel (1510 SW Harbor Way / 503-228-3233 / $239) is directly adjacent to the park. Visit *www.travelportland. com* for a further selection of hotels.

TICKETS

No admission fee. You'll need to purchase one $4 mug for the entire weekend and wooden tokens, at a price of $1 per token. Cash can be used to purchase food.

What to Pack
- Sealed water bottle—unsealed beverages are not allowed in
- Summer clothing
- Sunscreen
- Scottish cap
- Kazoo

party tip

The buzz beer of this festival is Watermelon Wheat, brewed by San Francisco's 21st Amendment Brewery. This delectable melon brew, made with fresh watermelon juice, has been a staple at the Oregon Brewer's Festival for years. Watermelon Wheat's increasing popularity has forced festival organizers to periodically stop serving it due to a fear of running dry. Get in line early for the event's version of liquid gold!

PENDLETON ROUNDUP

⭐ **Pendleton, Oregon**
First Saturday through the second Saturday in September
www.pendletonroundup.com

L et'er Buck! This four-day rodeo and week-long boot-stompin' party is the largest of its kind in the world. The buckshot hits the target each September in Pendleton, Oregon, a tiny town that's multiplied by three times its normal size during the famous Pendleton Roundup.

Located 200 miles east of Portland, Pendleton and its 15,000 inhabitants have played host to cowboy heaven since 1909. The Roundup is unique in the fact that it celebrates frontier life by continuing the traditions that inspired the rodeo so many years ago. American Indians play a huge role with flamboyantly colorful outfits and tomahawk mastery that could take the eyelash off a fly from fifty yards. You may be able to send a text message in under ten seconds, but can you catch a greased pig in under a minute? If you want to find out, then this celebration is for you.

The Roundup stretches between the first and second Saturdays in September. The first three days of the week include parades, concerts, and the PBR (Professional Bull Riders) Classic. The next four days, however, are when the rubber meets the wagon trail. Beginning on Wednesday, awaken to the Cowboy Breakfast at Stillman Park—just be sure your cholesterol levels can handle it. The late mornings are filled with events like the American Indian Beauty Contest, before the 1:15 P.M. rodeo start time. A slew of hair-raising rodeo events run the gamut—from bareback riding to steer wrestling to, yes, wild cow milking. Over 30,000 mustached madmen and denim-clad ladies pack the grandstands to witness the whiplash action that has sent many a fearless cowboy to the hospital.

The Roundup evenings are quirky, hilarious, and a ton of fun. After the rodeo you can head to the Happy Canyon Saloon, a wild-western-style jam-packed bar where you can gamble until the wee hours. The Happy Canyon Dance Hall begins thumping at around 9:00 P.M., with DJs spinning the hottest country dance songs while huge TVs display bull-riding videos—otherwise known as "cowboy porn." This scene repeats itself Wednesday though Saturday, although Friday and Saturday are the biggest party nights.

When attending the Pendleton Roundup it's important to look the part. You're better off dressing like the Outlaw Josey Wales than you are in khakis and a sweater vest. The crowd is classic and the experience is one of a kind.

TRANSPORTATION

✈ **AIR:** You can book a flight into Portland International Airport (PDX / *www.flypdx.com*), rent a car, and drive the 200 miles to Pendleton. Or you can fly directly to Pendleton Airport (PDT / *www.pendleton.or.us/airport.htm*). You'll probably connect on Horizon Air through a major northwest city. There is a Hertz Car Rental at the Pendleton Airport (541-276-3183)—book a car early due to crowding in the city. The difference in cost between this airport and Portland International is often minimal.

🚌 **SHUTTLE:** There are a couple of private shuttles that run back and forth from the Roundup grounds to the town, leaving every fifteen minutes.

The shuttle pickup / dropoff points are located at the Dairy Queen (1415 SW Court Ave.) and along Main Street. You can also walk, which takes approximately twenty minutes.

Ⓟ **PARKING:** If you need to park, try the Chamber of Commerce (501 S. Main St.), which has a large lot.

ACCOMMODATIONS

🛏 **HOTELS:** They fill very fast and many people make their reservations up to a year in advance. Hotels include Holiday Inn Express (600 SE Nye Ave. / 541-966-6520 / $109), Oxford Suites (2400 SW Court Pl. / 541-276-6000 / rate unavailable), America's Best Value Inn (201 SW Court Ave. / 541-276-1400 / $200), Best Western (400 SE Nye Ave. / 541-276-2135 / $86), and Red Lion Inn (304 SE Nye Ave. / 541-276-6111 / $191). For further hotel listings visit the Chamber of Commerce at *www.pendleton.thechamber.net/index.asp*.

🚐 **RV:** RV parks with hookups are also available. Try Mountain View RV Park (1375 SE Third St. / 541-276-1041), the Wild Rose RV Park (1500 SE Byers Ave. / 541-278-7805), and Wildhorse Resort & Casino RV Park (7277 Hwy 331 / 541-278-2274).

TICKETS

Rodeo tickets range from $14 to $21, depending on the date and type of seating. Tickets to Wednesday and Thursday rodeos are a couple of dollars less expensive than weekend tickets, and grandstand covered seating is a couple of dollars more than uncovered bleacher seating. Tickets do sell out, so it's a wise idea to purchase them ahead of time. Visit *www.ticketmaster.com* or call 503-224-4400. Tickets to the Happy Canyon night shows are sold separately for $9 to $15 and can also be purchased via Ticketmaster. For information and availability call the Pendleton Roundup at 800-45-RODEO.

party tip

You'll score major points if you know the Texas two-step before hitting the dance floor. Stand with your feet facing your partner, put your right hand on your partner's waist and take your partner's hand in your left. Step forward quickly with your left foot on the first beat of the song, step forward quickly with your right foot on the second beat, step forward slowly with your left foot on the third beat, pause on the fourth beat, step forward slowly with your right foot on the fifth beat, pause on the sixth beat, and then put your left foot even with the right. Repeat. If you get confused, slip a cheat sheet underneath your ten-gallon hat.

Washington

KENNEWICK HYDROPLANE RACES

⊛ Kennewick, Washington
Last full weekend in July
www.waterfollies.com

The focal point of this massive gathering in southern Washington is an exhilarating weekend full of hydroplane boat races and near-fatal crashes. The Pacific Northwesterners show up in droves to witness two full days of motorboat madness on the Columbia River, where the shoreline excitement matches the high-speed spectacle on the water. This is the aquatic equivalent of a NASCAR event, or more appropriately, to the Daytona 500.

Kennewick is part of the Tri-Cities, an area of Washington that's made up of three neighboring towns—Richland, Kennewick, and Pasco. The Tri-Cities are located where the Snake, Yakima, and Columbia Rivers converge, providing the perfect setting for boat racing and beer drinking. As many as 60,000 spectators pour into Columbia Park East at the end of July to witness this annual extravaganza and partake in its riverside festivities. The event is nationally broadcast to an audience of 3 million people.

Hydroplane fandom can be summed up fairly easily. There are rabid, full-fledged speedboat addicts who know the racers, know the engines, and can tell you the difference between horizontal stabilizers and single vertical tail propulsion. The majority of onlookers, however, come to party, troll for singles, and watch "really fast" boats. Unlimited Racing, the class that is seen in Kennewick, utilizes aviation engines to power the vessels. At full speed, only a small portion of the boat is actually in contact with the water!

The shores of the Columbia River are lined with beach clubs, bleacher seating, and beer gardens. A common practice is to spend one day on the Kennewick shore and the next day on the Pasco side.

The races begin at about 9:00 A.M. on Saturday and Sunday and go on until late afternoon; they are followed by a high-energy air show. Partygoers can purchase general admission tickets, watch from the bleachers, or stroll along the shores. Also available, and strongly recommended, are a variety of special Tri-City Water Follies passes. These limited viewing tickets provide access to the racer's pit area and include complimentary meals and admittance to keg spouts or private beer gardens. Many local corporations set up private tents with amenities of their own, and boat owners tie their vessels together at the far ends of the course, forming their own exclusive shindigs.

Head to either Kennewick or Richland after the day's events have concluded. The Tri-Cities area has recently become a hotbed for wine-loving retirees who have fallen in love with the climate, the landscape, and the abundance of delicious vino.

TRANSPORTATION

Tri-Cities is three and a half hours from Seattle and two hours from Spokane. You may save $50 or so by flying into Spokane, but fares to the Tri-Cities Airport are very reasonable. If you don't like flying into a small airport, then Spokane may be a better choice.

✈ **AIR:** Tri-Cities Airport (PSC / *www.portofpasco .org*) is a three-runway airport serviced by United and Delta. Many local hotels offer free shuttle service to and from the airport; however, taxis and car rentals are available. Book in advance. Spokane International Airport (GEG / *www.spokane airports.net*) is two hours away and has many car-rental agencies.

🛈 **TAXIS:** A-1 Tri-Cities Cab Co. (509-547-7777).

🚌 **SHUTTLE:** A number of shuttle buses run from throughout the Tri-Cities into Columbia Park, providing easy transportation into the races. Transit Center Service buses leave Knight Street Transit Center in Richland and Huntington Street Transit Center in Kennewick every hour from 8:00 A.M. to 11:00 A.M., departing fifteen minutes after the final race. If you want to leave early, hop on the Columbia Park Shuttle, which runs to the Transit Centers in Richland and Kennewick every hour from 11:00 A.M. to 3:00 P.M. Buses that service the Pasco side follow the same schedule.

🅿 **PARKING:** Onsite parking is available for $5 on Saturday and $10 on Sunday.

ACCOMMODATIONS

🏨 **HOTELS:** Stay in Kennewick or Richland for the most action and easy transport to the races. Book your hotel four months in advance to be safe. In Kennewick are Best Western (4001 W. Twenty-seventh Ave. / 509-586-1332 / $106), Comfort Inn (7801 W. Quinalt Ave. / 509-783-8396 / $85),

Fairfield Inn (7809 W. Quinalt Ave. / 509-783-2164 / $129), Guest House International Inn & Suites (5616 W. Clearwater Ave. / 509-735-2242 / $74), and Days Inn (2811 W. Second Ave. / 509 735-9511 / $100). In Richland are Hampton Inn (486 Bradley Blvd. / 509-943-4400 / $109), Red Lion (802 George Washington Way / 509-946-7611 / $130), Days Inn (615 Jadwin Ave. / 509-943-4611 / $57), Clarion Hotel (1515 George Washington Way / 509-946-4121 / $105), and Holiday Inn Express (1970 Center Parkway / 888-400-9714 / $131).

B&BS: The area has an assortment of wonderful and reasonably priced bed-and-breakfasts. In Kennewick try Cabin Suites (115 N. Yelm St. / 509-374-3966 / $75) and Cherry Chalet (8101 W. Tenth / 509-783-6406 / $85).

RV: For $350 you can park an RV on the Kennewick side, close to the pit area. This package includes event and pit passes for four people and campground access from Friday to Monday. Additional tickets cost $45, and there are no hookups. Visit the event website to download an application.

TICKETS

Two-day general admission tickets cost $25, go on sale in the beginning of July, and can be upgraded for $5 on race day for bleacher access. Saturday GA is $15 and Sunday GA costs $25. For $10 per day you can upgrade your GA tickets to include pit access. Special Viewing Area tickets go on sale at the beginning of May and sell out fast. The popular Hydro Hot Spot costs $99, includes two days admission and pit passes, a free lunch on Sunday, and access to a private cash bar. For $350 the Starting Line Club tickets include admission, breakfast, and lunch on both days for two people, as well as free keg beer and souvenirs. Roundtable Club is similar to Starting Line, but allows entrance and amenities for six people. Bulldog Beach Club, on the Pasco side, costs $225 for two people. Visit *www.waterfollies.com* to download and fill out a reservation form for special passes. Margarita Village, also on the Pasco shore, is a privately run party that charges a $10 cover.

What to Pack
- Binoculars
- Sunscreen
- Comfortable shoes
- Cheap sunglasses
- Detailed knowledge of the hull point design

---

party tip

Avoid showing up on a "Worst Accidents Caught on Video" cable special by keeping an eye on the water at all times. These speedboats are occasionally swept out of the water and into the crowd with the announcer screaming "can you believe this!" as disaster ensues. Avoid playing chicken with a mass of steel. Be on your toes and be prepared to move quickly while the races are underway.

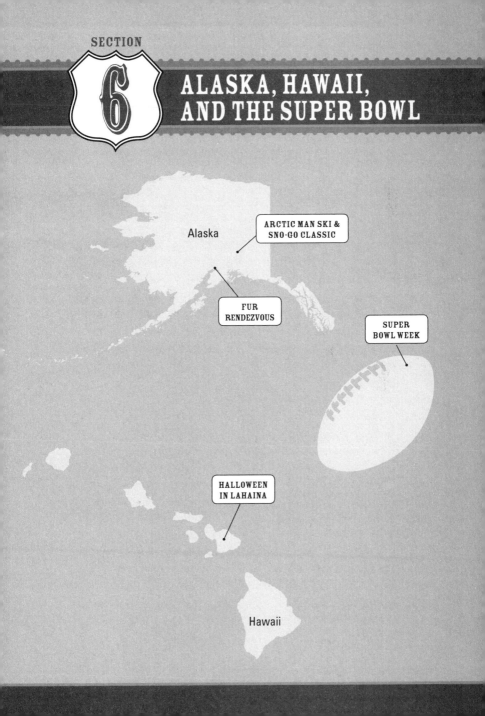

SECTION

6

ALASKA, HAWAII, AND THE SUPER BOWL

Alaska

ARCTIC MAN SKI & SNO-GO CLASSIC

FUR RENDEZVOUS

SUPER BOWL WEEK

HALLOWEEN IN LAHAINA

Hawaii

Alaska

FUR RENDEZVOUS

⊛ **Anchorage, Alaska**
Ten days, usually mid- to late February
www.furrondy.net

Over 65 percent of the city's residents, plus 10,000 out-of-towners, infiltrate the streets of Anchorage in mid-February for Alaska's version of Mardi Gras—on ice. Fur Rendezvous—the largest winter festival in North America—features outdoor winter recreational activities that range from the serious to the plain wacky, in a creative effort to unite the city and celebrate the tail end of a long, cold winter.

The history of the event dates back to the 1930s when a man named Vern Johnson realized that Anchorage citizens needed a winter carnival to break up the doldrums of shoveling snow and petting their dogs. He decided to stage the spectacle to coincide with the miners' and trappers' journey into town to auction off their goods. Sports like hockey, skiing, sled racing, and Native Alaskan blanket tossing were added into the mix, and the result was magical. In order to attract more visitors, the celebration leads into the world-famous Iditarod Trail Sled Dog Race. The Fur Rendezvous is the perfect opportunity to experience an off-the-beaten-trail celebration as well as one of the premier endurance contests in the world.

If you've ever wanted to play softball while wearing snowshoes (beerball), or have yearned to bowl on a frozen river with a cocktail in hand, then Fur Rondy is right up your icy alley. The festival begins on a Friday and ends ten days later on Sunday. A fireworks display and the crowning of Miss Fur Rondy kicks off the action in Small Boat Harbor, and the polar shenanigans ensue from there. The three-day long World Championship Dog

Sled Race (not the Iditarod) brings out the crowd in droves, as does the Frostbite Footrace, where costumed runners start and finish in front of Glacier Brewhouse (737 W. Fifth Ave.). Reindeer Races, the famous Grand Parade, Big Air Snowboard Challenges, and the never-ending Eskimo blanket tossing contests on Third Avenue and C Street are all daytime highlights. Calling all die-hard competitors—the Outhouse Races feature participants on skis dragging an outhouse down a hill while a teammate sits on the throne inside. Yes you can participate, but please resist the temptation to bring a magazine. The events never stop, and neither does the entertainment. Ice sculptures and Native Alaskan music fills the downtown area, as beefed-up huskies attempt to pull large objects during the canine feats of strength.

The Jim Beam Jam is the annual Fur Rondy opening-night dance party with live music and indoor displays of power—that is, Sumo Suit Wrestling. The location changes, so check the website. The Miners and Trappers Ball (Egan Center, 555 W. Fifth Ave.) is held on the second Saturday of the carnival, and is the second largest costume event in the state.

TRANSPORTATION

AIR: Book flights into Anchorage International Airport (ANC / *www.dot.state.ak.us/anc*), located eight miles from downtown Anchorage. Car-rental agencies are available. Anchorage is a three-hour flight from Seattle.

SHUTTLE / B BUS: The Municipality of Anchorage People Mover Bus runs from the airport to downtown every half hour from 6:00 A.M. to 11:00 P.M. Eagle River Shuttle (907-694-8888) and Airport-Valley Shuttle (907-373-4359) will take you back and forth from downtown. Call for a reservation.

TAXIS: Anchorage taxi companies include Alaska Yellow Cab (907-563-5353), Tommy's Cab Shop (907-272-5229), Alaska Cab Co. (907-562-6805), and Aaa Metro Cab (907-677-7000).

TRAIN: The Alaska Railroad travels to Anchorage from Fairbanks, Whittier, and Seward. Visit *www.akrr.com* for schedules and information.

ACCOMMODATIONS

HOTELS: Although the Fur Rendezvous is large, hotels do not sell out. You may want to consider staying at the Sheraton, as Fur Rondy events often take place there. Downtown Anchorage hotels include Sheraton (401 E. Sixth Ave. / 907-276-8700 / $117), Comfort Inn (111 Ship Creek Ave. / 907-277-6887 / $100), Hawthorn Suites (1110 W. Eighth Ave. / 800-527-1133 / $140), Inlet Tower Hotel & Suites (1200 L St. / 907-276-0110 / $109), Ramada Inn (115 E. Third Ave. / 907-272-7561 / $99), Marriott (820 W. Seventh Ave. / 907-279-8000 / $130), Howard Johnson Plaza Hotel (239 W. Fourth Ave. / 907-793-5500 / $89), and Days Inn (321 E. Fifth Ave. / 907-276-7226 / $69).

TICKETS

Anyone can enter the contests, and it's highly recommended that you do so. After all, this is not supposed to be a spectator event! Check the event website (*www.furrondy.net*) a couple of months in advance for an event schedule, timetable, and location information. Download a registration form, send it in with payment, and you'll be an official Fur Rondy "athlete." Snowshoe softball costs $225 per team, outhouse races cost $150 per team, and you can enter the ice sculpture competition for $35. Tickets to the Jim Beam Jam ($20) and Miners and Trappers Ball ($45) can be purchased prior to arrival or right at the door. Also, a number of buffets take place around town during the Rondy and at reasonable prices, too—an all-you-can-eat seafood buffet costs $10 and chili feeds are $5.

party tip

One of the more bizarre aspects of this party is a huge contingent of memorabilia collectors obsessed with Fur Rendezvous "pins." Each year since 1939, these typical promotional buttons have been sold to attendees to raise money for Fur Rendezvous—they're similar to pins given out to support political candidates. Some of the older ones fetch up to $1,000 on eBay. Make sure you hold on to yours—it may rise in value quicker than your 401(k).

ARCTIC MAN SKI & SNO-GO CLASSIC

⊛ **Summit Lake, Alaska**
Wednesday though Sunday in early April
www.arcticman.com

A slew of hardened wintry revelers assemble in Alaska for the state's largest snowmobile event, turning early April in Summit Lake into the biggest party across the Last Frontier. Getting to this frosty frolic may be difficult, but arctic action is intense, the partying is constant, and the experience creates memories to last a lifetime.

Arctic Man has been taking place near Paxson, 160 miles south of Fairbanks, for close to twenty-five years. Around 14,000 grizzly Alaskans leave Fairbanks and Anchorage in a mass entourage of campers, RVs, and trucks en route to the Hoodoo Mountains, aka "the middle of nowhere," for this highly anticipated yearly pilgrimage.

The core race of this five-day competition is a high-velocity feat of speed and endurance. Held on day three, the race features a team comprised of a skier or snowboarder plus a snowmobiler. The skier or snowboarder starts at a 5,800 foot elevation, and after zooming down the mountain for two miles he or she meets up with a snowmobile partner. The skier grabs hold of a towrope, and the duo flies back uphill at speeds of up to ninety miles per hour. At the peak of the second mountain, the skier lets go and burns 1,200 feet down to the finish line. The course record is just over four minutes and the event is billed as one of the most challenging ski races in the world.

Bringing a snowmobile to this event is recommended but not necessary, as the days are spent chewing up countless acreages of fresh powder, driving to and from the races, and sun bathing atop RVs. The evenings are madness at the Arctic Man parking lot; highlights include bonfire hopping, an incredible fireworks display over the desolate, snow-covered Hoodoo Mountains, and dancing at the massive "Bar Tent."

"Manufacturer's Row," located in the parking lot, is a great place to load up on new winter gear. Hopefully "bluebird" days are in the forecast, although some pretty nasty weather can blow through. Depending on visibility, the aurora borealis can be seen at night, lending added mysticism to the crisp Arctic Man experience.

This is obviously a camping party, although there are a couple of lodges close by. Attendees wrap themselves in goose down zero-degree bags, sleeping in their trucks, or if they're lucky, their RVs. You'll see camper vehicles from the 1960s and 1970s that look as though they've made the journey to each Arctic Man race since the beginning. The engine buzz from snowmobiles is nonstop, so bring earplugs. Men should grow a beard and women should leave their makeup kit at home.

TRANSPORTATION

Enjoying the Arctic Man experience to the fullest requires a fair share of organization and legwork for out-of-towners. You'll have to fill out a parking form, rent a camper and snowmobiles, pack the proper equipment, and make often icy treks into the Hoodoo Mountains.

AIR: Fairbanks International Airport (AKI / www.dot.state.ak.us/faiiap) is located three hours from Summit Lake. Anchorage International Airport (ANC / www.dot.state.ak.us/anc/aiawlcm) is located approximately four and a half hours away.

🚗 **AUTO RENTAL:** You can rent an SUV from car-rental agencies located at the airport. In this case you'll be without the comforts of home, but at least you'll have four-wheel drive, which is a necessity. It's possible to rent an RV in Fairbanks or Anchorage for approx $100 per day plus mileage charges. Make a reservation as far in advance as possible. Try USA RV Rentals (*www.usarvrentals.com* / 866-814-0253), Adventures in Alaska (*www.adventuresakrv.com* / 907-458-7368), or Canada Alaska USA Motorhomes (*www.canadamotorhomes.com*).

🅡 **SNOWMOBILE RENTAL:** Having your own snowmobile, or at least a couple for your group, is optimal. Although many outfits in Fairbanks or Anchorage offer snowmobile tours, we were only able to track down one snowmobile rental company. Unfortunately it's located in the farther of the two cities, Anchorage. Alaska Snow Safaris (888-414-7669 / *www.snowmobile-alaska.com*) has rates starting at $150 per day. A free trailer is included when you rent more than one machine, and multimachine trailers are available.

ACCOMMODATIONS

"PARKING PADS": These are 15' × 70' spaces. Up to twenty people have been known to cram themselves into a single parking pad during Arctic Man; the cost being $100. Pads include access to outhouses, dumpsters, medical care, and a plowed parking space. Send an e-mail to *arcticmn@gci.net* with your name, phone number, e-mail address, and the number of spaces you'd like to purchase. After being contacted by event organizers, visit *www.arcticman.com* and download a parking registration form. Mail the completed form, along with payment, to the address provided by March 15. Access to the snowmobile races is free.

🏨 **HOTELS:** If you crave the Arctic Man extravaganza minus the camping, try Denali Highway Cabins (HC 72 Box 7292 / 907-822-5972 / $150).

What to Pack
- Cooking supplies and food
- Ski socks
- Snow pants and ski coat
- Goggles, helmet, and a hat
- Gortex sleeping bag
- Camera with slow shutter speed to capture aurora borealis

---

party tip

Nothing beckons the ultimate in meat-headed displays of male testosterone like a high-speed recreational vehicle, and nothing will put a damper on your day like an avalanche. Avoid driving your snowmobile on slopes of thirty-five to forty-five degrees in an area where the wind has deposited a large amount of snow. If you're caught in a slide, drive toward the edges rather than straight down. Another trick, which hopefully you'll never have to use, is the "spit test." After being caught in an avalanche, it's difficult to know whether you're facing up or down. Dribble some spit, and the direction it moves will tell you where your head is.

Hawaii

HALLOWEEN IN LAHAINA

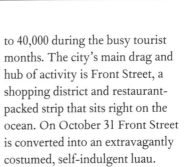

⭐ Maui, Hawaii
October 31
www.lahainahalloween.com

Most of the world tends to think of Hawaii as a little slice of paradise. Our blood pressure can drop twenty points simply by daydreaming of those enchanting islands with perfect beaches, seductive waterfalls, and divine sunsets. What most people fail to realize, however, is that when the sun goes down, Hawaiians like to party as much as those of us stuck on the mainland. Halloween in Lahaina, Maui, is an astounding celebration that has easily taken the rank of the Aloha State's wildest shindig. Not to mention the fact that anyone who attends is guaranteed to get leid.

Lahaina is the largest city in West Maui and the gateway to some popular resorts north of town. Although its population is around 10,000, Lahaina attracts up to 40,000 during the busy tourist months. The city's main drag and hub of activity is Front Street, a shopping district and restaurant-packed strip that sits right on the ocean. On October 31 Front Street is converted into an extravagantly costumed, self-indulgent luau.

If the ocean swells matched the swelling number of Halloween participants each year, then local surfers would be very happy. As many as 35,000 tourists and Hawaiians jam Front Street, forcing the area to close to vehicular traffic. Get to Lahaina early in the day if you need to park a car because finding a spot after 4:00 P.M. is nearly impossible, as is sitting down in a restaurant. The notorious Halloween Costume Contest begins at 7:00 P.M. in Banyan Tree Park, located in the heart of Lahaina. The Banyan tree was imported from India in 1873, stands sixty feet tall, and is 200 feet wide—you can't miss it. Two stages are set up for live music, while contestants compete fiercely over the $1,000 prize. This area may be your best bet for a meal without a huge line—delicious food booths are set up near the tree.

Back on Front Street the madness ensues as the witching hour approaches. You'll be hard-pressed to find someone without a costume—it's commonplace to see George Bush and Saddam Hussein sharing a few beers and laughs in a Front Street bar. Moose McGillycuddy's (844 Front St.) is a popular joint with the best happy-hour special in town. Any of the second story bars will suffice, just avoid bar-hopping as you may regret the time spent in line.

Nearby Kapalua Beach was voted "America's Best Beach" in 2006. Just head out of town on Highway 30 to mile marker thirty-two. Continue seven-tenths of a mile past the mile marker and turn down a steep, unmarked road on the left. The beach is 200 yards down the road—park on Highway 30 unless you have four-wheel drive.

TRANSPORTATION

AIR: Book flights into Maui's Kahului Airport (OGG / www.state.hi.us/dot/airports/faq.htm), located twenty-four miles from Lahaina. All major car-rental agencies are available.

TAXIS: Cabs are quite expensive: They charge $3 per mile, and a ride from the airport costs $74. On West Maui use Ali'i Cab (808-661-3688).

BUS: Maui has an inexpensive bus system made up of small van-like buses with seat belts and air-conditioning. The ride from the airport to Lahaina is $1, but you'll have to sit through a number of stops. Visit www.maui.gov/bus or call 808-871-4838.

MOPED/SCOOTER: These vehicles are fun and exciting ways to get about the island. They can cost anywhere between $50 and $150 per day. In Lahaina visit Aloha Toy Store (640 Front St. / 808-662-0888) or Wheels U.S.A. (150 Lahainaluna Rd. / 808-667-7751).

ACCOMMODATIONS

HOTELS: It is best to stay in the center of Lahaina. The city becomes extremely congested, parking is a nightmare, and drinking and driving is an issue. Even if you're sober, many other drivers will not be. The only beachfront hotel is reasonably priced Lahaina Shores Beach Resort (475 Front St. / 808-661-4835 / $179). Other beautiful and reasonable options include Outrigger Condominiums (660 Wainee St. / 866-253-9743 / $169), Lahaina Inn (127 Lahainaluna Rd. / 800-669-3444 / $145),

Best Western (658 Wharf St. / 808-661-3636 / $275, two-night min.), and the Plantation Inn (174 Lahainaluna Rd. / 808-667-9225 / $169).

party tip

While at the beach there's a very good chance that you or a friend will step on a Hawaiian sea urchin. These "hana," as the locals call them, have needle-like spines that jut out from the body and can easily become embedded in the foot of a swimmer. The needles are barbed, so pulling them out without causing damage to the surrounding tissue is impossible. There is, however, a local remedy that works like a charm. The acid in human urine will actually disintegrate the needles and relieve the throbbing pain caused by a sea urchin.

The Super Bowl

SUPER BOWL WEEK

⭐ **The year's host city**
Usually late January to early February
www.SuperBowl.com

This book provided guidance to the 101 greatest parties in America. Thus far, each party mentioned takes place in the same location year after year—that's the rule. But rules are made to be broken. There is no way to be true to the spirit of this travel guide without mentioning one mega-sized bash that rotates between U.S. cities each year.

Super Bowl Sunday does not appear as an official holiday on Hallmark's annual calendar. However, there is not a single event that so widely crosses the boundaries of religion, race, and class the way the National Football League championship game does. An estimated 140 million people tune in to the "Big Game," making it the number-one rated television broadcast each year.

The million-dollar question throughout the week leading up to game day is "What are you doing for the Super Bowl?" The best answer you can give is "I'm going."

The NFL provides three- to five-year notice on the location of each game. The 2009 game will be held in Tampa, and the 2010 game will be played in Miami. The average Super Bowl ticket's face value in 2007 was $600, and by 2011 they are projected to cost $900.

Don't let these projected prices deter you from planning to attend the big game in person. Buyers' remorse is an unfamiliar phrase to those lucky enough to get hold of a ticket. The Super Bowl is a once-in-a-lifetime party that turns the host city into a full week of wild times.

The host city pulls out all the stops in anticipation of the revenue that the game brings in. In 2008, Arizona got a $400 million boost to its economy. Every bar and nightclub takes advantage of the influx of fired-up visitors by throwing evening events from Wednesday to Sunday. The Bud Bowl party offers approximately 5,000 tickets through various promotions for both Friday and Saturday nights. The Coors Light Block Party rocks on the same nights, advertising to the "everyman," and selling tickets for $40—Otis Day and the Knights of *Animal House* fame are among recent performers. The NFL Players Association party opens to the public at 11:00 P.M. on Thursday, and Carmen Electra has been known to host the Leather & Laces charity event on Friday. *Playboy* and *Maxim* throw public galas, and superstars like P. Diddy and Fergie from the Black Eyed Peas often MC club extravaganzas of their own. Bands such as Velvet Revolver and REO Speedwagon play block parties while ESPN cameras capture the excitement. A myriad of private and public parties beckon visitors all week

long. Needless to say, the action is unavoidable.

Awaken by 10:00 A.M. on Super Bowl Sunday, grab some food, and stake your claim at a bar that you've scoped out on the days leading up to the game. Watering holes surrounding the stadium will be packed and rowdy, and your best bet is to beat the crowds.

Stadium tailgates provide for a game-day rush for both ticketed and unticketed fans. Contrary to popular opinion, not everyone who parks at the game actually goes into the game. You'll find a multitude of ticketless brethren who want to be as close to the gridiron as possible to root for their team.

TRANPORTATION

AIR: Air traffic into the host city is responsible for a large portion of the estimated 150,000 people who will arrive in town for the Super Bowl. Airline tickets can be quite reasonable during the Super Bowl—at the time of writing a round-trip ticket from Philadelphia to Phoenix cost $234 one month before the game. If you want to avoid the mass exodus, plan your flight home on Tuesday.

GROUND TRANSPORTATION: It is not recommended that you rent a car. Although car-rental agencies do not jack up rates too high ($47 a day average for an economy car), there really is no need for one. Super Bowl locations are metropolitan areas, and public transportation is quite efficient.

City buses and shuttles run much more frequently than usual, and they service every corner of the city and stadium. Write down some local taxi cab phone numbers in case you need a quick lift.

ACCOMMODATIONS

HOTELS: Here's where you'll pay. Hotels that don't offer frills (Days Inn / Econo Lodge) will raise their regular daily rates from $89 to $400 for the week before and the weekend of the Super Bowl. Your best bet is to book a room near the stadium, a year (or even two!) in advance. Depending on the city, rooms are available weeks beforehand, but your best shot at a decent rate is a ridiculously advanced reservation.

RENTAL HOMES: If you have a group of ten or twelve people, renting a condo or house may be the way to go. Local homeowners try to cash in when the Super Bowl comes to town, and they will rent out their homes in the ballpark of $750–$1,000 per night. Visit *www.vrbo.com*, as avoiding property management companies will save you some cash.

TICKETS

Super Bowl tickets are a highly sought-after commodity. A large bulk goes directly to corporations, and most average fans are forced to purchase them secondhand after the prices have been dramatically increased. If you find a ticket for $1,500, consider yourself lucky—nosebleed seating often sells for over $2,000. StubHub and brokers like TicketLiquidator and Go Tickets sell them online and are among the most reputable.

Entrance to the many block parties, concerts, and club events should be researched via the Internet. Many charge an entrance fee at the door, usually between $20 and $50, while others sell tickets online. The Coors Light Block Party is a great time—general admission is $40 and VIP entrance is $150. Do your homework before arriving in town.

What to Pack
- Team shirts for both teams
- Large foam finger
- Appetite for buffalo wings

---

party tip

Betting on the Super Bowl is as much a tradition as watching it. Office pools, "gentlemen's wagers," and online bookies have become an integral part of the big game. Take advantage of the jovial host city bar atmosphere and make friends with everyone by starting up a betting pool that relies solely on luck and has nothing to do with skill. The coin flip at the beginning of the game is the only true fifty-fifty bet you can make on the Super Bowl—it's either heads or tails. This gamble is always a crowd pleaser, and the bar contingent will be eager to take a piece of the action.

APPENDICES

PARTY TYPE BY REGION

Costume-Required Parties

MIDDLE AMERICA

THE WILD WEST

THE WEST COAST

ALASKA, HAWAII, AND THE SUPER BOWL

Spectator Sporting Events

THE NORTHEAST

THE SOUTHEAST

MIDDLE AMERICA

THE WILD WEST

THE WEST COAST

Optional Active Participation

Music-Based Events

MIDDLE AMERICA

THE WILD WEST

THE WEST COAST

Best for Camping

THE NORTHEAST

THE SOUTHEAST

MIDDLE AMERICA

THE WILD WEST

THE WEST COAST

ALASKA, HAWAII, AND THE SUPER BOWL

Not Exactly Family-Friendly

MONTHLY CALENDAR OF EVENTS

January

February

March

April

May

June

August

THE NORTHEAST

MIDDLE AMERICA

THE WILD WEST

September

THE NORTHEAST

MIDDLE AMERICA

THE WILD WEST

November

December

SUGGESTED SUMMER ROAD TRIPS

Northeast

ONE WEEK

Preakness Stakes in Pimlico, MD (third Saturday in May), to Figawi in Nantucket, MA (Memorial Day weekend)

Honfest in Baltimore, MD (second weekend in June), to Laconia Motorcycle Week in Laconia, NH (mid-June), to Mermaid Parade in Coney Island, NY (third Saturday in June)

Maine Lobster Festival in Rockland, ME (late July / early August), to Newport Folk Festival in Newport, RI (first weekend in August)

ONE MONTH

Figawi in Nantucket, MA (Memorial Day weekend), to Honfest in Baltimore, MD (second weekend in June), to Laconia Motorcycle Week in Laconia, NH (mid-June), to Mermaid Parade in Coney Island, NY (third Saturday in June)

THE ENTIRE SUMMER

Figawi in Nantucket, MA (Memorial Day weekend), to Honfest in Baltimore, MD (second weekend in June), to Laconia Motorcycle Week in Laconia, NH (mid-June), to Mermaid Parade in Coney Island, NY (third Saturday in June), to A Night in Venice in Ocean City, NJ (second or third Saturday in July), to Maine Lobster Festival in Rockland, ME (late July / early August), to Newport Folk Festival in Newport, RI (first weekend in August)

Southeast

ONE WEEK

National Hollerin' Contest in Spivey's Corner, NC (third Saturday in June), to Fourth of July in Wilmington, NC (July 4)

Or CMA Music Festival in Nashville, TN (first Thursday in June through Sunday), to Bonnaroo Music and Arts Festival in Manchester, TN (second full weekend in June)

ONE MONTH

CMA Music Festival in Nashville, TN (first Thursday in June through Sunday), to Bonnaroo Music and Arts Festival in Manchester, TN (second full weekend in June), to Hollerin' Contest in Spivey's Corner, NC (third Saturday in June), to Fourth of July in Wilmington, NC (July 4)

THE ENTIRE SUMMER

CMA Music Festival in Nashville, TN (first Thursday in June through Sunday), to Bonnaroo Music and Arts Festival in Manchester, TN (second full weekend in June), to Hollerin' Contest in Spivey's Corner, NC (third Saturday in June), to Fourth of July in Wilmington, NC (July 4), to Lebowski Fest in Louisville, KY (mid-July), to Bele Chere in Asheville, NC (last weekend in July)

Middle America

ONE WEEK

Party Cove in Lake of the Ozarks, MO (Memorial Day weekend), to Wakarusa Music and Camping Festival in Lawrence, KS (first weekend in June)

College Baseball World Series in Omaha, NE (middle two weeks of June), to Country Stampede Music and Camping Festival in Manhattan, KS (last weekend in June)

Taste of Chicago in Chicago, IL (late June / early July), to Summerfest in Milwaukee, WI (end of June / early July)

Or We Fest in Detroit Lakes, MN (first weekend in August), to Black Hills Motorcycle Rally in Sturgis, SD (first week in August)

ONE MONTH

Party Cove in Lake of the Ozarks, MO (Memorial Day weekend), to Wakarusa Music and Camping Festival in Lawrence, KS (first weekend in June), to College Baseball World Series in Omaha, NE (middle two weeks in June), to Country Stampede in Manhattan, KS (last weekend in June)

THE ENTIRE SUMMER

Party Cove in Lake of the Ozarks, MO (Memorial Day weekend), to Wakarusa Music and Camping Festival in Lawrence, KS (first weekend in June), to College Baseball World Series in Omaha, NE (middle two weeks in June), to Country Stampede in Manhattan, KS (last weekend in June), to Taste of Chicago in Chicago, IL (late June / early July), to Blissfest in Bliss, MI (second weekend in July), to RAGBRAI in IA (last full week in July), to We Fest in Detroit Lakes, MN (first weekend in August)

The Wild West

ONE WEEK

Cheyenne Frontier Days in Cheyenne, WY (last ten days in July), to Testicle Festival in Clinton, MT (first weekend in August)

Or Burning Man in Black Rock City, NV (week before Labor Day), to Jazz Aspen Snowmass Labor Day Festival in Aspen, CO (Labor Day weekend)

ONE MONTH

UFO Festival in Roswell, NM (first weekend in July), to Cheyenne Frontier Days in Cheyenne, WY (last ten days in July), to Testicle Festival in Clinton, MT (first weekend in August)

THE ENTIRE SUMMER

Hard Rock Rehab Party in Las Vegas, NM (Memorial Day weekend), to Telluride Bluegrass Festival in Telluride, CO (third weekend in June), to UFO Festival in Roswell, NM (first weekend in July), to Cheyenne Frontier Days in Cheyenne, WY (last ten days in July), to Testicle Festival in Clinton, MT (first weekend in August), to Burning Man in Black Rock City, NV (week before Labor Day), to Jazz Aspen Snowmass Labor Day Festival in Aspen, CO (Labor Day weekend)

The West Coast

ONE WEEK

Over the Line Tournament in San Diego, CA (middle two weekends in July), to Comic-Con in San Diego, CA (end of July)

Or Over the Line Tournament in San Diego, CA (middle two weekends in July), to Gilroy Garlic Festival in Gilroy, CA (last weekend in July)

Or Gay Pride Weekend in San Francisco, CA (last weekend in June), to Waterfront Blues Festival in Portland, OR (week of July 4)

ONE MONTH

Waterfront Blues Festival in Portland, OR (week of July 4), to Over the Line Tournament in San Diego, CA (middle two weekends in July), to Comic-Con in San Diego, CA (end of July).

Or Waterfront Blues Festival in Portland, OR (week of July 4), to Over the Line Tournament in San Diego, CA (middle two weekends in July), to Oregon Brewer's Festival in Portland, OR (last weekend in July)

THE ENTIRE SUMMER

Bay to Breakers 12K in San Francisco, CA (third Sunday in May), to Gay Pride Weekend in San Francisco, CA (last weekend in June), to Comic-Con in San Diego, CA (end of July), or Gilroy Garlic Festival in Gilroy, CA (last weekend in July)

ACKNOWLEDGMENTS

I'd like to start by thanking my agent, Alison Picard, for taking a chance. You saw the potential when this project was little more than an idea. Thank you also to my editor, Brendan O'Neill, for your guidance, approachability, coaching, and for always responding to my ranting e-mails in a timely fashion. Jennifer Kushnier, who helped to open the door for this project, is owed a tremendous debt of gratitude. Whoever sat in the Adams Media decision-making room and voted to give this party-hopping author a shot—many thanks!

I leaned on my brother Brian every day throughout this process. His willingness to proofread, edit, facilitate ideas, and insert humor resulted in a much higher-caliber book. I cannot express enough appreciation, Brian. I'm so fortunate to have a brother like you.

Erin Yemm is a lifesaver who spent a lot of time on this book. A heartfelt thanks for your tremendous research, data collection, and fact-checking. You came in at the nick of time and totally rocked.

My parents took us on plenty of family trips, which whetted my appetite for traveling, and therefore prompted this idea. Thank you for your love, Mom and Dad: Your sincere interest in our lives provides motivation to do and see rather than sit and wonder.

Kay and Larry Edwards are the greatest parents-in-law that a person could choose. Their encouragement and laughter were constant throughout the process, as it always is. Kay, your raving reviews of each chapter helped to push me through some bouts of doubt—thank you for being my most vocal fan.

Muchas gracias to the party people who provided excellent celebratory advice. They include Jason Bago, Judy Beghtol, Michelle Bell, Leslie Brunette, Mark Christy, Brandon and Katie Cutter, Patrick and T. J. DesMarais, Jono Edwards, Brendan Ferretti, Amy Gannon, Jonathan Gavetti, David Grimaldi, the Gross family, Erin Guerriero, Ryan Harms, Joanna Hoepner, Troy Jennings, Archie Kasnet, Mike Kelly, Brett Kemp, Ryan Kemp, Colleen and Ben Klimek, James Lobsenz, Ben Loeffler, Wendy Mader, Mike and Amber Mazurana, Brett McClintock, Jenny Metzler, Brooke Michaels, Damon Miele, Eryn Murphy, Chris Olson, Matt Olson, Billy and Susan Petersen, Scott Rice, Sarah Ryan, Troy Salazar, Russ Schumacher, Kelly Shanahan, Peter Stanfield, Meredith and Rob Steiner, Kristin Sullivan, Todd and Jasmine Trickel, Dan Veshi, and Dean Whalen. Special thanks to the greatest party dog around, Kenya, for taking me on long walks when I needed them.

Last, but certainly not least, thank you on behalf of partiers everywhere to the organizers and tireless volunteers who make these events happen. Their selfless hard work enables the rest of us to drink beer and relax. Many people don't realize that staging a mega-sized bash is a full-time job and a year-round effort. You guys rock.

ABOUT THE AUTHOR

Mike Guerriero is a native of Doylestown, Pennsylvania, who has been crossing the country on a party-seeking adventure for more than ten years. His passion for travel and for celebration served as the inspiration for this book. Mike lives with his wife, Jennifer, and their dog, Kenya, in Northern Colorado. His preferred footwear is flip-flops.

Visit *www.partyacrossamericabook.com* to share your own party experiences, to meet the author, and to blog about which celebrations you'd like to see in the next edition.